Steps to Writing an Argument

Use these steps to develop your own arguments.

Step 1 Find a Topic

Read your assignment and determine what type of argument is called for (see pages 25–26).

Find a topic that interests you by reading, talking, and exploring (see pages 28–34).

Step 2 Make a Claim and Support It with Good Reasons

Make a claim designed to change readers' views or persuade them to take action.

List your main points and think about the order of those points.

Step 3 Think About What's at Stake

What exactly is the problem or issue, what causes it, and who is most affected?

Has anyone tried to do anything about it? If so, why haven't they succeeded?

Step 4 Analyze Your Potential Readers

Who are your readers?

How familiar will they be with what you are arguing?

Which claims are they most likely to accept and which will they disagree with?

Step 5 Write a Draft

Introduction

Set out the issue or problem, and give some background if necessary.

Argue for the seriousness of the issue or problem.

Give your thesis in one sentence.

Body

Present and interpret your evidence and its significance.

Keep your focus narrow and make your structure clear to your readers.

If you are proposing a solution to a problem, state your solution and its benefits.

Take a few minutes to think about other views on your issue or problem.

Conclusion

Leave your readers with something interesting and provocative.

Issue a call to action—if your readers a   e action.

Step 6 Revise, Edit, Proofrea

For detailed instructions, see Chapter

For a checklist to use to evaluate your

Good Reasons

Researching and Writing Effective Arguments

SIXTH EDITION

Lester Faigley
University of Texas at Austin

Jack Selzer
The Pennsylvania State University

PEARSON

Boston   Columbus   Indianapolis   New York   San Francisco   Upper Saddle River
Amsterdam   Cape Town   Dubai   London   Madrid   Milan   Munich   Paris   Montréal   ⁷
Delhi   Mexico City   São Paulo   Sydney   Hong Kong   Seoul   Singapore   Taipei   T

In memory of our teacher and friend, James L. Kinneavy (1920–1999)

Editorial Director: Joseph Opiela
Senior Acquisitions Editor: Brad Potthoff
Director of Development: Mary Ellen Curley
Senior Development Editor: Linda Stern
Executive Marketing Manager: Roxanne McCarly
Senior Supplements Editor: Donna Campion
Senior Media Producer: Stefanie Snajder
Media Project Manager: Sara Gordus
Production/Project Manager: Eric Jorgensen
Project Coordination, Text Design, and Electronic Page Makeup: PreMediaGlobal
Senior Cover Design Manager: John Callahan
Cover Designer: John Callahan
Cover Images (clockwise from left): Courtesy of Lester Faigley, © Pixelbliss/Fotolia, © Igor S./Fotolia
Senior Manufacturing Buyer: Dennis Para
Printer/Binder: RR Donnelley/Crawfordsville
Cover Printer: Lehigh-Phoenix Color/Hagerstown

Credits and acknowledgments borrowed from other sources and reproduced, with permission, in this textbook appear on page 299.

Library of Congress Cataloging-in-Publication Data
Faigley, Lester, [date].
    Good reasons : researching and writing effective arguments / Lester Faigley, Jack Selzer. — Sixth edition.
        pages cm
    Includes index.
    ISBN-13: 978-0-321-90674-8
    ISBN-10: 0-321-90674-8
    1. English language—Rhetoric.   2. Persuasion (Rhetoric)   3. Report writing.   I. Selzer, Jack, author.
II. Title.
    PE1431.F35 2015
    808'.042—dc23
                                             2013034254

10 9 8 7 6 5 4—DOC—16 15

www.pearsonhighered.com

Student ISBN 10: 0-321-90674-8
Student ISBN 13: 978-0-321-90674-8
ALaCarte ISBN 10: 0-321-90806-6
ALaCarte ISBN 13: 978-0-321-90806-3

Detailed Contents

Analyzing Arguments 57

Writing Arguments   95

Designing and Presenting Arguments 207

Researching Arguments 221

Preface

Nothing you learn in college will prove to be more important to you than the ability to create an effective argument.

As a student you are already aware that campus life is itself filled with arguments. There are hot-button public issues that engage the academic community—how to deal with binge drinking, for example, or make the university more environmentally sustainable, or improve campus housing or study-abroad opportunities. Meanwhile, in the classroom and in research programs, you and your peers will present arguments on current controversies such as climate change and economic policy as well as on scholarly topics such as the structure of the human brain, the cultural achievements of ancient Egypt, or the means of determining the material composition of the planet Mercury.

After college, you will continue to need to communicate effectively your ideas and points of view. Your livelihood and your successful engagement in the life of your community will depend on it. Sometimes, as a citizen, you will be moved to register your views on how to improve your local school system or enhance local development; or as a member of a neighborhood group or a civic organization, you will be suggesting ways of making a positive difference. And certainly in the workplace you will often be making arguments to support your recommendations and to refute the flawed recommendations of others.

What This Book Offers You

For a number of years, we have studied arguments, taught students how to argue, and listened to others talk and write about the art of persuasion. Although there is no simple recipe for cooking up effective arguments, we've discovered there are definite strategies and tactics that writers can rely on in any situation to ensure that their ideas are considered seriously. However, we also know that regardless of the value of its content, a text will be ineffective if it cannot present its ideas in a way that is engaging, easy to use, and comprehensive. It has been our aim to create such a text in *Good Reasons*.

Lively, nontechnical language. We've pointedly avoided technical jargon in order to explain concepts and techniques as clearly as possible. Explanations, examples, captions, and exercises are all written with the goal of keeping language straightforward and accessible.

Emphasis on attractive design and visual arguments. *Good Reasons* is notable for its attention to visual as well as verbal arguments. In addition, the book itself demonstrates the value of visual argument in its attractive design that is liberally illustrated with graphics, photos, and other visuals.

Annotated student writing samples and numerous other examples. In line with our philosophy of showing rather than telling, chapters covering types of arguments include annotated student essays as well as annotated professional essays illustrating six basic types of arguments: definition, causal, evaluation, narrative, rebuttal, and proposal arguments.

Fresh, timely readings on current issues. These readings demonstrate how complex conversations develop around important issues of interest to students today. Readings span a range of material from canonical speeches to contemporary magazine articles. We've also taken care to select readings that give different points of view on issues such as the food industry, stem-cell research, gun control, and the college "gap" year.

New to This Edition

- **New Chapter 4 on drafting arguments,** offering advice on how to focus your thesis, organize your argument, and connect with readers

- **New Chapter 5 on revising and editing arguments** that provides a checklist for evaluating your draft, advice on revising your draft, and tips on how to edit and proofread effectively

- **Deeply revised Chapter 6 on analyzing written arguments** with a detailed example of how to analyze the text and context of an argument

- **Revised Chapter 7 on analyzing visual and multimedia arguments,** with an increased focus on using graphs

- **Additional examples of fallacies** and how to spot them in Chapter 2

- **New professional reading and annotated sample student essay in Chapter 10, "Evaluation Arguments"**

- **New annotated professional reading in Chapter 11, "Narrative Arguments"**

- **New annotated professional readings in Chapter 12, "Rebuttal Arguments"**

- **New professional readings in Chapter 13, "Proposal Arguments"**

- **Updated mini-arguments in Parts 1 and 3,** including many visual and multimodal examples

- **Updated guidance in Part 5 on how to gather information from database, Web,** and library sources and how to evaluate and cite that information
- **Updated MLA and APA coverage in Chapters 20 and 21,** including how to cite social media and *Twitter.*

Resources for Teachers and Students

Instructor's Manual

The **Instructor's Manual** that accompanies this text was revised by Brian Neff, of Colorado State University–Global Campus, and is designed to be useful for new and experienced instructors alike. The Instructor's Manual briefly discusses the ins and outs of teaching the material in each text chapter. Also provided are in-class exercises, homework assignments, discussion questions, and model paper assignments and syllabi.

Pearson MyLabs

MyWritingLab is an online homework, tutorial, and assessment program that provides engaging experiences to today's instructors and students. By incorporating rubrics into the writing assignments, faculty can create meaningful assignments, grade them based on their desired criteria, and analyze class performance through advanced reporting. For students who enter the course underprepared, MyWritingLab offers a diagnostic test and personalized remediation so that students see improved results and instructors spend less time in class reviewing the basics. Rich multimedia resources, including a Pearson eText, are built in to engage students and support faculty throughout the course. Visit www.mywritinglab.com for more information.

CourseSmart eTextbook

Good Reasons is also available as a CourseSmart eTextbook. This is an exciting new choice for students, who can subscribe to the same content online and search the text, make notes online, print out reading assignments that incorporate lecture notes, and bookmark important passages for later review. For more information, or to subscribe to the CourseSmart eTextbook, visit www.coursesmart.com.

Acknowledgments

We are much indebted to the work of many outstanding scholars of argument and to our colleagues who teach argument at Texas and at Penn State. In particular, we thank the following reviewers for sharing their expertise: Jen Hazel, Owens Community College; Danen Jobe, Pikes Peak Community College; Danizete Martínez, University of New Mexico–Valencia; Vasilka Maslanka, College of Lake County; Daniel Powell, Florida State College at Jacksonville; Eric Sack, Southeast Community College; and Michael Suwak, College of Southern Maryland. We are also grateful to the many students we've taught in our own classes, who have given us opportunities to test these materials in class and who have taught us a great deal about the nature of argument. Special thanks go the students whose work is included in this edition.

We have greatly benefited from working with Brad Potthoff, senior editor, and Linda Stern, senior development editor, whose talent and creativity continue to impress us and who contribute much to both the vision and the details of *Good Reasons*. They are the best, and we much enjoyed working with them on this and other books. Linda especially provided all kinds of expert advice and specific suggestions that we capitalized on in ways too numerous to mention. We appreciate Brian C. Neff's great work in preparing the Instructor's Manual. Andrea Stefanowicz at PreMediaGlobal and Eric Jorgensen at Pearson Longman did a splendid job in preparing our book for publication. We were quite fortunate to again have Elsa van Bergen as our copyeditor, who has no peer in our experience. Finally, we thank our families, who make it all possible.

Lester Faigley
Jack Selzer

Good Reasons

Researching and Writing Effective Arguments

Reading and Discovering Arguments

PART

1

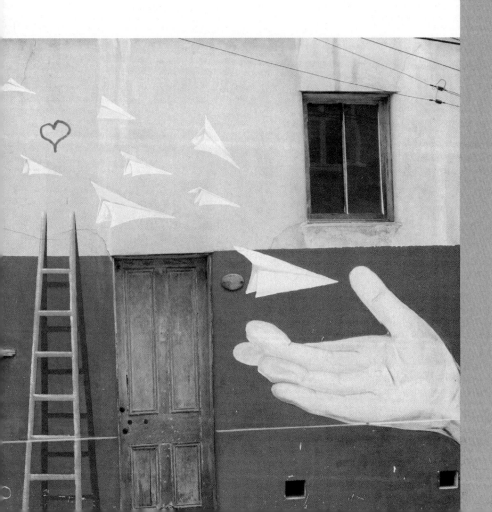

1 | Making an Effective Argument

MadV's *The Message* consists of a series of extremely short videos from *YouTube* members of words written on hands, similar to the one shown here.

What Exactly Is an Argument?

One of the best-known celebrities on *YouTube* is an anonymous video director who wears a Guy Fawkes mask and uses the name MadV. In November 2006 he posted a short video in which he held up his hand with the words "One World" written on his palm and invited viewers to take a stand by uploading a video to *YouTube*. They responded by the thousands, writing short messages written on their palms. MadV then compiled many of the responses in a 4-minute video titled *The Message* and posted it on *YouTube*.

MadV's project has been praised as a celebration of the values of the *YouTube* community. The common theme that we all should try to love and better understand other people is one that few oppose. Yet the video also raises the question of how any of the goals might be achieved. One hand reads "Stop Bigotry." We see a great deal of hatred in written responses to many *YouTube* videos. Slogans like "Open Mind," "Be Colorblind," "Love Is Stronger," "No More Racism," and "Yup One World" seem inadequate for the scope of the problem.

Like the ink-on-hand messages, bumper stickers usually consist of unilateral statements ("Be Green," "Save the Whales," or "Share the Road") but provide no supporting evidence or reasons for why anyone should do what they say. People committed to a particular cause or belief often assume that their reasons are self-evident, and that everyone thinks the same way. These writers know they can count on certain words and phrases to produce predictable responses.

In college courses, in public life, and in professional careers, however, written arguments cannot be reduced to signs or slogans. Writers of effective arguments do not assume that everyone thinks the same way or holds the same beliefs. They attempt to change people's minds by convincing them of the validity of new ideas or the superiority of a particular course of action. Writers of such arguments not only offer evidence and reasons to support their position but also examine the assumptions on which an argument is based, address opposing arguments, and anticipate their readers' objections.

Extended written arguments make more demands on their readers than most other kinds of writing. Like bumper stickers, these arguments often appeal to our emotions. But they typically do much more.

- They expand our knowledge with the depth of their analysis.
- They lead us through a complex set of claims by providing networks of logical relationships and appropriate evidence.
- They build on what has been written previously by providing trails of sources.

Finally, they cause us to reflect on what we read, in a process that we will shortly describe as critical reading.

Finding Good Reasons

Who's Using Up Earth's Resources?

ECOLOGICAL DEBTOR AND CREDITOR COUNTRIES, 1961 and 2005

Eco-debt: Footprint relative to biocapacity ■ more than 150% greater ■ 100-150% greater ■ 50-100% greater ■ 0-50% greater
Eco-credit: Biocapacity relative to footprint ■ 0-50% greater ■ 50-100% greater ■ 100-150% greater ■ more than 150% greater   ■ Insufficient data

1961 (2005 country boundaries)

2005

In the *Living Planet Report* for 2008, the World Wildlife Fund compared the ecological footprints from 1961 and 2005 for each country on Earth. The ecological footprint of a country is determined by its population, the amount of food, timber, and other resources consumed by its average citizen, the area required to produce food, fishing grounds, and the area required to absorb CO_2 emissions minus the amount absorbed by oceans.

Countries fall into four categories: ecological debtor nations (which consume more resources than they can produce), ecological creditor nations (which produce more than they consume), and two categories of ecologically balanced nations, where production and consumption are relatively balanced. In this map you can see that the United States, Mexico, Western Europe, China, India, Pakistan, Japan, and the nations of the Middle East have become ecological debtors with footprints more than 50 percent of their biocapacity—what they are able to produce. Nations such as Canada, Russia, Australia, New Zealand, and most nations in South America are ecological creditors, with footprints less than 50 percent of their biocapacity. In its entirety, the *Living Planet Report* makes the argument that nations should live in balance with what their land, rivers, lakes, and seas can support.

Write about it

1. What might be some of the causes of the differences among the ecological footprints of nations?

2. What is likely to happen in the future when some nations have enough resources (such as clean water and food) and others lack them?

3. Does the map succeed as an argument on its own? Does it contain any of the features of written arguments listed on pages 5–6?

Writing Arguments in College

Writing in college varies considerably from course to course. A lab report for a biology course looks quite different from a paper in your English class, just as a classroom observation in an education course differs from a case study report in an accounting class.

Nevertheless, much of the writing you will do in college will consist of arguments. Some common expectations about arguments in college writing extend across disciplines. For example, you could be assigned to write a proposal for a downtown light-rail system in a number of different classes—civil engineering, urban planning, government, or management. The emphasis of such a proposal would change depending on the course. In all cases, however, the proposal would require a complex argument in which you describe the problem that the light-rail system would improve, make a specific proposal that addresses the problem, explain the benefits of the system, estimate the cost, identify funding sources, assess alternatives to your plan, and anticipate possible opposition. That's a lot to think about.

Setting out a specific proposal or claim supported by reasons and evidence is at the heart of most college writing, no matter what the course. Some expectations of arguments (such as including a thesis statement) may be familiar to you, but others (such as the emphasis on finding alternative ways of thinking about a subject and finding facts that might run counter to your conclusions) may be unfamiliar.

WRITTEN ARGUMENTS...	WRITERS ARE EXPECTED TO...
State explicit claims	Make a claim that isn't obvious. The main claim is often called a **thesis**. (see pages 40–41)
Support claims with reasons	Express reasons in a **because clause** after the claim (We should do something *because* _____). (see pages 25–26)
Base reasons on evidence	Provide evidence for reasons in the form of facts, statistics, testimony from reliable sources, and direct observations. (see pages 37–38)
Consider opposing positions	Help readers understand why there are disagreements about issues by accurately representing differing views. (see pages 29–31)
Analyze with insight	Provide in-depth analysis of what they read and view. (see Chapters 6 and 7)

(continued)

WRITTEN ARGUMENTS . . .	WRITERS ARE EXPECTED TO . . .
Investigate complexity	Explore the complexity of a subject by asking "Have you thought about this?" or "What if you discard the usual way of thinking about a subject and take the opposite point of view?" (see pages 34–36)
Organize information clearly	Make the main ideas evident to readers and to indicate which parts are subordinate to others. (see pages 45–46)
Signal relationships of parts	Indicate logical relationships clearly so that readers can follow an argument without getting lost. (see page 54)
Document sources carefully	Provide the sources of information so that readers can consult the same sources the writer used. (see Chapters 20 and 21)

How can you argue responsibly?

In Washington, D.C., cars with diplomatic license plates are often parked illegally. Their drivers know they will not be towed or ticketed. People who abuse the diplomatic privilege are announcing, "I'm not playing by the rules."

When you begin an argument by saying "in my opinion," you are making a similar announcement. First, the phrase is redundant. A reader assumes that if you make a claim in writing, you believe that claim. More important, a claim is rarely *only* your opinion. Most beliefs and assumptions are shared by many people. If a claim truly is only your opinion, it can be easily dismissed. If your position is likely to be held by at least a few other people, however, then a responsible reader must consider your position seriously. You argue responsibly when you set out the reasons for making a claim and offer facts to support those reasons. You argue responsibly when you allow readers to examine your evidence by documenting the sources you have consulted. Finally, you argue responsibly when you acknowledge that other people may have positions different from yours.

How can you argue respectfully?

Our culture is competitive, and our goal often is to win. Professional athletes, top trial lawyers, or candidates for president of the United States either win big or lose. But most of us live in a world in which our opponents don't go away when the game is over.

Most of us have to deal with people who disagree with us at times but continue to work and live in our communities. The idea of winning in such situations can only be temporary. Soon enough, we will need the support of those who were on the other side of the most recent issue. You can probably think of times when a friendly argument resulted in a better understanding of everyone's views. And probably you can think of a time when an argument created hard feelings that lasted for years.

Usually, listeners and readers are more willing to consider your argument seriously if you cast yourself as a respectful partner rather than as a competitor. Put forth your arguments in the spirit of mutual support and negotiation—in the interest of finding the *best* way, not "my way." How can you be the person that your reader will want to join rather than resist? Here are a few suggestions both for your written arguments and for discussing controversial issues.

- **Try to think of yourself as engaged not so much in winning over your audience as in courting your audience's cooperation.** Argue vigorously, but not so vigorously that opposing views are vanquished or silenced. Remember that your goal is to invite a response that creates a dialogue and continuing partnership.

- **Show that you understand and genuinely respect your listener's or reader's position even if you think the position is ultimately wrong.** Remember to argue against opponents' positions, not against the opponents themselves. Arguing respectfully often means representing an opponent's position in terms that he or she would accept. Look for ground that you already share with your opponent, and search for even more. See yourself as a mediator. Consider that neither you nor the other person has arrived at a best solution. Then carry on in the hope that dialogue will lead to an even better course of action than the one you now recommend. Expect and assume the best of your listener or your reader, and deliver your best.

- **Cultivate a sense of humor and a distinctive voice.** Many textbooks about argument emphasize using a reasonable voice. But a reasonable voice doesn't have to be a dull one. Humor is a legitimate tool of argument. Although playing an issue strictly for laughs risks not being taken seriously, nothing creates a sense of goodwill quite as much as tasteful humor. A sense of humor can be especially welcome when the stakes are high, sides have been chosen, and tempers are flaring.

Arguments as Turns in a Conversation

Consider your argument as just one move in a larger process that might end up helping you. Most times we argue because we think we have something to offer. In the process of researching what has been said and written on a particular issue, however, often your own view is expanded and you find an opportunity to add your voice to the ongoing conversation.

A Case Study:The Microcredit Debate

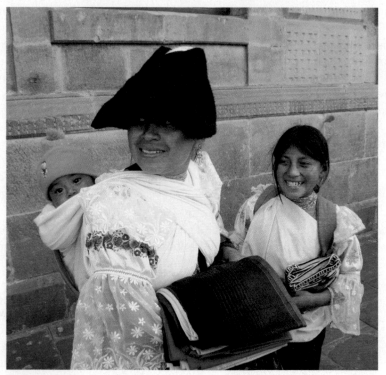

Two women financed by microcredit sell scarves in Quito, Ecuador.

World Bank researchers reported in 2009 that 1.4 billion people—over 20 percent of the then 6.7 billion people on earth—live below the extreme poverty line of $1.25 a day, with 6 million children starving to death every year. One cause of continuing extreme poverty is the inability of poor people to borrow money because they have no cash income or assets. Banks have seldom made loans to very poor people, who have had to turn to moneylenders that charge high interest rates sometimes exceeding 100 percent a month.

In 1976, Muhammad Yunus observed that poor women in Bangladesh who made bamboo furniture could not profit from their labor because they had to borrow money at high interest rates to buy bamboo. Yunus loaned $27 to forty-two women out of his pocket. They repaid him at an interest rate of two cents per loan. The success of the experiment eventually led to Yunus securing a loan from the government to create a bank to make loans to poor people. The Grameen Bank (Village Bank) became a model for other microfinancing projects in Bangladesh, serving 7 million people, 94 percent of whom are women. For his work with the Grameen initiative, Yunus received the Nobel Peace Prize in 2006.

Microcredit now has many supporters, including Hollywood stars like Natalie Portman and Michael Douglas, companies like Benetton and Sam's Club, and former President Bill Clinton. But the success in Bangladesh has not been replicated in many other poor countries. Many critics point to the shortcomings of microcredit. This debate can be better understood if you consider the different points of view on microcredit to be different voices in a conversation.

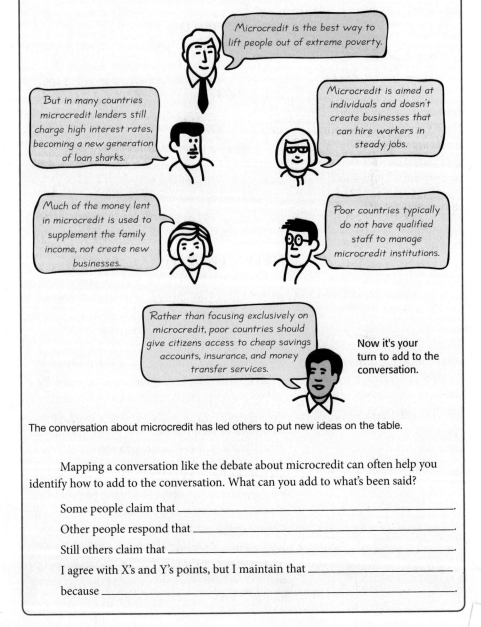

The conversation about microcredit has led others to put new ideas on the table.

Mapping a conversation like the debate about microcredit can often help you identify how to add to the conversation. What can you add to what's been said?

Some people claim that _____.

Other people respond that _____.

Still others claim that _____.

I agree with X's and Y's points, but I maintain that _____

because _____.

Build your credibility

Know what's at stake. What you are writing about should matter to your readers. If its importance is not evident, it's your job to explain why your readers should consider it important.

LESS EFFECTIVE:

We should be concerned about two-thirds of Central and South America's 110 brightly colored harlequin frog species becoming extinct in the last twenty years. (The loss of any species is unfortunate, but the writer gives us no other reason for concern.)

MORE EFFECTIVE:

The rapid decline of amphibians worldwide due to global warming may be the advance warning of the loss of cold-weather species such as polar bears, penguins, and reindeer.

Have your readers in mind. If you are writing about a specialized subject that your readers don't know much about, take the time to explain key concepts.

LESS EFFECTIVE:

Reduction in the value of a debt security, especially a bond, results from a rise in interest rates. Conversely, a decline in interest rates results in an increase in the value of a debt security, especially bonds. (The basic idea is here, but it is not expressed clearly, especially if the reader is not familiar with investing.)

MORE EFFECTIVE:

Bond prices move inversely to interest rates. When interest rates go up, bond prices go down, and when interest rates go down, bond prices go up.

Think about alternative solutions and points of view. Readers appreciate a writer's ability to see a subject from multiple perspectives.

LESS EFFECTIVE:

We will reduce greenhouse gas and global warming only if we greatly increase wind-generated electricity. (Wind power is an alternative energy source, but it is expensive and many people don't want windmills in scenic areas. The writer also doesn't mention using energy more efficiently.)

MORE EFFECTIVE:

If the world is serious about limiting carbon emissions to reduce global warming, then along with increasing efficient energy use, all non-carbon-emitting energy sources must be considered, including nuclear power. Nuclear power now produces about 20 percent of U.S. electricity with no emissions—the equivalent of taking 58 million passenger cars off the road.

Be honest. Readers also appreciate writers who admit what they aren't sure about. Leaving readers with unanswered questions can lead them to think further about your subject.

LESS EFFECTIVE:

The decline in violent crime during the 1990s was due to putting more people in jail with longer sentences.

MORE EFFECTIVE:

Exactly what caused the decline in violent crime during the 1990s remains uncertain. Politicians point to longer sentences for criminals, but the decrease in the population most likely to commit crimes—the 16-to-35 age group—may have been a contributing factor.

Write well. Nothing impresses readers more than graceful, fluent writing that is clear, direct, and forceful. Even if readers don't agree with you in the end, they still will appreciate your writing ability.

LESS EFFECTIVE:

*Nobody can live today without taking some risks, even very rich people. After all, we don't know what we're breathing in the air. A lot of food has chemicals and hormones in it. There's a big hole in the ozone, so more people will get skin cancer. And a lot of people have sexually transmitted diseases these days. (**The impact of the point is lost with unfocused writing.**)*

MORE EFFECTIVE:

We live in a world of risks beyond our control, to the extent that it is difficult to think of anything that is risk free down to the most basic human acts—sex in an era of AIDS, eating in an era of genetically altered food, walking outside in an ozone-depleted atmosphere, drinking water and breathing air laden with chemicals whose effects we do not understand.

2 Reading Arguments

QUICK TAKE

In this chapter, you will learn to

1. Recognize that controversies often involve many nuanced positions (see below)
2. Read an argument critically (see page 13)
3. Identify and define fallacies of logic, emotion, and language (see pages 16–19)
4. Map and summarize an argument (see pages 20–21)

Explore Controversies

People in general agree on broad goals for their society: clean water, abundant healthy food, efficient transportation, good schools, full employment, affordable health care, safe cities and neighborhoods, and peace with others near and far. However, people often disagree on how to define and achieve these goals. Controversies surround major issues and causes.

Often controversies are portrayed in the media as pro and con or even take on political labels. But if you read and listen carefully to what people have to say about a particular issue, you usually find a range of different positions on the issue, and you often discover nuances and complexities in the reasons people offer for their positions.

Find controversies

Online subject directories can help you identify the differing views on a large, general topic. Try the subject index of your library's online catalog. You'll likely find subtopics listed under large topics. Also, your library's Web site may have a link to the *Opposing Viewpoints* database.

One of the best Web subject directories for finding arguments is Yahoo's *Issues and Causes* directory. This directory provides subtopics for major issues and provides links to the Web sites of organizations interested in particular issues.

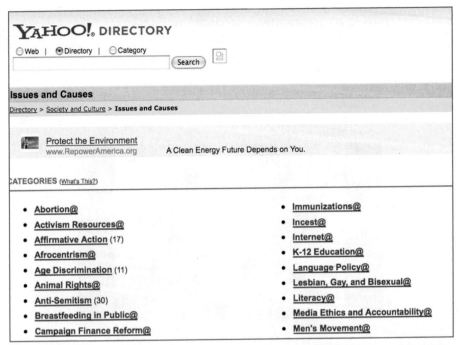

Yahoo! *Issues and Causes* directory (dir.yahoo.com/Society_and_Culture/Issues_and_Causes/)

Read Critically

After you survey the landscape of a particular issue, turn to careful reading of individual arguments, one at a time.

Before you begin reading, ask these questions

- Where did the argument first appear? Was it published in a book, newspaper, magazine, or electronic source? Many items in library databases and on the Web were published somewhere else first.
- Who wrote this argument? What do you know about the author?
- What does the title suggest that the argument might be about?

Read the argument once without making notes to gain a sense of the content

- When you finish, write one sentence that sums up the argument.

Finding Good Reasons

Everyone Is a Writer

Video blogs, known as vlogs, became a popular genre on *YouTube*.

Before the Internet was invented, readers had to make some effort to respond to writers by writing to them directly, sending a letter to the editor, or even scribbling or spray-painting a response. The Internet has changed the interaction between writers and readers by allowing readers to respond easily to writers and, in turn, changing readers into writers. Look, for example, at Amazon Web site. An incredible amount of writing surrounds any best-selling book—often an author's Web site and blog, newspaper reviews, and over a hundred readers' reviews. Or read a political, sports, culture, fashion, or parenting blog and the comments by readers of those blogs. Think about how the Internet has changed the relationship between readers and writers.

To find a blog that interests you, use a blog search engine such as *Bloglines*, *Google Blog Search*, *IceRocket*, or *Technorati*.

Write about it

1. Using a blog search engine or an online newspaper, find a blog by an author, politician, or news columnist. Answer as many of the questions for critical reading on page 15 as you can.

2. Write a summary of the blog entry.

3. What kinds of reasons do blog writers give for their responses to what they read?

4. How are blogs and online book reviews like or unlike traditional book reviews in print?

Read the argument a second and third time and make notes

- Go back through the text and underline the author's thesis.
- Do your sentence and the author's thesis match? If not, look at the text again and either adjust your sentence or check if you underlined the correct sentence.
- How is the argument organized? How are the major points arranged?
- What reasons or evidence does the writer offer in support of the thesis?
- How does the writer conclude the argument? Does the conclusion follow from the evidence presented?
- Who is the intended audience? What does the writer assume the readers know and believe?
- Do you detect a bias in the writer's position?
- Where do the writer's facts come from? Does the writer give the sources? Are the sources reliable?
- Does the writer acknowledge other views and unfavorable evidence? Does the writer deal fairly with the views of others?
- If there are images or graphics, are they well integrated and clearly labeled?

Annotate what you read

- **Mark major points and key concepts.** Sometimes major points are indicated by headings, but often you will need to locate them.
- **Connect with your experience.** Think about your own experiences and how they match up or don't match up with what you are reading.
- **Connect passages.** Notice how ideas connect to each other. Draw lines and arrows. If an idea connects to something from a few pages earlier, write a note in the margin with the page number.
- **Ask questions.** Note anything that puzzles you, including words you don't know and need to look up.

Map a controversy

Read broadly about an issue and identify three or more sources that offer different points of view on that issue. The sources may approach the issue from different angles or raise different questions instead of simply stating differing positions on the issue. Draw a map that represents the different views. The map on the next page shows some of the different positions on sustainable agriculture.

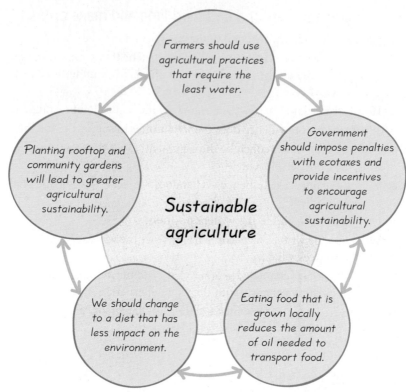

Map of different issues about sustainable agriculture.

Recognize Fallacies

Recognizing where good reasons go off track is one of the most important aspects of critical reading. What passes as political discourse is often filled with claims that lack evidence or substitute emotions for evidence. Such faulty reasoning often contains one or more **logical fallacies**. For example, politicians know that the public is outraged when the price of gasoline goes up, and they try to score political points by accusing oil companies of price gouging. This sounds good to angry voters—and it may well be true—but unless the politician defines what *price gouging* means and provides evidence that oil companies are guilty, the argument has no more validity than children calling each other bad names on the playground.

Following are some of the more common fallacies.

Fallacies of logic

- **Begging the question** *Politicians are inherently dishonest because no honest person would run for public office.* The fallacy of begging the question occurs when the claim is restated and passed off as evidence.

It's on the Internet

Although people at times use fallacies to score political points or to gain the attention of those who feel passionately about a topic, most fallacies occur because of faulty evidence. And while the Internet is a valuable research tool because of the wealth of information available, a lot of that information is misleading or factually incorrect.

Because anyone can post on the Internet, and because many Web sites repost information without attribution, bad information can spread quickly across the Web. You may have heard of videos going viral on the Web, but the same thing can happen with misinformation. One Web site posts a story that is then reposted on several other sites. Suddenly, because a story is available on several different Web sites, it becomes "true." If an argument uses such a story to prove a point, it is employing the *common knowledge fallacy*—a variation of the *bandwagon fallacy* in which "everyone does it" is replaced by "everyone knows it's true."

After Osama bin Laden was killed in May 2011, a quotation attributed to Martin Luther King, Jr., went viral, spreading across *Facebook* and other social media sites. Unfortunately, only part of the quotation was actually something King said. The error started with a *Facebook* post in which the poster began with her own thoughts on the situation and then quoted King. The original post was quoted and reposted, but as it spread, the entire quotation was attributed to King—not just the portion of the original post that contained his actual words. An argument that made use of the quotation would be based on a fallacy.

Although the speed with which information travels across social media may be to blame for the misattribution of the *Facebook* quotation to Martin Luther King, Jr., some bad information on the Internet proliferates because it is easy to commit the fallacy of *cherry-picking the evidence*—selectively using some information and suppressing facts that do not suit the argument. If you read many articles about the local food movement, you have probably come across the claim that the food on your plate travels, on average, 1,500 miles to get to you, a claim that is repeated in numerous places around the Web. However, the study that the claim came from focused on Chicago; the distance traveled would actually differ depending on where in the country you live, a fact that has not stopped the statistic from being used in a wide range of contexts.

One of the best ways to avoid fallacies in your own arguments is to carefully evaluate your sources—especially online sources—and the validity of the information you use to construct your arguments. Chapter 18 discusses how to evaluate the sources you use in a paper.

■ **Cherry-picking the evidence** *This small sedan is as highly rated in crash tests by the Insurance Institute for Highway Safety as the most highly rated SUV.* Cherry-picking the evidence means leaving out significant facts, usually because they do not support the argument being made. In this case, the writer omits the IIHS's warning that comparisons across vehicle size groups are invalid.

■ **Common knowledge fallacy** *We can't be doing that much harm to the environment. After all, alligators are thriving in the sewers of New York City.* The common knowledge fallacy assumes that stories and statistics that are widely disseminated or repeated are necessarily true. Here, the writer does not offer any facts to support the assertion about alligators.

■ **Either-or** *Either we eliminate the regulation of businesses or else profits will suffer.* The either-or fallacy suggests that there are only two choices in a complex situation. Rarely, if ever, is this the case. Consider, for example, the case of Enron, which was unregulated but went bankrupt.

■ **False analogies** *Japan quit fighting in 1945 when we dropped nuclear bombs on Hiroshima and Nagasaki. We should use nuclear weapons against other countries.* Analogies always depend on the degree of resemblance of one situation to another. In this case, the analogy fails to recognize that circumstances today are very different from those in 1945. Many countries now possess nuclear weapons, and we know their use could harm the entire world.

■ **Hasty generalization** *We have been in a drought for three years; that's a sure sign of climate change.* A hasty generalization is a broad claim made on the basis of a few occurrences. Climate cycles occur regularly over spans of a few years. Climate trends, however, must be established with more data than one drought cycle.

■ **Non sequitur** *A university that can raise a billion dollars from alumni should not have to raise tuition.* A non sequitur (a Latin term meaning "it does not follow") ties together two unrelated ideas. In this case, the argument fails to recognize that the money for capital campaigns is often donated for special purposes such as athletic facilities and is not part of a university's general revenue.

■ **Oversimplification** *No one would run stop signs if we had a mandatory death penalty for doing it.* This claim may be true, but the argument would be unacceptable to most citizens. More complex, if less definitive, solutions are called for.

■ **Post hoc fallacy** *The stock market goes down when the AFC wins the Super Bowl in even years.* The post hoc fallacy (from the Latin *post hoc, ergo propter hoc,* which means "after this, therefore because of this") assumes that events that follow in time have a causal relationship.

■ **Rationalization** *I could have finished my paper on time if my printer had been working.* People frequently come up with excuses and weak explanations for their own and others' behavior. These excuses often avoid actual causes.

- **Slippery slope** *We shouldn't grant citizenship to illegal immigrants now living in the United States because no one will want to obey our laws.* The slippery slope fallacy maintains that one thing inevitably will cause something else to happen.

Fallacies of emotion and language

- **Bandwagon appeals** *It doesn't matter if I copy a paper off the Web because everyone else does.* This argument suggests that everyone is doing it, so why shouldn't you? But on close examination, it may be that everyone really isn't doing it—and in any case, it may not be the right thing to do.
- **Name-calling** *Every candidate running for office in this election is either a left-wing radical or a right-wing ideologue.* Name-calling is frequent in politics and among competing groups. People level accusations using names such as *radical, tax-and-spend liberal, racist, fascist, ultra-conservative extremist.* Unless these terms are carefully defined, they are meaningless.
- **Polarization** *Feminists are all man-haters.* Like name-calling, polarization exaggerates positions and groups by representing them as extreme and divisive.
- **Straw man** *Environmentalists won't be satisfied until not a single human being is allowed to enter a national park.* A straw man argument is a diversionary tactic that sets up another's position in a way that can be easily rejected. In fact, only a small percentage of environmentalists would make an argument even close to this one.

Note fallacies while you read

Marta Ramos noted a fallacy in James McWilliams's argument against locavorism. You can read her rebuttal argument on pages 188–191.

Consider fruit and vegetable production in New York. The Empire State is naturally equipped to grow a wide variety of fruits, including pears, cherries, strawberries, and some peaches. But none of these compare to its ability to grow apples and grapes, which dominate production (accounting for 94 percent of all fruit grown).

At current levels of fruit production, apples are the only crop that could currently feed New Yorkers at a level that meets the U.S. Recommended Dietary Allowances. Every other fruit that the state produces is not being harvested at a level to provide all New Yorkers with an adequate supply. Other fruits such as bananas and oranges are not produced at all because conditions are unfavorable for growing them.

What does this situation mean in terms of feeding the state with the state's own produce?

In a nutshell, <u>it means citizens would have to give up tropical fruits altogether;</u> rarely indulge in a pear, peach, or basket of strawberries; and gorge on grapes and apples— most of them in processed form (either as juice, in a can, or as concentrate).

—James E. McWilliams. *Just Food: Where Locavores Get It Wrong and How We Can Truly Eat Responsibly.* (New York: Little, Brown, 2009), 44.

McWilliams makes a straw man argument. Locavores prioritize locally produced food but don't argue that it's only what people should eat.

Map and Summarize Arguments

When you finish annotating a reading, you might want to map it.

Draw a map

Marta Ramos drew a map of James McWilliams's argument.

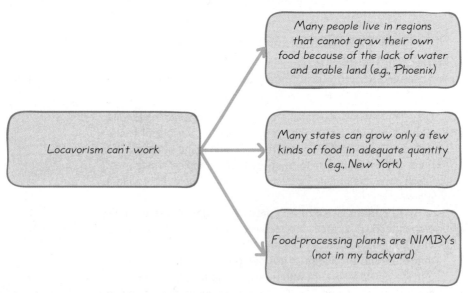

Map of the argument in James McWilliams's *Just Food*.

Write a summary

A summary should be a concise but thorough representation of the source.

- Begin your summary with the writer's name, the title of the argument, and the main point.
- Then report the key ideas. Represent the author's argument in condensed form as accurately as you can, quoting exact words for key points (see pages 254–255 for how to quote and integrate an author's words into your summary).
- Your aim is to give your readers an understanding of what the author is arguing for. Withhold judgment even if you think the author is dead wrong. Do not insert your opinions and comments. Stick to what the author is saying and what position the author is advocating.
- Usually summaries are no longer than 150 words. If your summary is longer than 150 words, delete excess words without eliminating key ideas.

McWilliams, James. *Just Food: Where Locavores Get It Wrong and How We Can Truly Eat Responsibly.* New York: Little Brown, 2009. Print.

Summary

In *Just Food,* James McWilliams argues that locavorism—the development of local food-supply systems—is an impractical goal. He offers three reasons why locavorism is not achievable. First, many people live in regions where they cannot grow their own food because of lack of water and arable land (for example, Phoenix). Second, many states can grow only a few kinds of food in adequate quantity (for example, New York), thus restricting food choices and limiting consumption to processed fruits and vegetables for much of the year. Third, many people will not like food processing plants near their homes.

3 | Finding Arguments

In this chapter, you will learn to

1. Distinguish arguments from other kinds of persuasion (see page 23)
2. Identify the basics of an argument (see page 24)
3. Find and explore a topic (see pages 25–34)
4. Develop good reasons and evidence for your point of view (see pages 34–38)

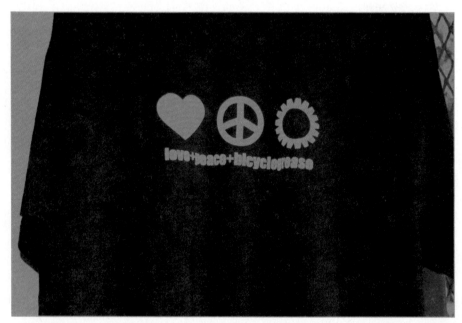

Although slogans printed on T-shirts often express the views of the people who wear them, the slogans usually cannot be considered arguments because they lack supporting reasons. Nevertheless, you can often supply reasons that are implied by the slogan. Think of reasons supporting the claim that bicycles make a community better.

Find Arguments in Everyday Conversations

Let's look at an example of a conversation. When the pain in his abdomen didn't go away, Jeff knew he had torn something while carrying his friend's heavy speakers up a flight of stairs. He went to the student health center and called his friend Maria when he returned home.

JEFF: I have good news and bad news. The pain is a minor hernia that can be repaired with day surgery. The bad news is that the fee we pay for the health center doesn't cover hospital visits. We should have health coverage.

MARIA: Jeff, you didn't buy the extra insurance. Why should you get it for nothing?

JEFF: Because health coverage is a right.

MARIA: No it's not. Not everyone has health insurance.

JEFF: Well, in some other countries like Canada, Germany, and Britain, they do.

MARIA: Yes, and people who live in those countries pay a bundle in taxes for the government-provided insurance.

JEFF: It's not fair in this country because some people have health insurance and others don't.

MARIA: Jeff, face the facts. You could have bought the extra insurance. Instead you chose to buy a new car.

JEFF: It would be better if the university provided health insurance because students could graduate in four years. I'm going to have to get a second job and drop out for a semester to pay for the surgery.

MARIA: Neat idea, but who's going to pay to insure every student?

JEFF: OK, all students should be required to pay for health insurance as part of their general fee. Most students are healthy, and it wouldn't cost that much more.

In this discussion, Jeff starts out by making a **claim** that students should have health coverage. Maria immediately asks him why students should not have to pay for health insurance. She wants a **reason** to accept his claim.

Distinguishing arguments from other kinds of persuasion

Scholars who study argument maintain that an argument must have a claim and one or more reasons to support that claim. Something less might be persuasive, but it isn't an argument.

A bumper sticker that says NO TOLL ROADS is a claim, but it is not an argument because the statement lacks a reason. Many reasons support an argument against building toll roads.

- We don't need new roads but should build light-rail instead.
- We should raise the gas tax to pay for new roads.
- We should use gas tax revenue only for roads rather than using it for other purposes.

When a claim has a reason attached, then it becomes an argument.

The basics of arguments

A reason is typically offered in a **because clause**, a statement that begins with the word *because* and that provides a supporting reason for the claim. Jeff's first attempt is to argue that students should have health insurance *because* health insurance is a right.

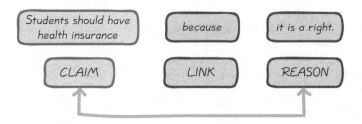

The word *because* signals a link between the reason and the claim. Every argument that is more than a shouting match or a simple assertion has to have one or more reasons. Just having a reason for a claim, however, doesn't mean that the audience will be convinced. When Jeff tells Maria that students have a right to health insurance, Maria replies that students don't have that right. Maria will accept Jeff's claim only if she accepts that his reason supports his claim. Maria challenges Jeff's links and keeps asking "So what?" For her, Jeff's reasons are not good reasons.

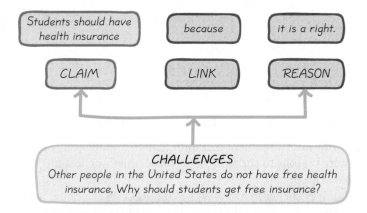

By the end of this short discussion, Jeff has begun to build an argument. He has modified his original claim and indicated how it might be implemented: All students should be required to pay for health insurance as part of their general fee. If he is to convince Maria, he will probably have to provide a series of claims that she will accept as linked to his primary claim. He will also need to find evidence to support these claims.

Benjamin Franklin observed, "So convenient a thing it is to be a rational creature, since it enables us to find or make a reason for every thing one has a mind to do." It is not hard to think of reasons. What *is* difficult is to convince your audience that your reasons are good reasons. In a conversation, you get immediate feedback that tells you whether your listener agrees or disagrees. When you are writing, you usually don't have someone you can question immediately. Consequently, you have to (1) be more specific about what you are claiming, (2) connect with the values you hold in common with your readers, and (3) anticipate what questions and objections your readers might have, if you are going to convince someone who doesn't agree with you or know what you know already.

When you write an argument, imagine a reader like Maria who is going to listen carefully to what you have to say but who is not going to agree with you automatically. Readers like Maria will expect the following.

- A **claim** that is interesting and makes them want to find out more about what you have to say
- At least one **good reason** that makes your claim worth taking seriously
- Some **evidence** that the good reason or reasons are valid
- Some acknowledgment of the **opposing views** and **limitations** of the claim

The remainder of this chapter will guide you through the process of finding a topic, making a claim, finding good reasons and evidence, and anticipating objections to your claim.

Find a Topic

When your instructor gives you a writing assignment, look closely at what you are asked to do. Assignments typically contain a great deal of information, and you have to sort through that information. First, circle all the instructions about the length, the due date, the format, the grading criteria, and anything else about the production and conventions of the assignment. This information is important to you, but it doesn't tell you what the paper is supposed to be about.

Read your assignment carefully

Often your assignment will contain key words such as *analyze, define, evaluate,* or *propose* that will assist you in determining what direction to take. *Analyze* can mean several things. Your instructor might want you to analyze a piece of writing (see Chapter 6), an image (see Chapter 7), or the causes of something (see Chapter 9).

Define usually means writing a **definition argument**, in which you argue for a definition based on the criteria you set out (see Chapter 8). *Evaluate* indicates an **evaluation argument**, in which you argue that something is good, bad, the best, or the worst in its class according to criteria that you set out (see Chapter 10). An assignment that contains the instructions *Write about an issue using your personal experience* indicates a **narrative argument** (see Chapter 11), while one that says *Take a position in regard to a reading* might lead you to write a **rebuttal argument** (see Chapter 12). *Propose* means that you should identify a particular problem and explain why your solution is the best one in a **proposal argument** (see Chapter 13).

What Is Not Arguable

- **Statements of fact.** Most facts can be verified through research. But even simple facts can sometimes be argued. For example, Mount Everest is usually acknowledged to be the highest mountain in the world at 29,028 feet above sea level. But if the total height of a mountain from base to summit is the measure, then the volcano Mauna Loa in Hawaii is the highest mountain in the world. Although the top of Mauna Loa is 13,667 feet above sea level, the summit is 31,784 above the ocean floor. Thus the "fact" that Mount Everest is the highest mountain on the earth depends on a definition of *highest*. You could argue for this definition.

- **Claims of personal taste.** Your favorite food and your favorite color are examples of personal taste. If you hate fresh tomatoes, no one can convince you that you actually like them. But many claims of personal taste turn out to be value judgments using arguable criteria. For example, if you think that *Alien* is the best science-fiction movie ever made, you can argue that claim using evaluative criteria that other people can consider as good reasons (see Chapter 10). Indeed, you might not even like science fiction and still argue that *Alien* is the best science-fiction movie ever.

- **Statements of belief or faith.** If someone accepts a claim as a matter of religious belief, then for that person, the claim is true and cannot be refuted. Of course, people still make arguments about the existence of God and which religion reflects the will of God. Whenever an audience will not consider an idea, it's possible but very difficult to construct an argument. Many people claim to have evidence that UFOs exist, but most people refuse to acknowledge that evidence as even being possibly factual.

If you remain unclear about the purpose of the assignment after reading it carefully, talk with your instructor.

Finding Good Reasons

Are Traffic Enforcement Cameras Invading Your Privacy?

Cameras that photograph the license plates and drivers of vehicles who run red lights or ride illegally in high-occupancy-vehicle (HOV) and bus lanes are currently in use in many U.S. cities and states. Cameras aimed at catching speeders, already common in Europe, are beginning to be installed in U.S. cities as well. Traffic cameras have become money machines for some communities, but they also have provoked intense public opposition and even vandalism—people have spray painted and shot cameras in attempts to disable them.

Write about it

1. How do you feel about using cameras to catch red-light runners? Illegal drivers in HOV and bus lanes? speeders? people who don't pay parking tickets? Make a list of as many possible topics as you can think of about the use of cameras to scan license plates.

2. Select one of the possible topics. Write it at the top of a sheet of paper, and then write nonstop for five minutes. Don't worry about correctness. If you get stuck, write the same sentence again.

3. When you finish, read what you have written and circle key ideas.

4. Put each key idea on a sticky note. If you think of other ideas, write them on separate sticky notes. Then look at your sticky notes. Put a star on the central idea. Put the ideas that are related next to each other. You now have the beginning of an idea map.

Thinking about what interests you

Your assignment may specify the topic you are to write about. If your assignment gives you a wide range of options and you don't know what to write about, look first at the materials for your course: the readings, your lecture notes, and discussion boards. Think about what subjects came up in class discussion.

If you need to look outside class for a topic, think about what interests you. Subjects we argue about often find us. There are enough of them in daily life. We're late for work or class because the traffic is heavy or the bus doesn't run on time. We can't find a place to park when we get to school or work. We have to negotiate through various bureaucracies for almost anything we do—making an appointment to see a doctor, getting a course added or dropped, or correcting a mistake on a bill. Most of the time we grumble and let it go at that. But sometimes we stick with a subject. Neighborhood groups in cities and towns have been especially effective in getting something done by writing about it—for example, stopping a new road from being built, getting better police and fire protection, and getting a vacant lot turned into a park.

Listing and analyzing issues

A good way to get started is to list possible issues to write about. Make a list of questions that can be answered "YES, because . . ." or "NO, because . . ." Think about issues that affect your campus, your community, the nation, and the world. Which issues interest you? About which issues could you make a contribution to the larger discussion?

Campus

- Should students be required to pay fees for access to computers on campus?
- Should smoking be banned on campus?
- Should varsity athletes get paid for playing sports that bring in revenue?
- Should admissions decisions be based exclusively on academic achievement?
- Should knowledge of a foreign language be required for all degree plans?
- Should your college or university have a computer literacy requirement?
- Is there any way to curb the dangerous drinking habits of many students on your campus?

Community

- Should people who ride bicycles and motorcycles be required to wear helmets?
- Should high schools be allowed to search students for drugs at any time?
- Should high schools distribute condoms?
- Should bilingual education programs be eliminated?
- Should bike lanes be built throughout your community to encourage more people to ride bicycles?
- Should more tax dollars be shifted from building highways to funding public transportation?

Nation/World

- Should talking on a cell phone while driving be banned?
- Should capital punishment be abolished?
- Should the Internet be censored?
- Should the government be allowed to monitor all phone calls and all e-mail to combat terrorism?
- Should assault weapons be outlawed?
- Should beef and poultry be free of growth hormones?
- Should a law be passed requiring that parents be informed before their teenage child has an abortion?
- Should people who are terminally ill be allowed to end their lives?
- Should the United States punish nations with poor human rights records?

Narrowing a list

1. Put a check beside the issues that look most interesting to write about or the ones that mean the most to you.
2. Put a question mark beside the issues that you don't know very much about. If you choose one of these issues, you will probably have to do in-depth research—by talking to people, by using the Internet, or by going to the library.
3. Select the two or three issues that look most promising. For each issue, make lists:
   - Who is most interested in this issue?
   - Whom or what does this issue affect?

- What are the pros and cons of this issue? Make two columns. At the top of the left one, write "YES, because." At the top of the right one, write "NO, because."
- What has been written about this issue? How can you find out what has been written?

Explore Your Topic

When you identify a potential topic, make a quick exploration of that topic, much as you would walk through a house or an apartment you are thinking about renting for a quick look. One way of exploring is to visualize the topic by making a map.

If you live in a state on the coast that has a high potential for wind energy, you might argue that your state should provide financial incentives for generating more electricity from the wind. Perhaps it seems like a no-brainer to you because wind power consumes no fuel and causes no air pollution. The only energy required is for the manufacture and transportation of the wind turbines and transmission lines. But your state and other coastal states have not exploited potential wind energy for three reasons:

1. **Aesthetics.** Some people think wind turbines are ugly and noisy.
2. **Hazard to wildlife.** A few poorly located wind turbines have killed birds and bats.
3. **Cost.** Wind power costs differ, but wind energy is generally more expensive than electricity produced by burning coal.

To convince other people that your proposal is a good one, you will have to answer these objections.

Possible objections to wind energy

ugly and noisy

hazard to wildlife

higher cost
$$$

The first two objections are relatively easy to address. Locating wind farms 10 kilometers offshore keeps them out of sight and sound of land and away from most migrating birds and all bats. The third objection, higher cost, is more difficult. One strategy is to argue that the overall costs of wind energy and energy produced by burning coal are comparable if environmental costs are included. You can analyze the advantages and disadvantages of each by drawing maps.

Advantages/disadvantages of coal-fired power plants

PLUS
Lower retail cost

MINUS
Coal mining
destroys forests

MINUS
Hot water
kills fish

MINUS
Solid wastes

MINUS
Fuel costs because
coal must be transported

MINUS
Air emissions include
• carbon dioxide
• sulphur dioxide
• mercury
• arsenic
• carbon monoxide

Advantages/disadvantages of wind energy

PLUS
No air emissions

PLUS
Offshore wind farms
out of sight and hearing

PLUS
Offshore wind farms
not a wildlife hazard

MINUS
Higher retail cost

PLUS
No hot water

PLUS
No wastes

PLUS
No impact from mining
and transporting fuel

These maps can help you organize an argument for providing financial incentives for wind energy.

Read About Your Topic

Much college writing draws on and responds to sources—books, articles, reports, and other material written by other people. Every significant issue discussed in today's world has an extensive history of discussion involving many people and various points of view. Before you formulate a claim about a significant issue, you need to become familiar with the conversation that's already happening by reading widely about it.

One of the most controversial and talked-about subjects in recent years is the outsourcing of white-collar and manufacturing jobs to low-wage nations. Since 2000 an estimated 400,000 to 500,000 American jobs each year have gone to cheap overseas labor markets. The Internet has made this migration of jobs possible, allowing companies to outsource not only low-skilled jobs but highly skilled jobs in fields such as software development, data storage, and even examining X-rays and MRI scans.

You may have read about this or another complex and controversial topic in one of your courses. Just as in a conversation with several people who hold different views, you may agree with some people, disagree with some, and with others agree with some of their ideas up to a point but then disagree.

Fox Business Network news anchor Lou Dobbs has been sharply critical of outsourcing. In *Exporting America: Why Corporate Greed Is Shipping American Jobs Overseas* (2006), Dobbs blames large corporations for putting profits ahead of the good of the nation. He accuses both Republicans and Democrats of ignoring the effects of a massive trade deficit and the largest national debt in American history, which Dobbs claims will eventually destroy the American way of life.

Thomas Friedman, columnist for the *New York Times*, takes a different viewpoint on outsourcing in *The World Is Flat: A Brief History of the Twenty-first Century* (2006). By *flat,* Friedman means that the nations of the world are connected as never before through the Internet and the lowering of trade barriers, which puts every nation in direct competition with all the others. Friedman believes that outsourcing is not only unstoppable but also desirable. He argues that Americans need to adapt to the new reality and rethink our system of education, or else we will be left hopelessly behind.

If you decide to write an argument about the issue of outsourcing, you might use either Dobbs's or Friedman's book as your starting point in making a claim. After doing additional research, you could begin by taking on the role of **skeptic**, disagreeing with the author; the role of **contributor**, agreeing with the author and adding another point; or the role of the **analyst**, finding some points to agree with while disagreeing with others.

The skeptic: Disagreeing with a source

It's easy to disagree by simply saying an idea is dumb, but readers expect you to be persuasive about why you disagree and to offer reasons to support your views.

X claims that _____, but this view is mistaken because
_____.

Example claim for arguing against outsourcing resulting from free trade policies

Thomas Friedman claims that the world is "flat," giving a sense of a level playing field for all, but it is absurd to think that the millions of starving children in the world have opportunities similar to those in affluent countries who pay $100 for basketball shoes made by the starving children.

Example claim for arguing in favor of outsourcing resulting from free trade policies

Lou Dobbs is a patriotic American who recognizes the suffering of manufacturing workers in industries like steel and automobiles, but he neglects that the major cause of the loss of manufacturing jobs in the United States and China alike is increased productivity—the 40 hours of labor necessary to produce a car just a few years ago has now been reduced to 15.

The contributor: Agreeing with a source with an additional point

Sources should not make your argument for you. With sources that support your position, indicate exactly how they fit into your argument with an additional point.

I agree with _____ and will make the additional point that
_____.

Example claim for arguing against outsourcing resulting from free trade policies

Lou Dobbs's outcry against the outsourcing of American jobs also has a related argument: We are dependent not only on foreign oil, but also on foreign clothing, foreign electronics, foreign tools, foreign toys, foreign cars and trucks—indeed, just about everything—which is quickly eroding the world leadership of the United States.

> **Example claim for arguing in favor of outsourcing resulting from free trade policies**
>
> Thomas Friedman's claim that the Internet enables everyone to become an entrepreneur is demonstrated by thousands of Americans, including my aunt, who could retire early because she developed an income stream by buying jeans and children's clothes at garage sales and selling them to people around the world on *eBay*.

The analyst: Agreeing and disagreeing simultaneously with a source

Incorporating sources is not a matter of simply agreeing or disagreeing with them. Often you will agree with a source up to a point, but you will come to a different conclusion. Or you may agree with the conclusions, but not agree with the reasons put forth.

> I agree with _____ up to a point, but I disagree with the conclusion _____ because _____.
>
> **Example claim for qualifying the argument against outsourcing resulting from free-trade policies**
>
> Lou Dobbs accurately blames our government for giving multinational corporations tax breaks for exporting jobs rather than regulating the loss of millions of jobs, but the real problem lies in the enormous appetite of Americans for inexpensive consumer products like smart phones, tablet computers, and HD televisions that is supported by borrowing money from overseas.
>
> **Example claim for qualifying the argument in favor of outsourcing resulting from free-trade policies**
>
> Thomas Friedman's central claim that the world is being "flattened" by globalization and there is not much we can do to stop this from happening is essentially correct, but he neglects the social costs of globalization around the world, where the banner of free trade has been the justification for devastating the environment, destroying workers' rights and the rights of indigenous peoples, and ignoring laws passed by representative governments.

Find Good Reasons

Get in the habit of asking these questions every time you are asked to write an argument.

Can you argue by definition?

Probably the most powerful kind of good reason is an argument from **definition**. You can think of a definition as a simple statement: _____ *is a* _____. You use these statements all the time. When you need a course to fulfill your social-science requirement, you look at the list of courses that are defined as social-science courses. You find out that the anthropology class you want to take is one of them. It's just as important when _____ *is not a* _____. Suppose you are taking College Algebra, which is a math course taught by the math department, yet it doesn't count for the math requirement. The reason it doesn't count is that College Algebra is not defined as a college-level math class. So you have to enroll next semester in Calculus I.

Many definitions are not nearly as clear-cut as the math requirement. If you want to argue that figure skaters are athletes, you will need to define what an athlete is. You start thinking. An athlete competes in an activity, but that definition alone is too broad, since many competitions do not require physical activity. Thus, an athlete must participate in a competitive physical activity and must train for it. But that definition is still not quite narrow enough, because soldiers also train for competitive physical activity. You decide to add that the activity must be a sport and that it must require special competence and precision. Your *because* clause turns out as follows: *Figure skaters are athletes because true athletes train for and compete in physical sporting competitions that require special competence and precision.*

If you can get your audience to accept your definitions, you've gone a long way toward convincing them of the validity of your claim. That is why the most controversial issues in our culture—abortion, affirmative action, gay rights, pornography, women's rights, privacy rights, gun control, the death penalty—are argued from definition. Is abortion a crime or a medical procedure? Is pornography protected by the First Amendment, or is it a violation of women's rights? Is the death penalty just or cruel and inhuman? You can see from these examples that definitions often rely on deeply held beliefs.

Because people have strong beliefs about controversial issues, they often don't care about the practical consequences. Arguing that it is much cheaper to execute prisoners who have been convicted of first-degree murder than to keep them in prison for life does not convince those who believe that it is morally wrong to kill. (See Chapter 8.)

Can you argue from value?

A special kind of argument from definition, one that often implies consequences, is the argument from value. You can support your claim with a "because clause" (or several of them) that includes a sense of evaluation. Arguments from value follow from claims like _____ *is a good* _____, or _____ *is not a good* _____.

    Evaluation arguments usually proceed from the presentation of certain criteria. These criteria come from the definitions of good and bad, of poor and not so poor, that prevail in a given case. A great burger fulfills certain criteria; so does an outstanding movie, an excellent class, or the best laptop in your price range. Sometimes the criteria are straightforward, as in the burger example. A great burger has to have tasty meat—tender and without gristle, fresh, never frozen—a fresh bun that is the right size, and your favorite condiments.

    But if you are buying a tablet computer and want to play the latest games along with doing your school tasks, you need to do some homework. The best tablet for games will have realistic graphics and a fast processor. The apps you want should be readily available. And while tablets have become affordable, you will want the best value for your money. The keys for evaluation arguments are finding the appropriate criteria and convincing your readers that those criteria are the right criteria (see Chapter 10).

Can you argue from consequence?

Another powerful source of good reasons comes from considering the possible consequences of your position: Can you sketch out the good things that will follow from your position? Can you establish that certain bad things will be avoided if your position is adopted? If so, you will have other good reasons to use.

    Causal arguments take the basic form of _____ *causes* _____ (or _____ *does not cause* _____). Very often, causal arguments are more complicated, taking the form _____ *causes* _____ *which, in turn, causes* _____ and so on. In one famous example, environmentalist Rachel Carson in *Silent Spring* makes powerful arguments from consequence. Rachel Carson's primary claim is that *DDT should not be sprayed on a massive scale because it will poison animals and people.* The key to her argument is the causal chain that explains how animals and people are poisoned. Carson describes how nothing exists alone in nature. When a potato field is sprayed with DDT, some of that poison is absorbed by the skin of the potatoes and some washes into the groundwater, where it contaminates drinking water. Other poisonous residue is absorbed into streams, where it is ingested by insect larvae, which in turn are eaten by fish. Fish are eaten by other fish, which are then eaten by waterfowl and people. At each stage, the poisons become more concentrated. (See Chapter 9 for additional examples of causal arguments.)

Proposal arguments are future-oriented arguments from consequence. In a proposal argument, you cannot stop with naming good reasons; you also have to show that these consequences would follow from the idea or course of action that you are arguing. For example, if you are proposing designated lanes for bicycles on the streets of your city, you must argue that they will encourage more people to ride bicycles to work and school, reducing air pollution and traffic congestion for everyone. (See Chapter 13.)

Can you counter objections to your position?

Another good way to find convincing good reasons is to think about possible objections to your position. If you can imagine how your audience might counter or respond to your argument, you will probably include in your argument precisely the points that will address your readers' particular needs and objections. If you are successful, your readers will be convinced that you are right. You've no doubt had the experience of mentally saying to a writer in the course of your reading, "Yeah, but what about this other idea?"—only to have the writer address precisely this objection.

You can impress your readers if you've thought about why anyone would oppose your position and exactly how that opposition would be expressed. If you are writing a proposal argument for a computer literacy requirement for all high school graduates, you might think about why anyone would object, since computers are critical for our jobs and lives. What will the practical objections be? What about philosophical ones? Why hasn't such a requirement been put in place already? By asking such questions in your own arguments, you are likely to develop robust because clauses.

Sometimes, writers pose rhetorical questions. You might say, "But won't paying for computers for all students make my taxes go up?" Stating objections explicitly can be effective if you make the objections as those of a reasonable person with an alternative point of view. But if the objections you state are ridiculous ones, then you risk being accused of setting up a **straw man**—that is, making the position opposing your own so simplistic that no one would likely identify with it. (See Chapter 12.)

Find Evidence to Support Good Reasons

Good reasons are essential ingredients of good arguments, but they don't do the job alone. You must support or verify good reasons with evidence. Evidence consists of hard data, examples, personal experiences, episodes, or tabulations of episodes (known as statistics) that are seen as relevant to the good reasons you are putting forward. Thus, a writer of arguments puts forward not only claims and good reasons but also evidence that those good reasons are true.

How much supporting evidence should you supply? How much evidence is enough? As is usual in the case of rhetoric, the best answer is "It depends." If a reader is likely to find one of your good reasons hard to believe, then you should be aggressive in offering support. You should present detailed evidence in a patient and painstaking way. As one presenting an argument, you have a responsibility not just to *state* a case but to *make* a case with evidence. Arguments that are unsuccessful tend to fail not because of a shortage of good reasons; more often, they fail because the reader doesn't agree that there is enough evidence to support the good reason that is being presented.

If your good reason isn't especially controversial, you probably should not belabor it. Think of your own experiences as a reader. How often do you recall saying to yourself, as you read a passage or listened to a speaker, "OK! OK! I get the point! Don't keep piling up all of this evidence for me because I don't want it or need it." However, such a reaction is rare, isn't it? By contrast, how often do you recall muttering under your breath, "How can you say that? What evidence do you have to back it up?" When in doubt, err on the side of offering too much evidence. It's an error that is seldom made and not often criticized.

When a writer doesn't provide satisfactory evidence to support a because clause, readers might feel that there has been a failure in the reasoning process. In fact, in your previous courses in writing and speaking, you may have learned about various fallacies associated with faulty arguments (pages 16–19).

Strictly speaking, there is nothing false about these so-called logical fallacies. The fallacies most often refer to failures in providing evidence; when you don't provide enough good evidence to convince your audience, you might be accused of committing a fallacy in reasoning. You will usually avoid such accusations if the evidence that you cite is both *relevant* and *sufficient.*

Relevance refers to the appropriateness of the evidence to the case at hand. Some kinds of evidence are seen as more relevant than others for particular audiences. On the one hand, in science and industry, personal testimony is seen as having limited relevance, while experimental procedures and controlled observations have far more credibility. On the other hand, in writing for the general public on controversial issues such as gun control, personal experience is often considered more relevant than other kinds of data.

Sufficiency refers to the amount of evidence cited. Sometimes a single piece of evidence or a single instance will carry the day if it is especially compelling in some way—if it represents the situation well or makes a point that isn't particularly controversial. More often, people expect more than one piece of evidence if they are to be convinced of something.

If you anticipate that your audience might not accept your evidence, face the situation squarely. First, think carefully about the argument you are presenting. If you cannot cite adequate evidence for your assertions, perhaps those assertions must be modified or qualified in some way. If you remain convinced of your assertions, then think about doing more research to come up with additional evidence.

4 Drafting Arguments

QUICK TAKE

In this chapter, you will learn to

1. Think about your purpose (see page 40)
2. State, focus, and evaluate your thesis (see page 40)
3. Appraise your readers' knowledge and attitudes (see page 42)
4. Organize your argument using a formal or working outline (see pages 45–46)
5. Write a title, an introduction, and a strong conclusion (see pages 47–48)

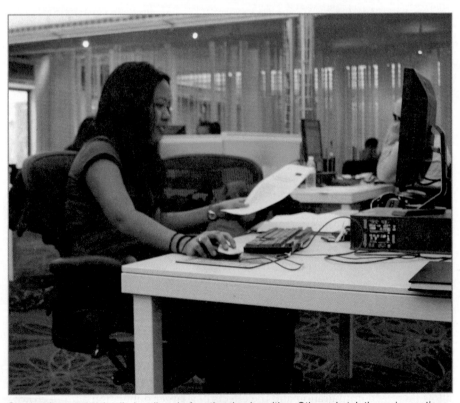

Some writers make detailed outlines before they begin writing. Others sketch the major sections and work from these notes. Still others start by freewriting and then identify key ideas and organize them. What is your most frequent planning strategy?

Think About Your Purpose

The first step in writing is to identify your purpose. When your instructor gives you a writing assignment, look closely at what you are being asked to do. Circle the information about the required length, the due dates, the format, and other requirements. You can attend to these details later.

Does your assignment contain words like *analyze, compare, define, evaluate, analyze causes,* or *propose* that signal your purpose? Identifying key terms can help you understand how to focus your argument. However, people rarely set out to define something in an argument just for the sake of definition, or to compare things simply for the sake of comparison. Instead, they have a purpose in mind, and they use the kinds of argument that are discussed in Chapters 8–13—most often in combination—as a means to an end. Most arguments use multiple approaches and multiple sources of good reasons.

State and Evaluate Your Thesis

Once you have identified a topic and purpose and have a good sense of how to develop your topic, the next critical step is to write a **working thesis**. Your **thesis** states your main claim. Much writing that you will do in college and later in your career will require an explicit thesis, usually placed near the beginning.

Focusing your thesis

The thesis can make or break your paper. If the thesis is too broad, you cannot do justice to the argument. Who wouldn't wish for fewer traffic accidents, better medical care, more effective schools, or a cleaner environment? Simple solutions for these complex problems are unlikely.

Stating something that is obvious to everyone isn't an arguable thesis. Don't settle for easy answers. When a topic is too broad, a predictable thesis often results. Narrow your focus and concentrate on the areas where you have the most questions. Those are likely the areas where your readers will have the most questions too.

The opposite problem is less common: a thesis that is too narrow. If your thesis simply states a commonly known fact, then it is too narrow. For example, the growth rate of the population in the United States has doubled since 1970 because of increased immigration. The U.S. Census Bureau provides reasonably accurate statistical information, so this claim is not arguable. But the policies that allow increased immigration and the effects of a larger population—more crowding and higher costs of health care, education, and transportation—are arguable.

Not arguable: The population of the United States grew faster in the 1990s than in any previous decade because Congress increased the rate of legal immigration and the government stopped enforcing most laws against illegal immigration in the interior of the country.

Arguable: Allowing a high rate of immigration helps the United States deal with the problems of an increasingly aging society and helps provide funding for millions of Social Security recipients.

Arguable: The increase in the number of visas to foreign workers in technology industries is the major cause of unemployment in those industries.

Evaluating your thesis

Once you have a working thesis, ask these questions.

- Is it arguable?
- Is it specific?
- Is it manageable given your length and time requirements?
- Is it interesting to your intended readers?

Example 1

Sample thesis

> *We should take action to resolve the serious traffic problem in our city.*

Is it arguable? The thesis is arguable, but it lacks a focus.

Is it specific? The thesis is too broad.

Is it manageable? Transportation is a complex issue. New highways and rail systems are expensive and take many years to build. Furthermore, citizens don't want new roads running through their neighborhoods.

Is it interesting? The topic has the potential to be interesting if the writer can propose a specific solution to a problem that everyone in the city recognizes.

When a thesis is too broad, it needs to be revised to address a specific aspect of an issue. Make the big topic smaller.

Revised thesis

> *The existing freight railway that runs through the center of the city should be converted to a passenger railway because this is the cheapest and quickest way to decrease traffic congestion downtown.*

Example 2

Sample thesis

> *Over 60 percent of Americans play computer games on a regular basis.*

Is it arguable? The thesis states a commonly acknowledged fact. It is not arguable.

Is it specific? The thesis is too narrow.

Is it manageable? A known fact is stated in the thesis, so there is little to research. Several surveys report this finding.

Is it interesting? The popularity of video games is well established. Nearly everyone is aware of the trend.

There's nothing original or interesting about stating that Americans love computer games. Think about what is controversial. One debatable topic is how computer games affect children.

Revised thesis

> *Computer games are valuable because they improve children's visual attention skills, literacy skills, and computer literacy skills.*

Think About Your Readers

Thinking about your readers doesn't mean telling them what they might want to hear. Instead, imagine yourself in a dialogue with your readers. What questions are they likely to have? How might you address any potential objections?

Understanding what your readers know—and do not know

Your readers' knowledge of your subject is critical to the success of your argument. If your readers are not familiar with the necessary background information, they probably won't understand your argument fully. If you know that your readers will be unfamiliar with your subject, you have to supply background information before attempting to convince them of your position. A good tactic is to tie your new information to what your readers already know. Comparisons and analogies can be very helpful in linking old and new information.

Finding Good Reasons

Should Talking While Driving Be Banned?

In a movement to improve driving safety, California, Connecticut, the District of Columbia, New Jersey, New York, Oregon, Utah, and Washington have passed laws banning the use of handheld cell phones while driving except for emergency workers and people making 911 calls. Several other states have banned cell phones while driving for drivers aged 18 and younger.

Proponents of the ban point to a National Highway Traffic Safety Administration study reporting that 25 to 30 percent of motor vehicle crashes—about 1.2 million accidents each year—are caused by driver distraction. Opponents of the ban argue that anything that distracts the driver—eating potato chips, talking with passengers, spilled coffee—can cause an accident. The answer, they say, is driver education.

Write about it

1. Write a thesis arguing in support of a ban on cell phones while driving, against a ban, or in support of a more limited position such as banning cell-phone use for drivers 18 and under.

2. Think about the audience that would tend to oppose your position. For example, if you support a ban on talking while driving, think about the likely responses of high school students, salespeople who spend much of their workday driving from place to place, and workers who receive assignments by phone. What good reasons would convince readers who hold an opposing view?

3. What reasons would people who oppose your position likely offer in response? What counterarguments could you give to answer these objections?

Understanding your readers' attitudes toward you

To get your readers to take you seriously, you must convince them that they can trust you. You need to get them to see you as

- **concerned:** Readers want you to be committed to your subject. They also expect you to be concerned about them. After all, if you don't care about them, why should they read what you write?
- **well informed:** Many people ramble on about any subject without knowing anything about it. College writing requires that you do your homework on a subject.
- **fair:** Many writers look at only one side of an issue. Readers respect objectivity and an unbiased approach.
- **ethical:** Many writers use only the facts that support their positions and often distort facts and sources. Critical readers often notice what is being left out. Don't try to conceal what doesn't support your position.

Understanding your readers' attitudes toward your subject

People have prior attitudes about controversial issues. You must take these attitudes into consideration as you write or speak. Imagine, for instance, that you are preparing an argument for a guest editorial in your college newspaper. You are advocating that your state government should provide parents with choices between public and private schools. You plan to argue that the tax dollars that now automatically go to public schools should go to private schools if parents so choose. You have evidence that the sophomore-to-senior dropout rate in private schools is less than half the rate in public schools. Furthermore, students from private schools attend college at nearly twice the rate of public school graduates. You intend to argue that one of the reasons private schools are more successful is that they spend more money on instruction and less on administration. And you believe that school choice speaks to the American desire for personal freedom.

Not everyone on your campus will agree with your position. How might the faculty at your college or university feel about this issue? How about the administrators, the staff, other students, and interested community members who read the student newspaper? What are their attitudes toward public funding of private schools? How are you going to deal with the objection that many students in private schools do better in school because they come from more affluent families?

Even when you write about a much less controversial subject, you must think carefully about your audience's attitudes toward what you have to say or write. Sometimes your audience may share your attitudes; other times, your audience may be neutral. At still other times, your audience will have attitudes that differ sharply from your own. Anticipate these various attitudes and act accordingly. If these attitudes are different from yours, you will have to work hard to counter them without insulting your audience.

Organize Your Argument

Asking a series of questions can generate a list of good reasons, but even if you have plenty, you still have to decide which ones to use and in what order to present them. Thinking about your readers' knowledge, attitudes, and values will help you to decide which reasons to present to your audience.

Writing plans often take the form of outlines, either formal outlines or working outlines. A **formal outline** typically begins with the thesis statement, which anchors the entire outline. Jenna Picchi created the following formal outline for an evaluation argument concerning organic foods. (You can read her final paper on pages 155–161.)

Organic Foods Should Come Clean

THESIS: The policy of producing and selling organic foods on a massive, industrial scale is not as good for the environment or consumers as producing and selling organic foods on a smaller scale. Although organic foods produced on an industrial scale are less expensive and more convenient, all industrial foods require massive use of fossil fuels to bring them to consumers and may be less sustainably produced.

   I. Open with personal anecdote about trying to shop organic near campus. End with claim.

  II. Give a specific example about issues related to industrial organic farming: the image of natural, healthy foods produced with traditional methods vs. reality of factory farms.

III. Look at industrial organic food industry:

    A. What is it?

    B. Why is it growing?

    C. What are its origins (the move from small organic to Big Organic)?

IV. State the first criterion: good organic food policy should produce healthy foods that are sustainably produced. Give reasons:

    A. Better for the environment.

    B. Better for individuals and public health.

    C. Better for taxpayers.

  V. State the second criterion: good policy should protect consumers and guarantee valid organic certifications.

    A. Organic standards are hard to police.

    B. Federal investigations have found major organic milk producers breaking rules.

    C. If the organic label isn't protected, customers won't trust it.

VI. State the third criterion: good policy avoids negative effects on small farms.
   A. Industrial organic companies help define organic standards.
   B. Industrial organic companies involved in setting prices.
   C. Local farms can be held accountable about standards and sustainability, earn consumer trust.
VII. Offer conclusion and perspective.

Alternatively, Picchi could have developed a **working outline**, which is a sketch of how to arrange an essay's major sections.

Organic Foods Should Come Clean

SECTION 1: Begin by discussing why consumers buy organic food. Describe the ways that organic foods are marketed to consumers and how the packaging on organic foods appeals to people's desire for better food. Contrast this common understanding of organic foods with the reality that organic foods are often produced by large industrial producers, owned by large corporations.

SECTION 2: One concern about the new trends in organic food production is that companies are using the organic label even when they don't support organic principles. The more agribusiness becomes a part of the organic food movement, the less the labels will mean. As the business evolves, the standards need to evolve to guarantee that the foods are sustainably produced and healthy and that consumers can trust organic labeling.

SECTION 3: As the organic standards change, they are hard to police, and there are several recent examples where the standards have been an issue. Many long-time organic farmers believe the large corporate farms are working to water down existing standards.

SECTION 4: Large corporate farms can outcompete smaller farms because they are more efficient, which means it is harder for consumers to find organic products that aren't produced by agribusiness.

SECTION 5: Good organic policy should have a positive impact on small producers, and small-scale farms have to be committed to sustainable practices. Consumers should be able to trust the producers of their food.

Write an Engaging Title and Introduction

Many writers don't think much about titles, but they are very important. A good title makes the reader want to see what you have to say. Be as specific as you can in your title, and if possible, suggest your stance.

Get off to a fast start in your introduction. Convince your reader to keep reading. Cut to the chase. Think about how you can get your readers interested. Consider using one of the following strategies.

- State your thesis concisely.
- Provide a hard-hitting fact.
- Ask a question.
- Give a vivid description of a problem.
- Discuss a contradiction or paradox.
- Describe a scenario.

Jenna Picchi decided to introduce her essay by using a personal anecdote in order to grab her readers' attention and develop her credibility by demonstrating her experience with her topic.

Organic Foods Should Come Clean

As a kid growing up not far from rural communities, I took for granted the access to local produce and the farm stands my family frequented. When I moved to a college town, I assumed I would have access to an even wider variety of foods and better choices. I wanted to continue eating organic as I had at home, even though it would be more work than a campus-dining plan. I learned quickly that even in a large college town, it takes determined searching in most supermarkets to find the organic produce, bread, meat, and dairy products that are scattered in less-trafficked corners of the store. Instead of shopping at the weekly farmer's market (which I cannot attend), I choose these supermarket fruits and vegetables from the lackluster and small display of things shipped in from California and Central America. Taking a recent look at these organic departments, I noticed that almost all the products are store or national brands. It never occurred to me that living in the middle of an agricultural state my choices would be so limited. After spending much time and energy seeking out organic products in stores all around town, I wondered whether the effort is worth it. How healthy are these foods in the local supermarket? And are these national brands as good for the environment as they seem?

Write a Strong Conclusion

Restating your thesis usually isn't the best way to finish a paper. Conclusions that offer only a summary bore readers. The worst endings say something like "in my paper I've said this." Effective conclusions are interesting and provocative, leaving readers with something to think about. Give your readers something to take away besides a straight summary. Try one of these approaches.

- Issue a call to action.
- Discuss the implications.
- Make recommendations.
- Project into the future.
- Tell an anecdote that illustrates a key point.

Picchi uses a call to action to conclude her essay on organic foods. Note how her conclusion also ties back to her introduction by mentioning college students.

> Small, local organic farmers are well positioned to deliver on the organic movement's original ideals of sustainably produced foods. Consumers should have a right to know where their food comes from and how organic standards are defined. In fact, as organic foods become more widely available to most consumers—even college students—it is worth questioning whether organic standards mean what they seem. Labeling foods organic cannot be just a marketing ploy, and the organic industry will continue to reach and inform more consumers if it can ensure this label has real meaning.

When you finish your conclusion, read your introduction again. The main claim in your conclusion should be closely related to the main subject, question, or claim in your introduction. If they do not match, revise the subject, question, or claim in the introduction to match the conclusion. Your thinking evolves and develops as you write, and often your introduction needs some adjusting if you wrote it first.

5 | Revising and Editing Arguments

QUICK TAKE

In this chapter, you will learn to

1. Evaluate your draft (see pages 49–51)
2. Respond to the writing of others (see pages 51, 53–54)
3. Revise your draft using outside feedback and your own analysis (see pages 54–55)
4. Edit and proofread carefully (see pages 55–56)

People frequently revise things that they own. What objects have you revised?

Evaluate Your Draft

To review and evaluate your draft, pretend you are someone who is either uninformed about your subject or informed but likely to disagree with you. If possible, think of an actual person and imagine yourself as that person.

Read your draft aloud all the way through. When you read aloud, you often hear clunky phrases and catch errors, but just put checks in the margins so you can return to them later. You don't want to get bogged down with the little stuff. What you are after in this stage is an overall sense of how well you accomplished what you set out to do.

Use the questions in the following Checklist to evaluate your draft. Note any places where you might make improvements. When you finish, make a list of your goals for the revision. You may have to write another draft before you move to the next stage.

Checklist for evaluating your draft

Does your paper or project meet the assignment?

- Look again at your assignment, especially at key words such as *analyze, define, evaluate,* and *propose.* Does your paper or project do what the assignment requires? If not, how can you change it?

- Look again at the assignment for specific guidelines including length, format, and amount of research. Does your work meet these guidelines? If not, how can you change it?

Do you have a clear focus?

- Underline your thesis. Think how you might make your thesis more precise.

- Underline the main idea of each paragraph. Check how each paragraph connects to your thesis. Think about how you can strengthen the connections.

Are your main points adequately developed?

- Put brackets around the reasons and evidence that support your main points.

- Can you explain your reasons in more detail?

- Can you add evidence to better support your main points?

Is your organization effective?

- Make a quick outline of your draft if you haven't already done so.

- Mark the places where you find abrupt shifts or gaps.

- Is the order of your main points clear?

- Are there sections or paragraphs that should be rearranged?

Do you consider your readers' knowledge and other points of view?

- Where do you acknowledge views besides your own?
- How can you make your discussion of opposing views more acceptable to readers who hold those views?
- Where do you give background if your readers are unfamiliar with your subject?
- Do you adequately define key terms that might be unfamiliar?

Do you represent yourself effectively?

- Forget for the moment that you wrote what you are reading. What is your impression of the writer?
- Is the tone of the writing appropriate for the subject?
- Are the sentences clear and properly emphatic?
- Did you choose words that convey the right connotations?
- Is the writing visually effective—easy to read with helpful headings and illustrations?

Respond to the Writing of Others

Your instructor may ask you to respond to the drafts of your classmates. Responding to other people's writing requires the same careful attention you give to your own draft. To write a helpful response, you should go through the draft more than once.

First reading

Read at your normal rate the first time through without stopping. When you finish, you should have a clear sense of what the writer is trying to accomplish. Try writing the following.

- **Main idea and purpose:** Write a sentence that summarizes what you think is the writer's main idea in the draft.
- **Purpose:** Write a sentence that states what you think the writer is trying to accomplish in the draft.

Finding Good Reasons

The Revision of Buildings and Places

The High Line operated from 1934 to 1980.

The High Line was unused for 25 years and fell into disrepair.

The first section of the new urban park opened in 2009.

In the 1930s, an elevated freight railway called the High Line was built in the industrial district of lower Manhattan to remove trains from New York City streets. The High Line cut through city blocks and ran directly through industrial buildings, where goods were loaded and unloaded without interrupting traffic. The rise of interstate trucking in the 1950s increasingly made the High Line obsolete, and in 1980, the High Line was used by a train for the last time. Some of the High Line was demolished, and surviving sections became overgrown with surprisingly adaptive weeds. In 1999, nearby residents formed Friends of the High Line and began lobbying to have the former railway converted to a park. The city, the state, and the railway owner eventually agreed to the development of the High Line as an urban park, and in 2009, the first section opened to the public. The park has been a huge success, bringing many people to visit and fostering new development in the surrounding Chelsea neighborhood.

The High Line is an example of a current trend of converting older structures such as warehouses, factories, railroads, airports, and docks that have outlived their usefulness to new uses. Rather than tearing down these structures, many are being converted to retail spaces, housing lofts, and museums. Likewise, many vacant parcels of land are being converted into parks.

Write about it

1. Identify an older building or space in your city, town, or campus that has been converted to a new use. How successful is the revision? One measure of success is how many people use the converted building or space. Not all revisions succeed. Go to the site and observe how many people visit and what they do when they get there.

2. Go to the oldest part of your city or town. Take a notebook or a tablet with you. Learn as much as you can about the history of a particular building or buildings through observing. Many buildings have visible signs of their past, such as the name of a former business on the front facade. Note as many details as you can identify. Then write about the history of the building or space from what you can infer from the details.

Second reading

In your second reading, you should be most concerned with the content, organization, and completeness of the draft. Make notes in pencil as you read.

- **Introduction:** Does the writer's first paragraph effectively introduce the topic and engage your interest?
- **Thesis:** What exactly is the writer's thesis? Is it clear? Note in the margin where you think the thesis is located.
- **Focus:** Does the writer maintain focus on the thesis? Note any places where the writer seems to wander off to another topic.
- **Organization:** Are the sections and paragraphs arranged effectively? Do any paragraphs seem to be out of place? Can you suggest a better order for the paragraphs?
- **Completeness:** Are there sections or paragraphs that lack key information or adequate development? Where do you want to know more?
- **Conclusion:** Does the last paragraph wrap up the discussion effectively?
- **Sources:** Are outside sources cited accurately? Are quotations used correctly and worked into the fabric of the draft?

Third reading

In your third reading, turn your attention to matters of audience, style, and tone.

- **Audience:** Who are the writer's intended readers? What does the writer assume the audience knows and believes?
- **Style:** Is the writer's style engaging? How would you describe the writer's voice?

- **Tone:** Is the tone appropriate for the writer's purpose and audience? Is the tone consistent throughout the draft? Are there places where another word or phrase might work better?

When you have finished the third reading, write a short paragraph on each bulleted item above. Refer to specific paragraphs in the draft by number. Then end by answering these two questions.

- What does the writer do especially well in the draft?
- What one or two things would most improve the draft in a revision?

Revise Your Draft

Once you have evaluated your draft and received feedback from others, it is time to revise. Revision is one of the most important steps in the writing process. Skilled writers know that the secret to writing well is rewriting. Work through your essay in detail looking for opportunities to address the issues you identified in your evaluation.

- **Keep your audience in mind.** Re-read the opening sentence of each paragraphs and ask yourself whether it is engaging enough to keep your readers interested. Rewrite accordingly.
- **Sharpen your focus whenever possible.** You may have started out with a large topic but now find that most of what you write concerns only one aspect. If so, revise your thesis and supporting paragraphs.
- **Check if key terms are adequately defined.** Locate your key terms. Are they defined precisely enough to be meaningful? Have you provided other necessary background information for your readers? Make the necessary adjustments.
- **Develop your ideas where necessary.** Key points and claims may need more explanation and supporting evidence. Look for new evidence that you can add without being redundant.
- **Check links between paragraphs.** Review any places where you make abrupt shifts and rewrite to make the transitions better. Make sure you signal the relationship from one paragraph to the next.
- **Consider your title.** Many writers don't think much about titles, but they are very important. A good title makes the reader want to see what you have to say. Be as specific as you can in your title, and if possible, suggest your stance.

- **Consider your introduction.** In the introduction you want to get off to a fast start and convince your reader to keep reading. Make sure your introduction cuts right to the chase.

- **Consider your conclusions.** Restating your thesis usually isn't the best way to finish; conclusions that offer only a summary bore readers. The words endings say something like "in my paper I've said this." Effective conclusions are interesting and provocative, leaving readers with something to think about. Rework your conclusion if necessary.

- **Improve the visual aspects of your text.** Is the font you selected easy to read? Would headings and subheadings help to identify key sections? If you include statistical data, would charts be effective? Would illustrations help to establish key points?

Edit and Proofread Carefully

When you finish revising, you are ready for one final careful reading with the goals of improving your style and eliminating errors.

Edit for style

- **Check connections between sentences and paragraphs.** Notice how your sentences flow within each paragraph and from paragraph to paragraph. If you need to signal the relationship from one sentence or paragraph to the next, use a transitional word or phrase (e.g., *in addition, moreover, similarly, however, nevertheless*).

- **Check your sentences.** Often you will pick up problems with individual sentences by reading aloud. If you notice that a sentence doesn't sound right, think about how you might rephrase it. If a sentence seems too long, consider breaking it into two or more sentences. If you notice a string of short sentences that sound choppy, consider combining them.

- **Eliminate wordiness.** Look for wordy expressions such as *because of the fact that* and *at this point in time*, which can easily be shortened to *because* and *now*. Reduce unnecessary repetition such as *attractive in appearance* or *visible to the eye* to *attractive* and *visible*. Remove unnecessary words like *very, really,* and *totally*. See how many words you can remove without losing the meaning.

- **Use active verbs.** Make your style more lively by replacing forms of *be* (*is, are, was, were*) or verbs ending in *-ing* with active verbs. Sentences that begin with *There is (are)* and *It is* can often be rewritten with active verbs.

Proofread carefully

In your final pass through your text, eliminate as many errors as you can. To become an effective proofreader, you have to learn to slow down. Some writers find that moving from word to word with a pencil slows them down enough to find errors. Others read backwards to force themselves to concentrate on each word.

You can get one-on-one help in developing your ideas, focusing your topic, and revising your paper or project at your writing center.

■ **Know what your spelling checker can and can't do.** Spelling checkers are the greatest invention since peanut butter. They turn up many typos and misspellings that are hard to catch. But spelling checkers do not catch wrong words (*to much* for *too much*), missing endings (*three dog*), and other similar errors.

■ **Check for grammar and punctuation.** Nothing hurts your credibility more than leaving errors in what you write. Many job application letters get tossed in the reject pile because of a single, glaring error. Readers probably shouldn't make such harsh judgments when they find errors, but often they do. Keep a grammar handbook beside your computer, and use it when you are uncertain about what is correct.

Analyzing Arguments

PART

2

6 Analyzing Written Arguments

QUICK TAKE

In this chapter, you will learn to

1. Define rhetorical analysis, including textual and contextual analysis (see below)
2. Analyze the rhetorical features of a specific argument (see page 59)
3. Analyze the appeals of logos, pathos, and ethos in a specific argument (pages 61–63)
4. Analyze the arrangement and style of a specific argument (see pages 63–64)
5. Appreciate how the rhetorical context shapes a specific argument (see pages 64–70)
6. Write an effective rhetorical analysis (see pages 70–72)

What Is Rhetorical Analysis?

To many people, the term *rhetoric* suggests speech or writing that is highly ornamental or deceptive or manipulative. You might hear someone say, "That politician is just using a bunch of rhetoric" or "The rhetoric of that advertisement is very deceiving." But *rhetoric* is also used these days in a positive or neutral sense to describe human communication; for instance, "*Silent Spring* is one of the most influential pieces of environmental rhetoric ever written." When we study rhetoric, we usually associate it with effective communication, following Aristotle's classic definition of rhetoric as "the art of finding in any given case the available means of persuasion."

Rhetoric is not just a means of *producing* effective communication. It is also a way of *understanding* communication. The two aspects mutually support one another: Becoming a better writer makes you a better interpreter, and becoming a better interpreter makes you a better writer.

Rhetorical analysis is the effort to understand how people attempt to influence others through language and more broadly through every kind of symbolic action—not only speeches, articles, and books, but also architecture, movies, television shows, memorials, Web sites, advertisements, photos and other images, dance, and popular songs. It might be helpful to think of rhetorical analysis as a kind of critical reading. Critical reading—rhetorical analysis, that is—involves studying carefully any kind of persuasive action in order to understand it better and to appreciate the tactics that it uses.

Build a Rhetorical Analysis

Rhetorical analysis examines how an idea is shaped and presented to an audience in a particular form for a specific purpose. There are many approaches to rhetorical analysis and no one "correct" way to do it. Generally, though, approaches to rhetorical analysis can be placed between two broad extremes—not mutually exclusive categories but extremes at the ends of a continuum.

At one end of the continuum are analyses that concentrate more on **texts** than on contexts. They typically use rhetorical concepts and terminologies to analyze the features of texts. Let's call this approach **textual analysis**. At the other extreme are approaches that emphasize **context** over text. These focus on reconstructing the cultural environment, or context, that existed when a particular rhetorical event took place. That reconstruction provides clues about the persuasive tactics and appeals. Those who undertake **contextual analysis** regard particular rhetorical acts as parts of larger communicative chains, or "conversations."

Now let's examine these two approaches in detail.

Analyze the Rhetorical Features: Textual Analysis

Just as expert teachers in every field of endeavor—from baseball to biology—devise vocabularies to facilitate specialized study, rhetoricians too have developed a set of key concepts to describe rhetorical activities. A fundamental concept in rhetoric is audience. But there are many others. Classical rhetoricians in the tradition of Aristotle, Quintilian, and Cicero developed a range of terms around what they called the canons of rhetoric in order to describe some of the actions of communicators: *inventio* (invention—the finding or creation of information for persuasive acts, and the planning of strategies), *dispostio* (arrangement), *elocutio* (style), *memoria* (the recollection of rhetorical resources that one might call upon, as well as the memorization of what has been invented and arranged), and *pronuntiatio* (delivery). These five canons generally describe the actions of any persuader, from preliminary planning to final delivery.

Over the years, as written discourse gained in prestige against oral discourse, four canons (excepting *memoria*) led to the development of concepts and terms useful for rhetorical analysis. Terms like *ethos*, *pathos*, and *logos*, all associated with invention, account for features of texts related to the trustworthiness and credibility of the writer or speaker (**ethos**), for the persuasive good reasons in an argument that derive from a community's mostly deeply held values (**pathos**), and for the good reasons that emerge from intellectual reasoning (**logos**). Fundamental to the classical approach to rhetoric is the concept of *decorum*, or "appropriateness": Everything within a persuasive act can be understood as reflecting a central rhetorical goal that governs consistent choices according to occasion and audience.

The statue of Castor stands at the entrance of the Piazza del Campidoglio in Rome. A textual analysis focuses on the statue itself. The size and realism of the statue makes it a masterpiece of classical Roman sculpture.

An example will make textual rhetorical analysis clearer. Let's look at the "Statement on the Articles of Impeachment" by Barbara Jordan at the end of this chapter, and at the student rhetorical analysis that follows it (pp. 73–80). In this chapter we use the fundamental concepts of rhetoric to better understand the presentation by Barbara Jordan.

Jordan's purpose and argument

What is the purpose of Jordan's speech? She presented it over forty years ago, but it remains compellingly readable because it concerns a perennial (and very contemporary) American issue: the limits of presidential power. In this case, Jordan argues in favor of bringing articles of impeachment against President Richard Nixon. She feels that the drastic step of impeachment is called for because President Nixon had violated the Constitution. Essentially, Jordan's argument comes down to this: Nixon, like any abuser of the Constitution, should be removed from office because he has been guilty of causing "the dimunition, the subversion, the destruction, of the Constitution" (para. 3 of Jordan's speech). The Founders of the nation established clear grounds for impeachment, and Nixon trespassed on those grounds by covering up crimes and by stonewalling efforts to investigate misdeeds. He "committed offenses, and planned and directed and acquiesced in a course of conduct which the Constitution will not tolerate" (para. 20). Jordan's speech amounts to a

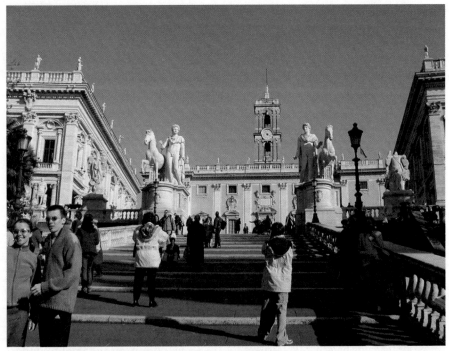

A contextual analysis focuses on the surroundings and history of the statue. According to legend, Castor (left of staircase) and his twin brother Pollux (right of staircase), the mythical sons of Leda, assisted Romans in an early battle. Romans built a large temple in the Forum to honor them. The statues were discovered in the sixteenth century and in 1583 were brought to stand at the top of the Cordonata, a staircase designed by Michelangelo as part of a renovation of the Piazza del Campidoglio commissioned by Pope Paul III Farnese in 1536.

definition of impeachment in general, based on the Constitution, which then calls for President Nixon's impeachment in particular. And she supports that overall argument with logical, emotional, and ethical appeals—logos, pathos, and ethos.

Logos

Jordan constructs her case in favor of impeachment through a carefully reasoned process. She begins by presenting a patient account of the meaning of impeachment as it appears in the Constitution, on which her "faith is whole; it is complete; it is total" (para. 3). The Constitution defines impeachment not as conviction but as a kind of indictment of a president for misconduct; once a president is impeached, a trial then follows, conducted by the House of Representatives and judged by the Senate. Only after conviction by two-thirds of the senators, after a fair trial, could the president be removed. (President Clinton was impeached while in office, but the Senate found him not guilty.) The Constitution offers grounds for impeachment only on very general terms: Article III, section 4, explains that presidents can be removed from office for treason, bribery, or other high crimes and misdemeanors.

Do Nixon's actions qualify as impeachable? Jordan must refer to the statements that the Founders made during the ratification process for the Constitution to lay out exactly what might be considered an impeachable high crime. After a lengthy explanation of what qualifies as impeachable—"the misconduct of public men" only in "occasional and extraordinary cases," and only "if the President be connected in any suspicious manner with any person and there [are] grounds to believe he will shelter him," and only if there are "great misdemeanors" and not simple "maladministration"—she then applies the definition to Nixon's actions. Carefully and systematically she offers the evidence. She ties "misconduct," the cover-up of crimes, and the sanctioning of other misdeeds to Nixon: "the President had knowledge that these funds were being paid" (para. 15); he consorted with a range of suspicious characters and "knew about the break-in of the psychiatrist's office" (para. 16); and he "engaged in a series of public statements and actions designed to thwart the lawful investigation of government prosecutors" (para. 17). The conclusion follows rationally and inevitably. The president must be impeached.

Pathos

The logical appeals in Jordan's speech are reinforced by her emotional appeals. Her repeated references to the Constitution have a strong emotional appeal. Because Americans have a deep respect for the Constitution, any attempt to undermine it must be resisted firmly and forcefully.

Perhaps the speech's most powerful emotional moment comes in the second paragraph. By bringing up the famous "We the people" opening of the Constitution early in the speech, Jordan rouses passions and brings listeners to her side. She calls attention to how she as an African American woman was originally left out of the Constitution because it defined citizens only as white males. The appeal to fair play certainly rouses emotions in her listeners; it gains considerable sympathy for Jordan.

You can probably note many other points in the speech that carry an emotional dimension. Jordan concludes her speech by rightly saying that "it is reason, and not passion, which must guide our deliberations, guide our debate, and guide our decision." But she also brings considerable pathos to bear on her argument. Jordan appeals to the whole person.

Ethos

Why do we take Jordan's word about the legal precedents and evidence that she cites? It is because she establishes her ethos, or trustworthiness, early in the essay and sustains it throughout. Jordan's scholarship establishes her credibility as a lawyer and as a citizen. Jordan comes through as a thorough professional, as an educated lawyer who has studied constitutional law and has done her homework, and as a deeply concerned citizen. Consequently, we can trust her word and trust her judgment. Particularly effective is her citation of the historical record on impeachment.

She has sifted the records to draw from the most respected of the framers of the Constitution—notably James Madison—and from authorities later in our national history. She buttresses her trustworthiness in other ways too:

- She quotes widely, if unobtrusively: by using precise quotations, she adds a trustworthy scholarly dimension to her presentation.
- She touches lightly on her own status as an African American woman to lend firsthand authority to what she has to say.
- She demonstrates a knowledge of history and constitutional law.
- She connects herself to America generally by linking herself to traditional American values such as freedom, ethnic pride, fair play, and tolerance.

Jordan knew that Nixon's supporters were depending on being able to make the case against Nixon into a partisan matter, Democrats vs. Republicans. So in her speech Jordan goes to great lengths to avoid being placed in a partisan camp and to be regarded as fair-minded. Overall, she comes off as hard-working, honest, educated and patriotic. And definitely credible.

Jordan's arrangement

We have already said some things about the arrangement of Jordan's speech. We especially noted how the overall structure follows the pattern of most definition arguments: Jordan offers her definition of impeachment and then in the final third of the talk applies that definition to the case of Richard Nixon. Note how she begins with an introductory comment about her personal situation; the tone of the first few sentences is light hearted as she offers gentle humor to "Mr. Chairman." And then she turns to a personal anecdote about her being left out of the Constitution "by mistake." In many ways, then, Jordan organizes very conventionally—she has a clear beginning, middle, and end.

And yet in other ways the arrangement is not so conventional. Rather than sticking with a light tone, Jordan turns deadly serious in paragraph 3. In the manner of a lawyer stating a legal case, a lawyer offering a final argument after evidence has been heard, she announces that her presentation will be based solely on constitutional law, and she then follows with point after point of a formal legal brief in favor of impeachment. Note that Jordan does not announce her conclusion early; just as if she were addressing a jury, she postpones her thesis ("If the impeachment provision in the Constitution will not reach the offenses charged here, then perhaps that 18th-century Constitution should be abandoned to a 20th-century paper shredder": para. 19) until the very end. Had she begun with such an explicit statement of her thesis, had she begun by stating her conclusion early, her speech might have been dismissed as a partisan speech and not a legal case.

Jordan's style

What about Jordan's style? How is it appropriate to her purposes? Would you describe it as "lawyerly" or not?

In one sense, Jordan speaks very much as a lawyer would speak to other lawyers. Her fourth paragraph, for example, consists solely of legal language—so legal that it is difficult for a layperson to understand where these quotations come from and what they mean. And further quotations from law cases show up as the speech continues. It is as if Jordan is addressing lawyers because she repeatedly uses legal terminology: "proceed forthwith"; "obfuscation"; "the powers relating to impeachment are an essential check in the hands of the body of the legislature against and upon the encroachments of the executive"; "the framers confided in the Congress the power, if need be, to remove the President"; "a narrowly channeled exception to the separation-of-powers maxim"; and so on.

And yet in another sense, Jordan is speaking in an accessible way to a larger audience of all Americans. Rather than sustaining the legal language, she speaks in simple sentences and simple cadences from beginning to the very end—from "Today I am an inquisitor. . . . My faith in the Constitution is whole; it is complete; it is total" to "That's the question. We know that. We know the question. . . . It is reason, not passion, which must guide our deliberations, guide our debate, and guide our decision." Whenever legal jargon threatens to take over, Jordan returns to everyday language accessible to all: "The Constitution doesn't say that"; "they [the framers] did not make the accusers and the judgers the same person"; "we are trying to be big because the task before us is a big one"; "we know the nature of impeachment. We've been talking of it awhile now." In sum, Jordan's style is in keeping with her ethos. Because she wishes to come off as both a concerned citizen and a legal expert, she chooses a style that is one part newspaper reporting—simple, straightforward, unadorned (in one spot she even misspeaks, substituting "attended" for "intended")—and one part legal brief, technical and jargony, full of convolutions and qualifications.

There is more to say about the rhetorical choices that Jordan made in crafting her "Statement on the Articles of Impeachment," but this analysis is enough to illustrate our main point. Textual rhetorical analysis employs rhetorical terminology—in this case, terms borrowed from the rhetorical tradition such as ethos, pathos, logos, arrangement, style, and tone—as a way of helping us to understand how a writer makes choices to achieve certain effects. And textual analysis cooperates with contextual analysis.

Analyze the Rhetorical Context

Communication as conversation

Notice that in the previous discussion, the fact that Barbara Jordan's "Statement on the Articles of Impeachment" was originally delivered before the House Judiciary Committee did not matter much. Nor did it matter when the speech was published

(July 24, 1974), who gave it, who exactly heard the speech, what their reactions were, or what other people were saying at the time. Textual analysis can proceed as if the item under consideration "speaks for all time," as if it is a museum piece unaffected by time and space. There's nothing wrong with museums, of course; they permit people to observe and appreciate objects in an important way. But museums often fail to reproduce an artwork's original context and cultural meaning. In that sense, museums can diminish understanding as much as they contribute to it. Contextual rhetorical analysis is an attempt to understand communications through the lens of their environments, examining the rough-and-tumble, real-world setting or scene out of which any communication emerges. Contextual analysis thus complements textual analysis; the two work together.

Contextual analysis, like textual analysis, may be conducted in any number of ways. But contextual rhetorical analysis always proceeds from a description of the **rhetorical situation** that motivated the event in question. It demands an appreciation of the social circumstances that call rhetorical events into being and that orchestrate the course of those events. It regards communications as anything but self-contained.

- Every communication is a response to other communications and to other social practices.
- Communications, and social practices more generally, reflect the attitudes and values of the living communities that sustain them.
- Analysts seek evidence of how those other communications and social practices are reflected in texts.

Rhetorical analysis from a contextualist perspective understands individual pieces as parts of ongoing conversations.

The challenge is to reconstruct the conversation surrounding a specific piece of writing or speaking. Sometimes it is easy to do so. For example, sometimes there are obvious references to the context in the very words of an argument. Or sometimes you may have appropriate background information on the topic, as well as a feel for what is behind what people are writing or saying about it. People who have strong feelings these days about the environment, stem cell research, college sports, or any number of other current issues are well informed about the arguments that are converging around those topics.

But other times it takes some research to reconstruct the conversations and social practices related to a particular issue. If the issue is current, you need to study how the debate is conducted in current blogs, magazines, newspapers, talk shows, movies and TV shows, Web sites, and so forth. If the issue is from an earlier time, you must do archival research into historical collections of newspapers, magazines, books, letters, and other documentary sources in order to develop a feel for the rhetorical situation that generated the argument under analysis. Archival research usually involves libraries, special research collections, or film and television archives where it is possible to learn quite a bit about context.

Let's return now to a discussion of Jordan's "Statement" on pages 73–76. With a bit of research it is possible to reconstruct some of the "conversations" that Jordan was participating in, and the result will be an enhanced understanding of her speech as well as an appreciation for how you might do a contextual rhetorical analysis yourself. As you will see, contextual analysis will permit you to understand the challenge that any writer or speaker was facing so that you can then discover what strategies and tactics were used in order to meet that challenge. What issues and questions were swirling about in the minds of the audience members when Jordan spoke, and how did she address those issues and questions?

Jordan's life and works

You can begin by learning more about Jordan herself because ethos is not simply a textual presence; ethos also can be something that a writer or speaker brings to a performance. The headnote to her speech on page 73 "Statement on the Articles of Impeachment" provides some facts about her (e.g., that she was African American, that she went to law school, that she was elected to the U.S. House of Representatives at the age of just 36; that she came to prominence during the Watergate hearings). The speech itself suggests a few additional details: that protecting the Constitution was a special passion of hers, and that she had a reputation for doing her homework. You can learn more about Jordan by using the Internet and your library's Web site. Jordan's credibility, her ethos, is established not just by the decisions she made within her speech but also by her prior reputation.

Perhaps the most relevant information concerning Jordan that is available online is about her early political career. Jordan was a relative unknown when she gave her speech; even her colleagues in Congress did not know her well. She had recently been elected to Congress as a young woman in part because of the support of Lyndon Johnson, a fellow Texan who preceded Richard Nixon as president. Johnson then advocated for her placement on the House Judiciary Committee, chaired by Democrat Peter Rodino of New Jersey; this was a highly prized, prestigious appointment that rarely goes to someone new. Thus Jordan came to her speech with a reputation as being beholden to Johnson and the Democratic party. Her challenge therefore was to avoid the appearance of partisanship—as we will show below, that explains many of her rhetorical choices. Then again, few Americans outside Washington and Texas knew of her reputation. She essentially delivered her speech to the nation and to her congressional colleagues as a relative unknown. (Incidentally, Jordan continued to serve in Congress until 1978, when she stepped down voluntarily, for health reasons.)

The context of the speech

In one sense, the audience of Jordan's speech consisted of the other thirty-four members of the House Judiciary Committee, gathered together to decide whether or not to recommend impeachment. And yet Jordan was not at all speaking to a closed committee meeting. Her speech was heard by a national audience watching on television.

The Senate Watergate hearings had been televised the summer before Jordan's speech, from May through July of 1973. Millions of Americans had become accustomed to watching sensational testimony presented by a host of witnesses. The hearings produced charges that President Nixon may well have authorized break-ins at Democratic campaign headquarters in Washington during the 1972 election season, that he and members of his leadership team covered up their sponsorship of the break-ins, and that the White House was involved in all sorts of other dirty tricks and improprieties.

Americans remained deeply divided about these accusations until it was discovered that Nixon had himself collected possible hard evidence. He had taped many conversations in the Oval Office, tapes that could support or refute the charges against the president. But for the next year, Nixon engaged in a protracted legal battle to keep the tapes from being disclosed, on the grounds that they were private conversations protected under "executive privilege." During that time Nixon's vice president, Spiro Agnew, was forced to resign, and a number of his advisers were indicted and convicted on charges of obstructing justice. Partial and edited transcripts of the tapes were produced sporadically by the president, under pressure, but those produced only further rancor, particularly when eighteen minutes of a key conversation were mysteriously erased.

These events created a continuing national uproar and sustained headlines that fueled discussion. The House Judiciary Committee opened hearings into whether the president should be impeached beginning on May 9 of 1974. Those closed meetings moved slowly, deliberately, and inconclusively through the entire summer. On July 24, 1974, the courts ruled that Nixon had to turn over all his remaining tapes. That same day, knowing that hard evidence was now at hand, the House Judiciary Committee immediately went into session to vote whether to impeach Nixon. In keeping with the Senate Watergate hearings, these sessions were open and televised to the nation. Each member of the committee was given fifteen minutes to make an opening statement that would be carried on television to the nation. Barbara Jordan was therefore speaking not just to congressional colleagues but to millions of citizens who had never heard of her but who were very interested in what she would have to say.

Jordan was scheduled to speak at 9 p.m.—prime time. The nation was ready to listen to her argument, and she was ready to deliver: she would call for impeachment, and she would do so in a way that was absolutely principled and nonpartisan.

The larger conversation

We could offer much more contextualizing background here. We could cite a host of articles, books, news reports, and TV broadcasts in order to establish the nature of the conversation about impeachment that was raging in the nation from the summer of 1973 until President Nixon finally resigned on August 8, 1974. Such an account would establish a rather simple point: The country was bitterly divided on three related issues.

The first was a question of partisanship. His fellow Republicans naturally gave the benefit of the doubt to President Nixon, and that benefit was quite considerable, given that Nixon had won the 1972 election over George McGovern in a landslide. By contrast, Democrats controlled the Senate and the House of Representatives, and they were aggressive in pursuing a case against the president because they stood to gain politically. (Indeed, Jimmy Carter would win the presidency in the 1976 election largely because he stood as an honest antidote to the scandal of Watergate.) But partisanship was not supposed to be an issue in an impeachment. When Andrew Johnson was impeached by the House during 1867–1868 (and narrowly acquitted by the Senate), it was apparent that his impeachment was politically motivated. In subsequent years, it therefore was understood that impeachment should never be partisan, should never be politically motivated but based on "treason, bribery, or high crimes and misdemeanors." In the weeks leading up to July 24, supporters of President Nixon, led by his lawyer James D. St. Clair, constantly charged that his adversaries were motivated by purely political purposes. Representative David Dennis of Indiana spoke explicitly of "a political lynching," Representative Charles Sandman of New Jersey and other Republicans had emphasized partisanship earlier in the day during their own 15-minute presentations, and millions of average citizens also suspected that opponents of Nixon wanted to remove him simply to gain political power. On a practical level, since Nixon could be convicted in the Senate only by a two-thirds majority, it was essential that some Republicans come to support conviction. A purely partisan vote—Democratic vs. Republicans—could not succeed.

Barbara Jordan's task was therefore formidable. She had to take the majority, Democratic position—without seeming to take it *because* she was a Democrat. And she had to do so even though she was indeed a committed Democrat, recently installed in part through the intercession of Lyndon Johnson and embodying her Democratic credentials because of her black skin. (Nixon had swept the Southern states in the 1972 election in part because he appealed directly to white voters there.) If you scan issues of *Newsweek*, *Time*, the *Washington Post*, or the *New York Times* from the summer of 1974, you will see how frequently the Republicans were claiming that President Nixon was the victim of a "partisan vendetta." It was the strategy of his defense team to do so. By contrast, Democrats needed to get at least a half-dozen Republican members of the House Judiciary Committee to support impeachment if the actual impeachment were to succeed in the Senate.

Jordan consequently adopted a number of tactics to establish her nonpartisanship. She begins by identifying herself as a youthful, junior member of the committee, not a Democratic member, and quickly follows by claiming particular and fervent allegiance to the Constitution, not to any political party. Speaking as a custodian of "the public trust," she quotes the Constitution, its framers, and respected authorities such as Alexander Hamilton, Woodrow Wilson, James Madison of them southerners—and avoids names with a partisan identification. And she consistently and frequently uses the pronoun *we* to refer to the entire committee, Republicans and Democrats alike. In all these ways Jordan sought to address the nation on nonpartisan grounds. (And she must have succeeded: over the next three days, when the House Judiciary Committee voted in favor of three articles of impeachment—obstruction of justice, abuse of presidential power, and contempt of Congress—six of the seventeen Republican committee members voted in favor of the first, six in favor of the second, and two supported the third article. Only ten of the seventeen Republicans opposed all three articles.)

The second concern in the nation on July 24, 1974, was about hard evidence. The president's former lawyer, John Dean, had accused Nixon of obstructing justice and conspiring to give hush money to Watergate burglars; Watergate gangster Charles Colson at his sentencing hearing had recently claimed that the president obstructed justice; and many other charges had been raised. But supporting evidence was seen as circumstantial; it all appeared to be the president's word against the word of others. The conversation swirling around Barbara Jordan, therefore, was very much concerned with hard evidence, or a so-called "murder weapon" or "smoking gun." Supporters of the president, including Representatives Trent Lott and Charles Wiggins on the Judiciary Committee, constantly claimed that while the charges against Nixon were serious, they were not corroborated by irrefutable evidence. (This claim was ultimately addressed by the tapes that Nixon had collected: earlier on the very day that Jordan spoke, the Supreme Court in an 8–0 vote demanded that Nixon turn over sixty-four tapes to investigators, and those tapes provided the damning evidence that finally brought Nixon to resign two weeks later. The Supreme Court decision is alluded to in the first sentence of paragraph 13, when Jordan mentions the "new evidence that would be forthcoming" because of what happened "today.")

In her speech, Jordan addresses the evidence question explicitly, beginning in paragraph 11: "we were told that the evidence which purports to support the allegations . . . is thin . . . [and] insufficient." The paragraphs that follow rehearse hard evidence already established—evidence about the break-ins and other crimes committed by Howard Hunt as well as payments to Hunt; evidence about the payment of hush money (para. 15); evidence cited in paragraphs 16 and 17, including that "the President has made public announcements and assertions bearing on the Watergate case which . . . he knew to be false." The emphasis on evidence in Jordan's speech definitely derives from the conversations that she was enmeshed in during July 1974.

The third national concern that Jordan addressed in her speech had to do with a legal issue, one that as a lawyer Jordan was especially qualified to address: Were the actions of President Nixon serious enough to be "impeachable offenses"? As the evidence of presidential wrongdoing piled up, many Americans could see that Nixon had committed all sorts of transgressions. But were they serious enough to justify impeachment? Everyone agreed that if the president had committed a felony, he should be removed; but what about lesser offenses—how high did a crime have to reach in order to be a "high crime," and what "misdemeanors" justified impeachment? As we have already shown in our textual analysis, Jordan in paragraph 6 defines the circumstances of impeachment by quoting the framers of the Constitution directly, and in paragraph 7 concedes that a president should not be removed for incompetence (i.e., "maladministration"). The following paragraphs indicate that public officials should not be removed for "petty reasons" but only for "the grossest offenses." By agreeing that a president should be removed only for very serious offenses, and by establishing that there was indeed hard evidence of the president's guilt in serious offenses, Jordan in just ten or twelve minutes summed up for the nation the case for impeachment. And as we have seen, she did it in a language that was convincing both to her congressional colleagues and to the millions of citizens watching at home.

Barbara Jordan's specific contribution to the conversation about impeachment in 1974 could be extended for a long time—indefinitely, in fact. There is no need to belabor the point, however; our purpose has been simply to illustrate that contextual analysis of a piece of rhetoric can enrich our understanding of it.

Write a Rhetorical Analysis

Effective rhetorical analysis, as we have seen, can be textual or contextual in nature. But we should emphasize again that these two approaches to rhetorical analysis are not mutually exclusive. Indeed, many if not most analysts operate between these two extremes; they consider the details of the text, but they also attend to the particulars of context. Textual analysis and contextual analysis inevitably complement each other. Getting at what is at stake in Barbara Jordan's speech on impeachment or any other sophisticated argument takes patience and intelligence. Rhetorical analysis, as a way of understanding how people argue, is both enlightening and challenging.

Try to use elements of both kinds of analysis whenever you want to understand a rhetorical event more fully. Rhetoric is "inside" texts, but it is also "outside" them: specific rhetorical performances are an irreducible mixture of text and context, and so interpretation and analysis of those performances must account for both text and context. Remember, however, the limitations of your analysis. Realize that your analysis will always be somewhat partial and incomplete, ready to be deepened, corrected, modified, and extended by the insights of others. Rhetorical analysis can itself be part of an unending conversation—a way of learning and teaching within a community.

Steps to Writing a Rhetorical Analysis

Step 1 Select an Argument to Analyze

Find an argument to analyze—a speech or sermon, an op-ed in a newspaper, an ad in a magazine designed for a particular audience, or a commentary on a talk show.

Examples

- Editorial pages of newspapers (but not letters to the editor unless you can find a long and detailed letter)
- Opinion features in magazines such as *Time*, *Newsweek*, and *U.S. News & World Report*
- Magazines that take political positions such as *National Review*, *Mother Jones*, *New Republic*, *Nation*, and *Slate*
- Web sites of activist organizations (but not blog or newsgroup postings unless they are long and detailed)

Step 2 Analyze the Context

Who is the author?

Through research in the library or on the Web, learn all you can about the author.

- How does the argument you are analyzing repeat arguments previously made by the author?
- What motivated the author to write? What is the author's purpose for writing this argument?

Who is the audience?

Through research, learn all you can about the publication and the audience.

- Who is the anticipated audience?
- How do the occasion and forum for writing affect the argument?

What is the larger conversation?

Through research, find out what else was being said about the subject of your selection. Track down any references made in the text you are examining.

- When did the argument appear?
- What other concurrent pieces within the "cultural conversation" (e.g., TV shows, other articles, speeches, Web sites) does the item you are analyzing respond to or "answer"?
- Think of the author of the item you are analyzing as facing a "challenge": what difficulties does the author have to overcome in order to persuade his or her audience?

Step 3 Analyze the Text

Summarize the argument

- What is the main claim?
- What reasons are given in support of the claim?

- How is the argument organized? What are the components, and why are they presented in that order?

What is the medium and genre?

- What is the medium? A newspaper? a scholarly journal? a Web site?
- What is the genre? An editorial? an essay? a speech? an advertisement? What expectations does the audience have about this genre?

What appeals are used?

- Analyze the ethos. How does the writer represent himself or herself? Does the writer have any credentials as an authority on the topic? How does the writer establish reliability and trust—or fail to do so?
- Analyze the logos. Where do you find facts and evidence in the argument? What kinds of facts and evidence does the writer present? Direct observation? statistics? interviews? surveys? quotations from authorities?
- Analyze the pathos. Does the writer attempt to invoke an emotional response? Where do you find appeals to important shared values? ·

How would you characterize the style?

- Is the style formal, informal, satirical, or something else?
- Are any metaphors or other rhetorical figures used?

Step 4 Write a Draft

Introduction

- Describe briefly the argument you are analyzing, including where it was published, how long it is, and who wrote it.
- If the argument is about an issue unfamiliar to your readers, supply the necessary background.

Body

- Analyze the context, following Step 2.
- Analyze the text, following Step 3.

Conclusion

- Do more than simply summarize what you have said. You might, for example, end with an example that typifies the argument.
- You don't have to end by either agreeing or disagreeing with the writer. Your task in this assignment is to analyze the strategies the writer uses.

Step 5 Revise, Edit, Proofread

For detailed instructions, see Chapter 5.
For a checklist to evaluate your draft, see pages 50–51.

Barbara Jordan

Statement on the Articles of Impeachment

Barbara Jordan (1936–1996) grew up in Houston and received a law degree from Boston University in 1959. Working on John F. Kennedy's 1960 presidential campaign stirred an interest in politics, and in 1966 Jordon became the first African American woman elected to the Texas State Senate. In 1972 she was elected to the United States House of Representatives and thus became the first African American woman from the South ever to serve in Congress. Jordan was appointed to the House Judiciary Committee. Soon she was in the national spotlight when that committee considered articles of impeachment against President Richard Nixon, who had illegally covered up a burglary of Democratic Party headquarters during the 1972 election. When Nixon's criminal acts reached the Judiciary Committee, Jordan's opening speech on July 24, 1974, set the tone for the debate and established her reputation as a moral beacon for the nation. Nixon resigned as president on August 9, 1974, when it was evident that he would be impeached.

Thank you, Mr. Chairman.

Mr. Chairman, I join my colleague Mr. Rangel in thanking you for giving the junior members of this committee the glorious opportunity of sharing the pain of this inquiry. Mr. Chairman, you are a strong man and it has not been easy, but we have tried as best we can to give you as much assistance as possible.

2   Earlier today, we heard the beginning of the Preamble to the Constitution of the United States: "We, the people." It's a very eloquent beginning. But when that document was completed on the seventeenth of September in 1787, I was not included in that, the people." I felt somehow for many years that George Washington and Alexander Hamilton just left me out by mistake. But through the process of amendment, interpretation, and court decision, I have finally been included in "We, the people."

3   Today I am an inquisitor. Any hyperbole would not be fictional and would not overstate the solemnness that I feel right now. My faith in the Constitution is whole; it is complete; it is total. And I am not going to sit here and be an idle spectator to the diminution, the subversion, the destruction, of the Constitution.

4   "Who can so properly be the inquisitors for the nation as the representatives of the nation themselves?" "The subjects of its jurisdiction are those offenses which proceed from the misconduct of public men." And that's what we're talking about. In other words, [the jurisdiction comes] from the abuse or violation of some public trust.

5   It is wrong, I suggest, it is a misreading of the Constitution for any member here to assert that for a member to vote for an article of impeachment means that that member must be convinced that the President should be removed from office. The Constitution doesn't say that. The powers relating to impeachment are an essential check in the hands of the body of the legislature against and upon the encroachments of the executive. [By creating] the division between the two branches of the legislature, the House and the Senate, assigning to the one the right to accuse and to the other the right to judge, the framers of this Constitution were very astute. They did not make the accusers and the judgers the same person.

6   We know the nature of impeachment. We've been talking about it awhile now. It is chiefly designed for the President and his high ministers to somehow be called into account. It is designed to "bridle" the executive if he engages in excesses. "It is designed as a method of national inquest into the conduct of public men." The framers confided in the Congress the power, if need be, to remove the President in order to strike a delicate balance between a President swollen with power and grown tyrannical, and preservation of the independence of the executive.

7   The nature of impeachment: [it is] a narrowly channeled exception to the separation-of-powers maxim. The Federal Convention of 1787 said that. It limited impeachment to high crimes and misdemeanors and discounted and opposed the term *maladministration*. "It is to be used only for great misdemeanors," so it was said in the North Carolina ratification convention. And in the Virginia ratification convention: "We do not trust our liberty to a particular branch. We need one branch to check the other."

8   "No one need be afraid"—the North Carolina ratification convention—"No one need be afraid that officers who commit oppression will pass with immunity." "Prosecutions of impeachments will seldom fail to agitate the passions of the whole community," said Hamilton in the Federalist Papers, number 65. "We divide into parties more or less friendly or inimical to the accused." I do not mean political parties in that sense.

9   The drawing of political lines goes to the motivation behind impeachment; but impeachment must proceed within the confines of the constitutional term "high crime[s] and misdemeanors." Of the impeachment process, it was Woodrow Wilson who said that "Nothing short of the grossest offenses against the plain law of the land will suffice to give them speed and effectiveness. Indignation so great as to overgrow party interest may secure a conviction; but nothing else can."

10   Common sense would be revolted if we engaged upon this process for petty reasons. Congress has a lot to do: Appropriations, Tax Reform, Health Insurance, Campaign Finance Reform, Housing, Environmental Protection, Energy Sufficiency, Mass Transportation. Pettiness cannot be allowed to stand in the face of such overwhelming problems. So today we are not being petty. We are trying to be big, because the task we have before us is a big one.

11   This morning, in a discussion of the evidence, we were told that the evidence which purports to support the allegations of misuse of the CIA by the President is thin.

We're told that that evidence is insufficient. What that recital of the evidence this morning did not include is what the President did know on June the 23rd, 1972.

12   The President did know that it was Republican money, that it was money from the Committee for the Re-Election of the President, which was found in the possession of one of the burglars arrested on June the 17th. What the President did know on the 23rd of June was the prior activities of E. Howard Hunt, which included his participation in the break-in of Daniel Ellsberg's psychiatrist, which included Howard Hunt's participation in the Dita Beard ITT affair, which included Howard Hunt's fabrication of cables designed to discredit the Kennedy Administration.

13   We were further cautioned today that perhaps these proceedings ought to be delayed because certainly there would be new evidence forthcoming from the President of the United States. There has not even been an obfuscated indication that this committee would receive any additional materials from the President. The committee subpoena is outstanding, and if the President wants to supply that material, the committee sits here. The fact is that only yesterday, the American people waited with great anxiety for eight hours, not knowing whether their President would obey an order of the Supreme Court of the United States.

14   At this point, I would like to juxtapose a few of the impeachment criteria with some of the actions the President has engaged in. Impeachment criteria: James Madison, from the Virginia ratification convention: "If the President be connected in any suspicious manner with any person and there be grounds to believe that he will shelter him, he may be impeached."

15   We have heard time and time again that the evidence reflects the payment to the defendants of money. The President had knowledge that these funds were being paid and these were funds collected for the 1972 presidential campaign. We know that the President met with Mr. Henry Petersen 27 times to discuss matters related to Watergate, and immediately thereafter met with the very persons who were implicated in the information Mr. Petersen was receiving. The words are: "If the President is connected in any suspicious manner with any person and there be grounds to believe that he will shelter that person, he may be impeached."

16   Justice Story: "Impeachment is intended for occasional and extraordinary cases where a superior power acting for the whole people is put into operation to protect their rights and rescue their liberties from violations." We know about the Huston plan. We know about the break-in of the psychiatrist's office. We know that there was absolute complete direction on September 3rd when the President indicated that a surreptitious entry had been made in Dr. Fielding's office, after having met with Mr. Ehrlichman and Mr. Young. "Protect their rights." "Rescue their liberties from violation."

17   The Carolina ratification convention impeachment criteria: those are impeachable "who behave amiss or betray their public trust." Beginning shortly after the Watergate break-in and continuing to the present time, the President has engaged in a series of public statements and actions designed to thwart the lawful investigation by government prosecutors. Moreover, the President has made public announcements and assertions bearing on the Watergate case, which the evidence will show he knew to be false. These assertions, false assertions, impeachable, those who misbehave. Those who "behave amiss or betray the public trust."

18   James Madison again at the Constitutional Convention: "A President is impeachable if he attempts to subvert the Constitution." The Constitution charges the President
with the task of taking care that the laws be faithfully executed, and yet the President
has counseled his aides to commit perjury, willfully disregard the secrecy of grand jury
proceedings, conceal surreptitious entry, attempt to compromise a federal judge, while
publicly displaying his cooperation with the processes of criminal justice. "A President is
impeachable if he attempts to subvert the Constitution."

19   If the impeachment provision in the Constitution of the United States will not
reach the offenses charged here, then perhaps that 18th-century Constitution should
be abandoned to a 20th-century paper shredder.

20   Has the President committed offenses, and planned, and directed, and acquiesced in a course of conduct which the Constitution will not tolerate? That's the question. We know that. We know the question. We should now forthwith proceed to answer
the question. It is reason, and not passion, which must guide our deliberations, guide
our debate, and guide our decision.

21   I yield back the balance of my time, Mr. Chairman.

Sample Student Rhetorical Analysis

T. Jonathan Jackson

Dr. Netaji

English 1102

11 October 2013

An Argument of Reason and Passion: Barbara Jordan's

"Statement on the Articles of Impeachment"

Barbara Jordan's July 24, 1974 speech before the U.S. House
Judiciary Committee helped convince the House of Representatives,
and the American public, that President Richard Nixon should be
impeached. Nixon was under investigation for his role in the cover-up of
the Watergate scandal. He knew about the burglary of Democratic Party
headquarters, but denied having any knowledge of it and illegally shielded
those responsible. Jordan used her speech to argue that the president
should be impeached because his actions threatened the Constitution and
the people of the United States; however, Jordan never explicitly states
this position in her speech. Instead, she establishes her credibility
and then uses logic to set out the evidence against the president.

> Jackson provides background information in the first paragraph and his thesis at the end.

In one sense, the audience of Jordan's speech consisted of the
other 34 members of the House Judiciary Committee, gathered together
to decide whether or not to recommend impeachment. And yet Jordan was
not speaking just to a committee meeting; her speech was very public.

The Senate Watergate hearings had been televised during the
months before her speech, and millions of Americans watched sensational
testimony by a host of witnesses. The Senate hearings produced charges
that Nixon authorized break-ins at Democratic campaign headquarters
in Washington during the 1972 election and that the White House was
involved in many political dirty tricks and improprieties.

But the accusations remained only accusations—and Americans
remained deeply divided about them—until it was discovered that
Nixon had himself collected possible hard evidence: he had taped many
conversations in the Oval Office, tapes that could support or refute the
charges against the president. Nixon engaged in a protracted legal battle to
keep the tapes from being disclosed, on the grounds that they were private

Jackson 2

conversations protected under "executive privilege," and he released only partial and edited transcripts. Finally on July 24, 1974, the courts ruled that Nixon had to turn all his remaining tapes over. That same day, knowing that hard evidence was now at hand, the House Judiciary Committee immediately went into session to vote whether to impeach Nixon. Each member of the committee was given fifteen minutes for an opening statement.

Nixon was a Republican and Jordan, like the majority of the committee, was a Democrat. Jordan had to convince her audience she was not biased against the president simply because of her party affiliation. Jordan was also new to Congress, relatively unknown outside of Texas, and a low-ranking member of the committee. Consequently, she had to establish her ethos to the committee as well as to the television audience. She had to present herself as fair, knowledgeable, and intellectually mature.

> Jackson observes that Jordan had a formidable assignment in establishing her ethos in a short speech.

At the heart of Jordan's argument is her faith in the Constitution. She begins her speech from a personal perspective, pointing out that the Constitution is not perfect because it originally excluded African Americans like her. But now that the Constitution recognizes her as a citizen, Jordan says, her faith in it "is whole; it is complete; it is total." She even implies that, as a citizen, she has a moral duty to protect the Constitution, saying, "I am not going to sit here and be an idle spectator to the diminution, the subversion, the destruction of the Constitution." Jordan's emotional connection to the Constitution shows the audience that she is motivated by a love of her country, not by party loyalty. She establishes herself as someone fighting to defend and protect American values.

> Jackson analyzes how Jordan's fervent allegiance to the Constitution made her appear unbiased.

Jordan describes the Constitution as the accepted authority on the laws related to impeachment. She shows the audience how the Constitution gives her the authority to act as an "inquisitor," or judge. She depicts the Constitution and the American people as potential victims, and the president as the potential criminal. She warns of the need to remove "a President swollen with power and grown tyrannical."

The appeals to pathos and ethos in the opening of the speech establish Jordan's motivations and credibility, allowing her to next lay out her logical arguments. Jordan proceeds to explain how the Constitution defines impeachment, and she fleshes out this brief definition with

Jackson 3

evidence from several state Constitutional Conventions. She also quotes Supreme Court Justice Joseph Story. Using evidence from the North Carolina and Virginia Constitutional Conventions, Jordan shows that impeachment was intended only for "great misdemeanors," and that the branches of government were intended to act as a check upon one another.

Next Jordan uses quotations from James Madison, Justice Story, and others to define impeachable offenses. For each offense, Jordan provides an example of an act that President Nixon was known to have committed, and she shows how his actions meet the definition of impeachable offenses. She compares Nixon's meetings with Watergate suspects to Madison's statement that "if the President is connected in any suspicious manner with any person and there be grounds to believe that he will shelter that person, he may be impeached." She pairs Justice Story's statement that impeachment should "protect [citizens'] rights and rescue their liberties from violation" with Nixon's knowledge of the burglary of a private psychiatrist's office. She links Nixon's attempts to bribe a judge and thwart grand jury proceedings with Madison's statement that "a President is impeachable if he attempts to subvert the Constitution."

> Jordan uses quotations from respected figures in American history to apply to Nixon's misdeeds.

> Jordan had to confront a legal issue: Were the actions of President Nixon serious enough to justify impeachment?

Throughout this section, Jordan repeats the historical quotes before and after her descriptions of the president's acts. This repetition makes the connections stronger and more memorable for the audience. Jordan also contrasts the formal, high-toned language of the Founders and the Constitution with descriptions that make President Nixon's actions sound sordid and petty: He knew about money "found in the possession of one of the burglars arrested on June the 17th," about "the break-in of Daniel Ellsberg's psychiatrist," about "the fabrication of cables designed to discredit the Kennedy Administration." Words like "burglars," "arrested," "break-in," and "fabrication" sound like evidence in a criminal trial. These words are not the kind of language Americans want to hear describing the actions of their president.

Jordan then adds another emotional appeal, implying that the Constitution is literally under attack. "If the impeachment provisions will not reach the offenses charged here," she says, "then perhaps that 18th-century Constitution should be abandoned to a 20th-century paper

Jackson 4

shredder." This dramatic image encourages the audience to imagine President Nixon shredding the Constitution just as he had destroyed other evidence implicating him in the Watergate scandal. It implies that if the president is not stopped, he will commit further abuses of power. Jordan also makes the American people responsible for this possible outcome, saying that "we" may as well shred the Constitution if it cannot be used to impeach Nixon. This emotional appeal has the effect of shaming those who say they cannot or should not vote for impeachment.

> Jackson notes that the metaphor of the paper shredder adds emotional force.

Jordan concludes her speech not by calling for impeachment, but by calling for an answer to the question, "Has the President committed offenses, and planned, and directed, and acquiesced in a course of conduct which the Constitution will not tolerate?" It almost seems like Jordan is being humble and trying not to judge by not stating her position outright. However, the reverse is true: Jordan doesn't state her position because she doesn't need to. The evidence she presented led Congress and the American public inescapably to one conclusion: President Nixon had committed impeachable offenses. Just two weeks later, Nixon resigned from office. Jordan had made her point.

> In his conclusion Jackson points out how Jordan shifts the focus to her audience in her conclusion.

Jackson 5

Works Cited

Jordan, Barbara. "Statement on the Articles of Impeachment." *American Rhetoric: Top 100 Speeches*. American Rhetoric, 25 July 1974. Web. 25 Sept. 2013.

7 | Analyzing Visual and Multimedia Arguments

QUICK TAKE

In this chapter, you will learn to

1. Distinguish how visual arguments are similar to and different from verbal arguments (see below)
2. Critically evaluate photos and videos, charts and graphs, and informational graphics used as evidence (see page 85)
3. Evaluate any specific visual argument by analyzing its context and its visual and textual elements (see pages 87–92)
4. Write an effective visual analysis (see page 92)

What Is a Visual Argument?

We live in a world flooded with images. They pull on us, compete for our attention, push us to do things. But how often do we think about how they work?

Can there be an argument without words?

Arguments in written language are visual in one sense: we use our eyes to read the words on the page. But without words, can there be a visual argument? Certainly some visual symbols take on conventional meanings. Signs in airports or other public places, for example, are designed to communicate with speakers of many languages.

Some visual symbols even make explicit claims. A one-way street sign says that drivers should travel only in the one direction. But are such signs arguments? In Chapter 3, we point out that scholars of argument do not believe that every-thing *is* an argument. Most scholars define an argument as a claim supported by one or more reasons. A one-way sign has a claim: All drivers should go in the same direction. But is there a reason? We all know an unstated reason the sign carries: Drivers who go the wrong way violate the law and risk a substantial fine (plus they risk a head-on collision with other drivers).

Visual arguments require viewer participation

The *Deepwater Horizon* oil spill (also known as the BP oil spill) was the largest off-shore oil spill in the history of the United States. Caused by an explosion on April 20, 2010, the spill dumped millions of gallons of oil every day for months in spite of efforts to contain it. People around the world were reminded of the spill when they turned on their televisions and saw video of the oil gushing from the well, and nearly everyone was outraged.

People interpreted the oil flowing from the pipe quite differently, inferring multiple *because* clauses. Citizens were angry for different reasons.

The *Deepwater Horizon* oil spill was a disaster because

- eleven workers were killed and seventeen were injured.
- enormous harm was done to Gulf wetlands, birds, fish, turtles, marine mammals, and other animals.
- the tourism industry suffered another major blow just five years after Hurricane Katrina.
- the fishing and shrimping industries suffered huge losses.

The main oil leak from the *Deepwater Horizon* wellhead.

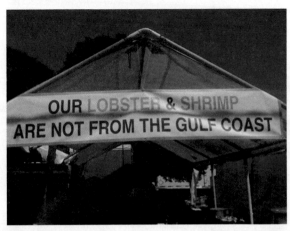

A photo of this booth at the Taste of Chicago sent on *Twitter* enraged people in New Orleans.

- President Obama declared a moratorium on deep-water drilling, threatening the loss of jobs.
- BP and its partners were negligent in drilling the well.
- the spill was an unfortunate act of God like Hurricane Katrina.

Differing interpretations of visual arguments extended beyond the spill itself. A news producer in Chicago took a photo (above) of a booth at the Taste of Chicago festival and sent it to a friend in New Orleans, who sent it to a food writer, who posted it on *Twitter*. The mayor of New Orleans called it "disgraceful."

Talks shows in both Chicago and New Orleans ranted for a few days about the other city. One comment was perhaps telling about the source of the rage: A menu disclaimer would have been acceptable, but a prominent visual argument, even in text form, was hitting below the belt.

What Is a Multimedia Argument?

Multimedia describes the use of multiple content forms including text, voice and music audio, video, still images, animation, and interactivity. Multimedia goes far back in human history (texts and images were combined at the beginnings of writing), but digital technologies and the Web have made multimedia the fabric of our daily lives. But what exactly are multimedia arguments?

For example, games provide intense multimedia experiences, but are they arguments? Game designers such as Jane McGonigal believe they are arguments. McGonigal maintains that games make people more powerful because they connect them into larger wholes.

Images from Michael Wesch's *A Vision of Students Today.*

Thousands of multimedia arguments have been posted on *YouTube*. One frequently viewed video is Michael Wesch's *A Vision of Students Today*, posted in October 2007. Wesch's point is that today's education is ill-suited for most students. He enlisted his students to make the point with text and video.

Analyze Visual Evidence

Videos without narration, images, and graphics seldom make arguments on their own, but they are frequently used to support arguments.

Evaluate photographs and videos as evidence

Almost from the beginnings of photography, negatives were manipulated but realistic results required a high skill level. In the digital era anyone can alter photographs. Perhaps there's nothing wrong with using Photoshop to add absent relatives to family photographs or remove ex-boyfriends and ex-girlfriends. But where do you draw the line? Not only do many videos on *YouTube* use outright deception, but newsmagazines and networks have also been found guilty of these practices.

Ask questions about what you view.

- Who created the image or video? What bias might the creator have?
- Who published the image or video? What bias might the publisher have?
- Who is the intended audience? For example, political videos often assume that the viewers hold the same political views as the creators.
- What is being shown, and what is not being shown? For example, a video ad promoting tourism for the Gulf of Mexico will look very different from a video showing sources of pollution.
- Who is being represented, and who is not being represented? Who gets left out is as important as who gets included.

The ease of cropping digital photographs reveals an important truth about photography: A photograph represents reality from a particular viewpoint. A high-resolution picture of a crowd can be divided into many smaller images each of which says something different about the event. The act of pointing the camera in one direction and not in another shapes how photographic evidence will be interpreted. (See the examples on page 86.)

Evaluate charts and graphs

Statistical information is frequently used as evidence in arguments. The problem with giving many statistics in sentence form, however, is that readers shortly lose track of the numbers. Charts and graphs present statistics visually, allowing readers to take in trends and relationships at a glance.

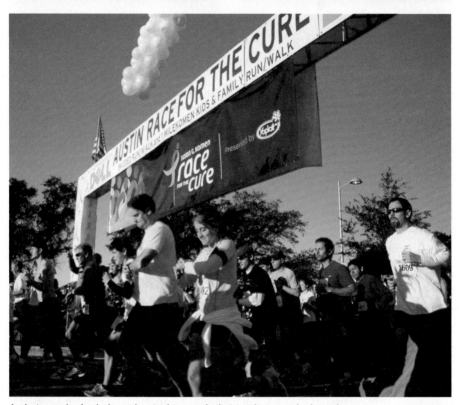

A photographer's choices about whom and what to photograph shape how we see an event.

However, charts and graphs can also be misleading. For example, a chart that compares the amounts of calories in competing brands of cereal might list one with 70 calories and another with 80 calories. If the chart begins at zero, the difference looks small. But if the chart starts at 60, the brand with 80 calories appears to have twice the calories of the brand with 70. Furthermore, the chart is worthless if the data are inaccurate or come from an unreliable source. Creators of charts and graphs have an ethical obligation to present data as fairly and accurately as possible and to provide the sources of the data.

Ask these questions when you are analyzing charts and graphs

- Is the type of chart appropriate for the information presented?

 Bar and column charts make comparisons in particular categories. If two or more charts are compared, the scales should be consistent.

 Line graphs plot variables on a vertical and a horizontal axis. They are useful for showing proportional trends over time.

 Pie charts show the proportion of parts in terms of the whole. Segments must add up to 100 percent of the whole.

- Does the chart have a clear purpose?
- Does the title indicate the purpose?
- What do the units represent (dollars, people, voters, percentages, and so on)?
- What is the source of the data?
- Is there any distortion of information?

Evaluate informational graphics

Informational graphics more sophisticated than standard pie and bar charts have become a popular means of conveying information. Many are interactive, allowing viewers of a Web site to select the information they want displayed. These information graphics are a form of narrative argument, and the stories they tell have a rhetorical purpose. (See the examples on page 88.)

Build a Visual Analysis

It's one thing to construct a visual argument yourself; it's another thing to analyze visual arguments that are made by someone else. Fortunately, analyzing arguments made up of images and graphics is largely a matter of following the same strategies for rhetorical analysis that are outline in Chapter 6—except that you must analyze images instead of (or in addition to) words. To put it another way, when you analyze

Education: East Side vs. West Side

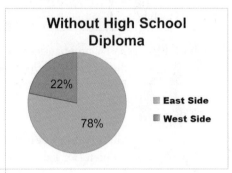

Without High School Diploma

22%

78%

East Side

West Side

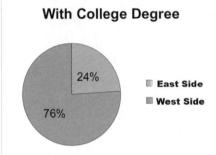

With College Degree

24%

76%

East Side

West Side

Starbucks Locations: East Side vs. West Side

West Side

East Side

As of April 2012

Charts can make points vividly. In a comparison of the east side and west side of a city, the unequal number of Starbucks locations has a high correlation with the education level of the residents.

Ad for Hofstra University, 1989

a visual argument, think about the image itself as well as its relationship to other images (and discourses). The arguments implied by visual images, like the arguments made through text alone, are carried both by the context and by the image.

Analyze context

A critical analysis of a visual image, like the analyses of written arguments that we discuss in the previous chapter, must include a consideration of context. Consider, for example, the above advertisement for Hofstra University. The context for the ad is not difficult to uncover through a bit of research. The ad appeared in 1989 and 1990, when Hofstra, located on Long Island 25 miles from New York City, was celebrating its fiftieth anniversary and hoping to use the occasion to enhance its esteem. At the time, Hofstra enjoyed a good reputation for its professional programs, particularly in education and business (which one-third of the 7,500 students were majoring in). However, it was not as highly regarded in the core science and humanities disciplines that are often associated with institutional prestige. In addition, Hofstra was quite well known in the New York metropolitan area—half its students were commuting to school rather than living in dormitories—but it was not attracting many students from outside the region, and its campus life was consequently regarded as mediocre. Its student body was generally well prepared, hardworking, and capable, but its most outstanding applicants were too often choosing other universities.

Feeling that its performance was exceeding its reputation and that it was capable of attracting a more diverse and talented student body, Hofstra developed a national ad campaign designed to change the opinions of prospective students and their parents, as well as the general public. It placed the ads—the ad reproduced here is one of a series—in several magazines and newspapers in order to persuade people that Hofstra was an outstanding university not just in the professions but in all fields, and that the opportunities available to its students were varied and valuable.

Analyze visual and textual elements

Ads make arguments, and the message of the Hofstra ad is something like this: "Hofstra is a prestigious, high-quality institution that brings out the best in students because of its facilities, its academic reputation, its student body, and the strength of its faculty and academic programs." The text of the Hofstra ad expresses that argument specifically: "The best" and "we teach success" are prominently displayed; the size of the print visually reinforces the message; and the fine print supports the main thesis by mentioning Hofstra's facilities (the large library with "a collection [of volumes] larger than that of 95% of American universities," the "television facility . . . with broadcast quality production capability"); its reputation (its ranking in *Barron's Guide to the Most Prestigious Colleges* and its "professionally accredited programs"); and its faculty and students. The ad works by offering good reasons and supporting arguments that are based on logical reasoning and evidence, as well as appeals to our most fervently held values. By placing the ad in prestigious publications, Hofstra enhanced its credibility even further.

In this chapter, however, we are emphasizing visuals in arguments. What kind of argument is made and supported by the image of the young girl with the flute? The photo of the girl is black and white, so that it can be printed easily and inexpensively in newspapers and magazines. But the black and white format also contributes a sense of reality and truthfulness, in the manner of black and white photos or documentary films. (Color images, on the other hand, can imply flashiness or commercialism.) Even in black and white, the image is quite arresting. In the context of an ad for Hofstra, the image is particularly intriguing. The girl is young—does she seem about 10 or 12 years of age?—and her readiness for distinguished performance suggests that she is a prodigy, a genius—in other words, the kind of person that Hofstra attracts and sustains. The ad implies that you might encounter her on the Hofstra campus sometime: if she is not a student at Hofstra now, she soon will be. Come to Hofstra, and you too can acquire the traits associated with excellence and success.

The girl is dressed up for some kind of musical performance, and the details of her costume imply that the performance is of a high order: It is not just any costume, but one associated with professional performances of the most rarefied kind, a concert that calls for only the best musicians. The delicacy and refinement of the girl are implied by the posture of her fingers, the highly polished flute that she holds with an upright carriage, and the meticulousness of her tie, shirt, and coat. The girl's expression suggests that she is serious, sober, disciplined, but comfortable—the kind of student (and faculty member) that Hofstra features. (The layout and consistent print style used in the ad reinforce that impression; by offering a balanced and harmonious placement of elements and by sticking to the same type style throughout, the ad stands for the values of balance, harmony, consistency, and order.) The girl is modest and unpretentious in expression, yet she looks directly at the viewer with supreme self-confidence. Her age suggests innocence, yet her face proclaims ambition; her age and the quasi-masculine costume (note that she wears neither a ring nor earrings) give her a sexual innocence that is in keeping with the contemplative life. Come to Hofstra, the image proclaims, and you will meet people who are sober and graceful, self-disciplined and confident, ambitious without being arrogant. The ad is supporting its thesis with good reasons implied by its central image—good reasons that we identified with logos and pathos in the previous chapter.

Speaking of pathos, what do you make of the fact that the girl is Asian? On one hand, the Asian girl's demeanor reinforces cultural stereotypes. Delicate, small, sober, controlled, even humorless, she embodies characteristics that recall other Asian American icons (particularly women), especially icons of success through discipline and hard work. On the other hand, the girl speaks to the Asian community. It is as if she is on the verge of saying, "Come and join me at Hofstra, where you too can reach the highest achievement. And read the copy below me to learn more about what Hofstra has to offer." In this way the girl participates in Hofstra's ambition to attract highly qualified, highly motivated, and high-performing minority students—as well as any other high-performing student, regardless of ethnicity or gender, who values hard work, academic distinction, and the postponement of sensual gratification in return for long-term success.

If she is Asian, the girl is also thoroughly American. She appears not to be an international student but an American of immigrant stock. Her costume, her controlled black hair, and her unmarked face and fingers identify her as achieving the American dream of material success, physical health and well being, and class advancement. If her parents or grandparents came to New York or California as immigrants, they (and she) are now naturalized—100 percent American, completely successful. The social class element to the image is unmistakable: The entire ad speaks of Hofstra's ambition to be among the best, to achieve an elite status. When the ad appeared in 1989, Hofstra was attracting few of the nation's elite students. The girl signals a change. She displays the university's aspiration to become among the nation's elite—those who enjoy material success as well as the leisure, education, and sophistication to appreciate the finest music. That ambition is reinforced by the university's emblem in the lower right-hand corner of the ad. It resembles a coat of arms and is associated with royalty. Hofstra may be a community that is strong in the professions, but it also values the arts.

No doubt there are other aspects of the image that work to articulate and to support the complex argument of the ad. There is more to be said about this ad, and you may disagree with some of the points we have offered. But consider this: By 2009, twenty years after the ad was run, Hofstra's total enrollment had climbed above 12,000, with 7,500 undergraduates. Its admissions were more selective, its student body was more diverse and less regional in character, its graduation rate had improved, its sports teams had achieved national visibility, and its minority student population had grown. Many factors contributed to the university's advancement, but it seems likely that this ad was one of them.

Write a Visual Analysis

Like rhetorical analysis, effective visual analysis takes into account the context of the image as well as its visual elements and any surrounding text. When you analyze a visual image, look carefully at its details and thoroughly consider its context. What visual elements grab your attention first, and how do other details reinforce that impression—what is most important and less important? How do color and style influence impressions? How does the image direct the viewer's eyes and reinforce what is important? What is the relationship between the image and any text that might accompany it? Consider the shapes, colors, and details of the image, as well as how the elements of the image connect with different arguments and audiences.

Consider also what you know or can learn about the context of an image and the design and text that surround it. Try to determine why and when it was created, who created it, where it appeared, and the target audience. Think about how the context of its creation and publication affected its intended audience. What elements have you seen before? Which elements remind you of other visuals?

Sample Student Visual Analysis

Discussion board posts are a frequent assignment in writing classes. Usually they are short essays, no more than 300 words. Sources of any information still need to be cited.

The assignment for this post was to find and analyze an example of a visual metaphor.

Thread: "Use Only What You Need": The Denver Water Conservation
Campaign
Author: Chrissy Yao
Posted Date: March 1, 2013 1:12 PM

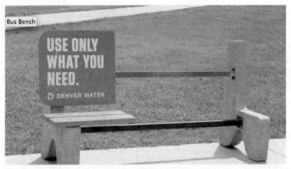

Partial bus bench from Denver Water's conservation campaign

In 2006, Denver Water, the city's oldest water utility, launched
a ten-year water conservation plan based on using water efficiently
("Conservation"). Denver Water teamed up with the Sukle Advertising
firm and produced the "Use Only What You Need" campaign to help
alleviate the water crisis that the city was enduring (Samuel). The
campaign uses billboard advertising, magazine ads, and even stripped-
down cars to impart messages of water conservation and efficiency.

> Yao describes the ad campaign that uses the partial bus bench.

Clever visual metaphors are at the heart of the campaign. One
example is a park bench with available seating for only one individual.
The words, "USE ONLY WHAT YOU NEED," are stenciled on the back of the
bench. The bench, which can actually be used for sitting, conveys the
idea that if only one person were using the bench, that person would
only need a small area to sit on, not the whole thing. The bench makes
concrete the concept of water conservation.

> Yao analyzes the visual metaphor.

The innovative ad campaign that uses objects in addition to
traditional advertising has proven successful. The simplicity and
minimalist style of the ads made a convincing argument about using
resources sparingly. The average water consumption of Denver dropped
between 18% and 21% annually from 2006 to 2009.

Works Cited

"Conservation." *Denver Water*. Denver Water, 2010. Web. 23 Feb. 2013.

Samuel, Frederick. "Denver Water." *Ad Goodness*. N.p., 16 Nov. 2006.
    Web. 24 Feb. 2013.

Writing Arguments

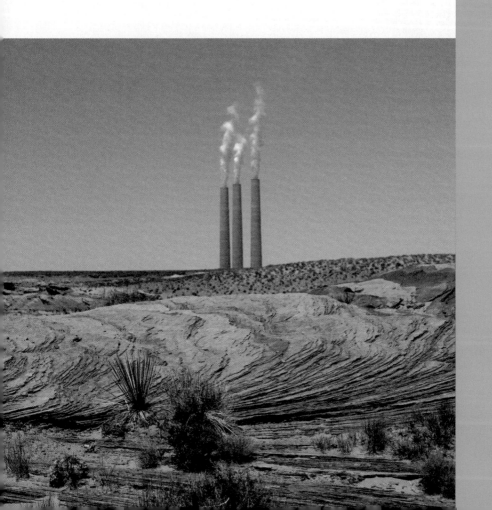

8 | Definition Arguments

QUICK TAKE

In this chapter, you will learn to

1. Use definition arguments that set out criteria and then argue that something meets or doesn't meet those criteria (see page 96)

2. Recognize formal definitions, operational definitions, and definitions by example (see pages 96–99)

3. Analyze a definition argument (see pages 99–102)

4. Write an effective definition argument (see pages 104–105)

Graffiti dates back to the ancient Egyptian, Greek, Roman, and Mayan civilizations. Is graffiti vandalism? Or is it art? The debate has gone on for three decades. In the 1980s New York City's subways were covered with graffiti. Many New Yorkers believe that removing graffiti from subway cars was a first step toward the much-celebrated social and economic recovery of the city. For them graffiti was a sign that the subways were not safe. But at the same time, Martha Cooper and Henry Chalfant released a book titled *Subway Art*—a picture book that celebrated graffiti-covered subways as an art form. Should we appreciate graffiti as the people's art. Or should graffiti be removed as quickly as possible, as a destructive eyesore?

Understand How Definition Arguments Work

Definition arguments set out criteria and then argue that whatever is being defined meets or does not meet those criteria.

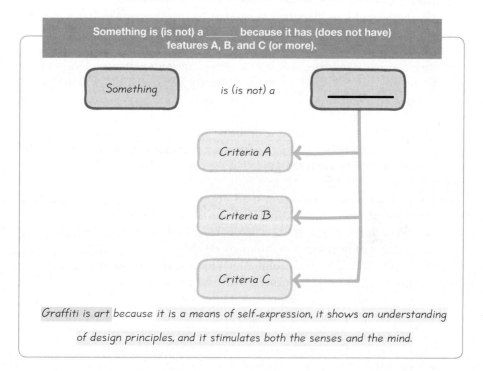

Something is (is not) a _____ because it has (does not have) features A, B, and C (or more).

Something **is (is not) a** _____

Criteria A

Criteria B

Criteria C

Graffiti is art because it is a means of self-expression, it shows an understanding of design principles, and it stimulates both the senses and the mind.

Recognize Kinds of Definitions

Rarely do you get far into an argument without having to define something. Imagine that you are writing an argument about the decades-old and largely ineffective "war on drugs" in the United States. We all know that the war on drugs is being waged against drugs that are illegal, like cocaine and marijuana, and not against the legal drugs produced by the multibillion-dollar drug industry. Our society classifies drugs into two categories: "good" drugs, which are legal, and "bad" drugs, which are illegal.

How exactly does our society arrive at these definitions? Drugs would be relatively easy to define as good or bad if the difference could be defined at the molecular level. Bad drugs would contain certain molecules that define them as bad. The history of drug use in the United States, however, tells us that this is not so simple. In the twentieth century alcohol was on the list of illegal drugs for over a decade, while opium was considered a good drug and was distributed in many patent medicines by pharmaceutical companies. Similarly, LSD and MDMA (methylenedioxymethamphetamine, better known by its street name *ecstasy*) were developed by the pharmaceutical industry but later made illegal. In a few states marijuana is now legal in small quantities and for medicinal use.

If drugs cannot be classified as good or bad by their molecular structure, then perhaps society classifies them by their effects. It might be reasonable to assume that addictive drugs are illegal, but that's not the case. Nicotine is highly addictive and is a legal drug, as are many prescription medicines. Drugs taken for the purpose of pleasure are not necessarily illegal (think of alcohol and Viagra), nor are drugs that alter consciousness or change personality (such as Prozac).

How a drug is defined as legal or illegal apparently is determined by example. The nationwide effort to stop Americans from drinking alcohol during the first decades of the twentieth century led to the passage of the Eighteenth Amendment and the ban on sales of alcohol from 1920 to 1933, known as Prohibition. Those who argued for Prohibition used examples of drunkenness, especially among the poor, to show how alcohol broke up families and left mothers and children penniless in the street. Those who opposed Prohibition initially pointed to the consumption of beer and wine in many cultural traditions. Later they raised examples of the bad effects of Prohibition—the rise of organized crime, the increase in alcohol abuse, and the general disregard for laws.

When you make a definition argument, it's important to think about what kind of definition you will use. Descriptions of three types follow.

Formal definitions

Formal definitions typically categorize an item into the next-higher classification and provide criteria that distinguish the item from other items within that classification. Most dictionary definitions are formal definitions. For example, fish are cold-blooded aquatic vertebrates that have jaws, fins, and scales and are distinguished from other cold-blooded aquatic vertebrates (such as sea snakes) by the presence of gills. If you can construct a formal definition with a specific classification and differentiating criteria that your audience will accept, then likely you will have a strong argument. The key is to get your audience to agree to your classification and criteria. Often your argument will amount to revising your audience's view of the classification or criteria (or both). For instance, imagine that you want to change your audience's view of contemporary universities. You might construct a thesis statement something like this: "While most people still think of universities as institutions of higher learning [classification] that prepare people for citizenship and the workplace [differentiating criteria], they are actually nothing more than big businesses" [revised classification].

Operational definitions

Many concepts cannot be easily defined by formal definitions. Researchers in the natural and social sciences must construct **operational definitions** that they use for their research. For example, researchers who study binge drinking among college students define a binge as five or more drinks in one sitting for a man, and four or more drinks for a woman. Some people think this standard is too low and should be raised to six to eight drinks to distinguish true problem drinkers from the general college population. No matter what the number, researchers must argue that the particular definition is one that suits the concept.

Definitions from example

Many human qualities such as honesty, courage, creativity, deceit, and love must be defined by examples that the audience accepts as representative of the concept. Few would not call the firefighters who entered the World Trade Center on September 11, 2001, courageous. Most people would describe someone with a diagnosis of terminal cancer who refuses to feel self-pity as courageous. But what about a student who declines to go to a concert with her friends so she can study for an exam? Her behavior might be admirable, but most people would hesitate to call it courageous. The key to arguing a **definition from example** is that the examples must strike the audience as typical of the concept, even if the situation is unusual.

Build a Definition Argument

Because definition arguments are so powerful, they are found at the center of some of the most important debates in American history. Definition arguments were at the heart of the abolition of slavery, for example, and many of the major arguments of the civil rights movement were based on definitions. Martin Luther King, Jr.'s, "Letter from Birmingham Jail" is one eloquent example.

King was jailed in April 1963 for leading a series of peaceful protests in Birmingham, Alabama. While he was being held in solitary confinement, Rev. King wrote a letter to eight white Birmingham clergymen. These religious leaders had issued a statement urging an end to the protests in their city. King argued that it was necessary to act now rather than wait for change. His purpose in writing the argument was to win acceptance for the protests and protestors and to make his audience see that the anti-segregationists were not agitators and rabble-rousers, but citizens acting responsibly to correct a grave injustice. A critical part of King's argument is his definition of "just" and "unjust" laws.

U.S. National Guard troops block off Beale Street in Memphis, Tennessee, as striking sanitation workers wearing placards reading "I *AM* A MAN" pass by on March 29, 1968. Rev. Martin Luther King, Jr., returned to Memphis to lead the march and was assassinated a week later on April 4.

Supporters of segregation in Birmingham had obtained a court order forbidding further protests, and the eight white clergymen urged King and his supporters to obey the courts. Our society generally assumes that laws, and the courts that enforce them, should be obeyed. King, however, argues that there are two categories of laws, and that citizens must treat one category differently from the other. Morally just laws, King argues, should be obeyed, but unjust ones should not. But how are just laws to be distinguished from unjust ones? By distinguishing two different kinds of laws, King creates a rationale for obeying some laws and disobeying others.

His argument rests on the clear moral and legal criteria he uses to define just and unjust laws. Without these criteria, people could simply disobey any law they chose, which is what King's detractors accused him of advocating. King had to show that he was in fact acting on principle, and that he and his supporters wanted to establish justice, not cause chaos. First, King states that a "just law is a man-made code that squares with the moral law of God" and "an unjust law is a code that is out of harmony with the moral law." Second, King notes that "any law that degrades human personality is unjust." Finally, King states that just laws are ones that hold for everyone because they were arrived at through democratic processes, while unjust laws are those that are inflicted on a minority that, because they were not permitted to vote, had no participation in approving them.

The definitions that King offers promote his goals. He maintains in his famous "Letter" that people have a moral responsibility to obey just laws, and, by the same logic, "a moral responsibility to disobey unjust laws." He then completes his definitional argument by showing how segregation laws fit the definition of "unjust" that he has laid out. Once his audience accepts his placement of segregation laws in the "unjust" category, they must also accept that King and his fellow protestors were right to break those laws. He answers his critics effectively through a powerful definition argument.

Note how King's three definitions all fit the structure described at the beginning of this chapter:

Something is (or is not) a ___ because it has (does not have) features A, B, and C.

Building an extended definition argument like King's is a two-step process. First, you have to establish the criteria for the categories you wish to define. In

Martin Luther King, Jr., speaking in New York City in 1967.

King's letter, consistency with moral law and uplifting of the human spirit are set forth as criteria for a just law. King provides arguments from St. Thomas Aquinas, a religious authority likely to carry significant weight with Birmingham clergymen and others who will read the letter.

Second, you must convince your audience that the particular case in question meets or doesn't meet the criteria. King cannot simply state that segregation laws are unjust; he must provide evidence showing how they fail to meet the criteria for a just law. Specifically, he notes that segregation "gives the segregator a false sense of superiority and the segregated a false sense of inferiority." These false senses of self are a distortion or degradation of the human personality.

Sometimes definition arguments have to argue for the relevance and suitability of the criteria. King, in fact, spent a great deal of his letter laying out and defending his criteria for just and unjust laws. While he addressed his letter to clergymen, he knew that it would find a wider audience. Therefore, he did not rely solely on criteria linked to moral law, or to Thomas Aquinas, or the "law of God." People who were not especially religious might not be convinced by those parts of his argument. So King presents two additional criteria for just laws that he knows will appeal to those who value the democratic process.

When you build a definition argument, often you must put much effort into identifying and explaining your criteria. You must convince your readers that your criteria are the best ones for what you are defining and that they apply to the case you are arguing.

King's Extended Definition Argument

After establishing criteria for two kinds of laws, *just* and *unjust*, King argues that citizens must respond differently to laws that are unjust, by disobeying them. He then shows how the special case of *segregation laws* meets the criteria for unjust laws. If readers accept his argument, they will agree that segregation laws belong in the category of unjust laws, and therefore must be disobeyed.

Criteria for Just Laws	Criteria for Unjust Laws	Segregation Laws
Consistent with moral law	Not consistent with moral law	✓
Uplift human personality	Damage human personality	✓
Must be obeyed by all people	Must be obeyed by some people, but not others	✓
Made by democratically elected representatives	Not made by democratically elected representatives	✓
Appropriate Response to Just Laws	**Appropriate Response to Unjust Laws**	
All citizens should obey them.	All citizens should disobey them.	✓

Finding Good Reasons

What Is Parody?

William Jennings Bryan depicted as Don Quixote in his campaign against powerful trusts in 1899.

During the 2007–2010 global financial crisis, the slogan "too big to fail" expressed anger over the government bailout of big banks at a time when individuals were losing their jobs and homes. A century earlier, Democratic presidential candidate William Jennings Bryan campaigned against *trusts*—powerful groups of companies that dominated markets. This cartoon represents Bryan as Miguel de Cervantes's character Don Quixote, fruitlessly charging windmills. The novel *Don Quixote*, published in 1605 with a sequel in 1615, is itself a parody of contemporary chivalric romances, so the cartoon is a parody using a parody.

Downfall, a German film released in 2004 about Hitler's last days, has been the basis for thousands of popular *YouTube* parodies. Every parody uses the same scene of a defeated Hitler, played by Bruno Ganz, unleashing a furious speech to his staff in German with YouTubers adding subtitles on politics, sports, popular culture, and everyday life. The owner of the rights to the film, Constantin Films, demanded that *YouTube* take down the parodies in April 2010, and *YouTube* complied for a few months. Critics of the move successfully argued that fair-use law allows a film clip, a paragraph from an article, or a short piece of music to be adapted if the purpose is to create commentary or satire.

Write about it

1. Which of the following criteria do you think must be present for a work to be considered a parody? Are there any criteria you might change or add?
   - The work criticizes a previous work
   - The work copies the same structure, details, or style of the previous work
   - The connections to the previous work are clear to the audience
   - The work is humorous
   - The title is a play on the previous work

2. Do the various uses of the *Downfall* clip meet the criteria above? Would you define them as parodies? Why or why not?

Steps to Writing a Definition Argument

Step 1 Make a Claim

Make a definitional claim on a controversial issue that focuses on a key term.

Template

_____ is (or is not) a _____ because it has (or does not have) features A, B, and C (or more).

Examples

- Hate speech (or pornography, literature, films, and so on) is (or is not) free speech protected by the First Amendment because it has (or does not have) these features.
- Hunting (or using animals for cosmetics testing, keeping animals in zoos, wearing furs, and so on) is (or is not) cruelty to animals because it has (or does not have) these features.

Step 2 Think About What's at Stake

- Does nearly everyone agree with you? If so, then your claim probably isn't interesting or important. If you can think of people who disagree, then something is at stake.
- Who argues the opposite of your claim?
- Why or how do they benefit from a different definition?

Step 3 List the Criteria

- Which criteria are necessary for _____ to be a _____?
- Which are the most important?
- Does your case in point meet all the criteria?

Step 4 Analyze Your Potential Readers

- Who are your readers?
- How does the definitional claim you are making affect them?
- How familiar are they with the issue, concept, or controversy that you're writing about?
- Which criteria are they most likely to accept with little explanation, and which will they disagree with?

Step 5 Write a Draft

Introduction

- Set out the issue, concept, or controversy.
- Give the background that your intended readers need.

Body

- Set out your criteria and argue for the appropriateness of the criteria.
- Anticipate where readers might question either your criteria or how they apply to your subject.
- Address opposing viewpoints by acknowledging how their definitions differ and by showing why your definition is better.

Conclusion

- Do more than simply summarize. You can, for example, go into more detail about what is at stake or the implications of your definition.

Step 6 Revise, Edit, Proofread

- For detailed instructions, see Chapter 5.
- For a checklist to use to evaluate your draft, see pages 50–51.

Michael Pollan

Eat Food: Food Defined

Michael Pollan is a journalism professor at the University of California, Berkeley, and the author of *In Defense of Food: An Eater's Manifesto* (2008), from which this excerpt is taken. *In Defense of Food* received many prizes and was named one of the ten best books of the year by the *New York Times* and the *Washington Post*. Pollan is also the author of *Second Nature* (1991), *A Place of My Own* (1997), *The Botany of Desire: A Plant's Eye View of the World* (2001), *The Omnivore's Dilemma: A Natural History of Four Meals* (2006), *Food Rules* (2010), and *Cooked: A Natural History of Transformation* (2013). He is also a contributing writer for the *New York Times Magazine*.

Pollan asks why Americans worry so much about nutrition and yet seem so unhealthy. The title *In Defense of Food* is one of the many paradoxes that Pollan examines in the book excerpted here. After all, why should food need defending if it is plentiful and we eat so much of it? Pollan argues that the answer lies in how we define food.

Pollan begins by asking, Why does food need to be defined?

The first time I heard the advice to "just eat food" it was in a speech by Joan Gussow, and it completely baffled me. Of course you should eat food—what else is there to eat? But Gussow, who grows much of her own food on a flood-prone finger of land jutting into the Hudson River, refuses to dignify most of the products for sale in the supermarket with that title. "In the thirty-four years I've been in the field of nutrition," she said in the same speech, "I have watched real food disappear from large areas of the supermarket and from much of the rest of the eating world." Taking food's place on the shelves has been an unending stream of foodlike substitutes, some seventeen thousand new ones every year—"products constructed largely around commerce and hope, supported by frighteningly little actual knowledge." Ordinary food is still out there, however, still being grown and even occasionally sold in the supermarket, and this ordinary food is what we should eat.

Pollan claims that everything that pretends to be food really isn't food, thus establishing the need for a definition.

2 But given our current state of confusion and given the thousands of products calling themselves food, this is more easily said than done. So consider these related rules of thumb. Each proposes a different sort of map to the contemporary food landscape, but all should take you to more or less the same place.

Don't eat anything your great grandmother wouldn't recognize as food.

3 Why your great grandmother? Because at this point your mother and possibly even your grandmother is as confused as the rest of us; to be safe we need to go back at least a couple generations,

to a time before the advent of most modern foods. So depending on your age (and your grandmother), you may need to go back to your great- or even great-great grandmother. Some nutritionists recommend going back even further. John Yudkin, a British nutritionist whose early alarms about the dangers of refined carbohydrates were overlooked in the 1960s and 1970s, once advised, "Just don't eat anything your Neolithic ancestors wouldn't have recognized and you'll be OK."

Pollan's first criterion of what is food offers a simple concept.

4   What would shopping this way mean in the supermarket? Well, imagine your great grandmother at your side as you roll down the aisles. You're standing together in front of the dairy case. She picks up a package of Go-Gurt Portable Yogurt tubes—and has no idea what this could possibly be. Is it a food or a toothpaste? And how, exactly, do you introduce it into your body? You could tell her it's just yogurt in a squirtable form, yet if she read the ingredients label she would have every reason to doubt that that was in fact the case. Sure, there's some yogurt in there, but there are also a dozen other things that aren't remotely yogurt like, ingredients she would probably fail to recognize as foods of any kind, including high-fructose corn syrup, modified corn starch, kosher gelatin, carrageenan, tri-calcium phosphate, natural and artificial flavors, vitamins, and so forth. (And there's a whole other list of ingredients for the "berry bubblegum bash" flavoring, containing everything but berries or bubblegum.) How did yogurt, which in your great grandmother's day consisted simply of milk inoculated with a bacterial culture, ever get to be so complicated? Is a product like Go-Gurt Portable Yogurt still a whole food? A food of any kind? Or is it just a food product?

Another way of defining food is to define what isn't food, but what Pollan calls "food products."

5   There are in fact hundreds of foodish products in the supermarket that your ancestors simply wouldn't recognize as food: breakfast cereal bars transected by bright white veins representing, but in reality having nothing to do with, milk; "protein waters" and "nondairy creamer"; cheeselike food-stuffs equally innocent of any bovine contribution; cakelike cylinders (with creamlike fillings) called Twinkies that never grow stale. Don't eat anything incapable of rotting is another personal policy you might consider adopting.

6   There are many reasons to avoid eating such complicated food products beyond the various chemical additives and corn and soy derivatives they contain. One of the problems with the products of food science is that, as Joan Gussow has pointed out, they lie to your body; their artificial colors and flavors and synthetic sweeteners and novel fats confound the senses we rely on to assess new foods and prepare our bodies to deal with them. Foods that lie leave us with little choice but to eat by the numbers, consulting labels rather than our senses.

7   It's true that foods have long been processed in order to preserve them, as when we pickle or ferment or smoke, but

industrial processing aims to do much more than extend shelf life. Today foods are processed in ways specifically designed to sell us more food by pushing our evolutionary buttons—our inborn preferences for sweetness and fat and salt. These qualities are difficult to find in nature but cheap and easy for the food scientist to deploy, with the result that processing induces us to consume much more of these ecological rarities than is good for us. "Tastes great, less filling!" could be the motto for most processed foods, which are far more energy dense than most whole foods: They contain much less water, fiber, and micronutrients, and generally much more sugar and fat, making them at the same time, to coin a marketing slogan, "More fattening, less nutritious!"

8   The great grandma rule will help keep many of these products out of your cart. But not all of them. Because thanks to the FDA's willingness, post–1973, to let food makers freely alter the identity of "traditional foods that everyone knows" without having to call them imitations, your great grandmother could easily be fooled into thinking that that loaf of bread or wedge of cheese is in fact a loaf of bread or a wedge of cheese. This is why we need a slightly more detailed personal policy to capture these imitation foods; to wit:

What food is can also be defined by what it isn't, hence a list of criteria for what isn't food.

Avoid food products containing ingredients that are a) unfamiliar set, b) unpronounceable, c) more than five in number, or that include d) high-fructose corn syrup.

9   None of these characteristics, not even the last one, is necessarily harmful in and of itself, but all of them are reliable markers for foods that have been highly processed to the point where they may no longer be what they purport to be. They have crossed over from foods to food products.

10   Consider a loaf of bread, one of the "traditional foods that everyone knows" specifically singled out for protection in the 1938 imitation rule. As your grandmother could tell you, bread is traditionally made using a remarkably small number of familiar ingredients: flour, yeast, water, and a pinch of salt will do it. But industrial bread—even industrial whole-grain bread—has become a far more complicated product of modern food science (not to mention commerce and hope). Here's the complete ingredients list for Sara Lee's Soft & Smooth Whole Grain White Bread. (Wait a minute—isn't "Whole Grain White Bread" a contradiction in terms? Evidently not any more.)

Pollan points out that the language used for food products is as convoluted as the ingredients.

Enriched bleached flour [wheat flour, malted barley flour, niacin, iron, thiamin mononitrate (vitamin B), riboflavin (vitamin B_2), folic acid], water, whole grains [whole wheat flour, brown rice flour (rice flour, rice bran)], high fructose corn syrup [hello!], whey, wheat gluten, yeast, cellulose. Contains 2% or less of each of the following: honey, calcium sulfate, vegetable oil (soybean and/or cottonseed oils), salt, butter (cream, salt), dough conditioners (may contain one or more of the following: mono- and diglycerides, ethoxylated mono- and diglycerides, ascorbic acid, enzymes, azodicarbonamide), guar gum, calcium propionate (preservative), distilled vinegar, yeast nutrients (monocalcium phosphate, calcium sulfate, ammonium sulfate), corn starch, natural flavor, beta-carotene (color), vitamin D$_3$, soy lecithin, soy flour.

11   There are many things you could say about this intricate loaf of "bread," but note first that even if it managed to slip by your great grandmother (because it is a loaf of bread, or at least is called one and strongly resembles one), the product fails every test proposed under rule number two: It's got unfamiliar ingredients (monoglycerides I've heard of before, but ethoxylated monoglycerides?); unpronounceable ingredients (try "azodicarbonamide"); it exceeds the maximum of five ingredients (by roughly thirty-six); and it contains high-fructose corn syrup. Sorry, Sara Lee, but your Soft & Smooth Whole Grain White Bread is not food and if not for the indulgence of the FDA could not even be labeled "bread."

12   Sara Lee's Soft & Smooth Whole Grain White Bread could serve as a monument to the age of nutritionism. It embodies the latest nutritional wisdom from science and government (which in its most recent food pyramid recommends that at least half our consumption of grain come from whole grains) but leavens that wisdom with the commercial recognition that American eaters (and American children in particular) have come to prefer their wheat highly refined—which is to say, cottony soft, snowy white, and exceptionally sweet on the tongue. In its marketing materials, Sara Lee treats this clash of interests as some sort of Gordian knot—it speaks in terms of an ambitious quest to build a "no compromise" loaf—which only the most sophisticated food science could possibly cut.

13   And so it has, with the invention of whole-grain white bread. Because the small percentage of whole grains in the bread would render it that much less sweet than, say, all-white Wonder Bread—which scarcely waits to be chewed before transforming itself into glucose—the food scientists have added high-fructose corn syrup and honey to make up the difference; to overcome the problematic heft and toothsomeness of a real whole grain bread, they've deployed "dough conditioners," including guar gum and the aforementioned azodicarbonamide, to simulate the texture of supermarket white bread. By incorporating certain varieties of albino wheat, they've managed to maintain that deathly but apparently appealing Wonder Bread pallor.

14   Who would have thought Wonder Bread would ever become an ideal of aesthetic and gustatory perfection to which bakers would actually aspire—Sara Lee's Mona Lisa?

15   Very often food science's efforts to make traditional foods more nutritious make them much more complicated, but not necessarily any better for you. To make dairy products low fat, it's not enough to remove the fat. You then have to go to great lengths to preserve the body or creamy texture by working in all kinds of food additives. In the case of low-fat or skim milk that usually means adding powdered milk. But powdered milk contains oxidized cholesterol, which scientists believe is much worse for your arteries than ordinary cholesterol, so food makers sometimes compensate by adding antioxidants, further complicating what had been a simple one-ingredient whole food. Also, removing the fat makes it that much harder for your body to absorb the fat-soluble vitamins that are one of the reasons to drink milk in the first place.

16   All this heroic and occasionally counterproductive food science has been undertaken in the name of our health—so that Sara Lee can add to its plastic wrapper the magic words "good source of whole grain" or a food company can ballyhoo the even more magic words "low fat." Which brings us to a related food policy that may at first sound counterintuitive to a health-conscious eater:

Avoid Food Products That Make Health Claims.

17   For a food product to make health claims on its package it must first have a package, so right off the bat it's more likely to be a processed than a whole food. Generally speaking, it is only the big food companies that have the wherewithal to secure FDA-approved health claims for their products and there trumpet them to the world. Recently, however, some of the tonier fruits and nuts have begun boasting about their health-enhancing properties, and there will surely be more as each crop council scrounges together the money to commission its own scientific study. Because all plants contain antioxidants, all these studies are guaranteed to find something on which to base a health oriented marketing campaign.

18   But for the most part it is the products of food science that make the boldest health claims, and these are often founded on incomplete and often erroneous science—the dubious fruits of nutritionism. Don't forget that trans-fat-rich margarine, one of the first industrial foods to claim it was healthier than the traditional food it replaced, turned out to give people heart attacks. Since that debacle, the FDA, under tremendous pressure from industry, has made it only easier for food companies to make increasingly doubtful health claims, such as the one Frito-Lay now puts on some of its chips—that eating them is somehow good for your heart. If you bother to read the health claims closely (as food marketers make sure consumers seldom do), you will find that there is often considerably less to them than meets the eye.

19   Consider a recent "qualified" health claim approved by the FDA for (don't laugh) corn oil. ("Qualified" is a whole new category

of health claim, introduced in 2002 at the behest of industry.) Corn oil, you may recall, is particularly high in the omega-6 fatty acids we're already consuming far too many of. Very limited and preliminary scientific evidence suggests that eating about one tablespoon (16 grams) of corn oil daily may reduce the risk of heart disease due to the unsaturated fat content in corn oil.

20   The tablespoon is a particularly rich touch, conjuring images of moms administering medicine, or perhaps cod-liver oil, to their children. But what the FDA gives with one hand, it takes away with the other. Here's the small-print "qualification" of this already notably diffident health claim:

> [The] FDA concludes that there is little scientific evidence supporting this claim.
>
> To achieve this possible benefit, corn oil is to replace a similar amount of saturated fat and not increase the total number of calories you eat in a day.

Close reading of labels undercuts health claims of food products.

21   This little masterpiece of pseudoscientific bureaucratese was extracted from the FDA by the manufacturer of Mazola corn oil. It would appear that "qualified" is an official FDA euphemism for "all but meaningless." Though someone might have let the consumer in on this game: The FDA's own research indicates that consumers have no idea what to make of qualified health claims (how would they?), and its rules allow companies to promote the claims pretty much any way they want—they can use really big type for the claim, for example, and then print the disclaimers in teeny-tiny type. No doubt we can look forward to a qualified health claim for high-fructose corn syrup, a tablespoon of which probably does contribute to your health—as long as it replaces a comparable amount of, say, poison in your diet and doesn't increase the total number of calories you eat in a day.

22   When corn oil and chips and sugary breakfast cereals can all boast being good for your heart, health claims have become hopelessly corrupt. The American Heart Association currently bestows (for a fee) its heart-healthy seal of approval on Lucky Charms, Cocoa Puffs, and Trix cereals, Yoo-hoo lite chocolate drink, and Healthy Choice's Premium Caramel Swirl Ice Cream Sandwich—this at a time when scientists are coming to recognize that dietary sugar probably plays a more important role in heart disease than dietary fat. Meanwhile, the genuinely heart-healthy whole foods in the produce section, lacking the financial and political clout of the packaged goods a few aisles over, are mute. But don't take the silence of the yams as a sign that they have nothing valuable to say about health.

Pollan adds a playful touch by echoing the title of a popular movie to make a point.

Sample Student Definition Argument

Conley 1

Patrice Conley

Professor Douglas

English 101

15 Nov. 2013

Flagrant Foul: The NCAA's Definition of Student Athletes as Amateurs

Every year, thousands of student athletes across America sign the National Collegiate Athletic Association's Form 08-3a, the "Student-Athlete" form, waiving their right to receive payment for the use of their name and image (McCann). The form defines student athletes as amateurs, who cannot receive payment for playing their sports. While their schools and coaches may make millions of dollars in salaries and endorsement deals and are the highest-paid public employees in many states, student athletes can never earn a single penny from their college athletic careers. Former Nike executive Sonny Vacarro sums it up: "Everyone has a right except for the player. The player has no rights" ("Money").

> Patrice Conley sets out the definition she is attempting to rectify: amateurs are athletes who aren't paid.

Make no mistake: college athletics are big business. The most visible college sports—big-time men's football and basketball—generate staggering sums of money. For example, the twelve universities in the Southeastern Conference receive $205 million each year from CBS and ESPN for the right to broadcast their football games (Smith and Ourand). Even more money comes in from video games, clothing, and similar licenses. In 2010, the *New York Times* reported that "the NCAA's licensing deals are estimated at more than $4 billion" per year (Thamel). While the staggering executive pay at big corporations has brought public outrage, coaches' salaries are even more outlandish. Kentucky basketball coach John Calipari is paid over $4 million a year for a basketball program that makes about $35-40 million a year, more than 10% of the entire revenue. Tom Van Riper observes that no corporate CEO commands this large a share of the profits. He notes that if Steve Ballmer, the CEO at Microsoft, had Calipari's deal, Ballmer would make over $6 billion a year.

> Conley identifies what's at stake.

> Conley disputes the definition that college sports are amateur sports.

> The huge salaries paid to college coaches are comparable to those in professional sports.

How can colleges allow advertisers, arena operators, concession owners, athletic gear manufacturers, retailers, game companies, and media moguls, along with coaches and university officials, to make millions and pay the stars of the show nothing? The answer is that colleges define

Conley 2

Conley argues
that colleges
use the defini-
tion of athletes
as amateurs to
refuse to pay
them.

athletes as amateurs. Not only are student athletes not paid for playing
their sport, they cannot receive gifts and are not allowed to endorse
products, which may be a violation of their right to free speech. The NCAA,
an organization of colleges and schools, forces student athletes to sign
away their rights because, it says, it is protecting the students. If student
athletes could accept money from anyone, the NCAA argues, they might
be exploited, cheated, or even bribed. Taking money out of the equation
is supposed to let students focus on academics and preserve the amateur
status of college sports.

Conley shows in
this paragraph
how the defini-
tion of college
athletes as un-
paid amateurs
is based on out-
dated notions.

The definition of amateur arose in the nineteenth century in Britain,
when team sports became popular. Middle-class and upper-class students
in college had ample time to play their sports while working-class
athletes had only a half-day off (no sports were played on Sundays in
that era). Teams began to pay top working-class sportsmen for the time
they had to take off from work. Middle-class and upper-class sportsmen
didn't want to play against the working-class teams, so they made
the distinction between amateurs and professionals. The definition of
amateur crossed the Atlantic to the United States, where college sports
became popular in the 1880s. But it was not long until the hypocrisy of
amateurism undermined the ideal. Top football programs like Yale's had
slush funds to pay athletes, and others used ringers—players who weren't
students—and even players from other schools (Zimbalist 7). The Olympic
Games maintained the amateur-professional distinction until 1988, but
it was long evident that Communist bloc nations were paying athletes
to train full-time and Western nations were paying athletes through
endorsement contracts. The only Olympic sport that now requires amateur

Conley argues
that everyone
else has dis-
carded that
old idea of
"amateurism as
unpaid," so why
won't the NCAA
discard it?

status is boxing. The college sports empire in the United States run by
the NCAA is the last bastion of amateurism for sports that draw audiences
large enough to be televised.

Colleges might be able to defend the policy of amateurism if they
extended this definition to all students. A fair policy is one that treats
all students the same. A fair policy doesn't result in some students
getting paid for professional work, while other students do not. Consider
the students in the Butler School of Music at the University of Texas at

Conley 3

Austin, for example. Many student musicians perform at the professional level. Does the school prevent them from earning money for their musical performances? No. In fact, the school runs a referral service that connects its students with people and businesses who want to hire professional musicians. The university even advises its students on how to negotiate a contract and get paid for their performance ("Welcome").

> Comparisons show that colleges do not apply the definition of amateur consistently.

Likewise, why are student actors allowed to earn money from their work and images, while student athletes are not? Think about actor Emma Watson, who enrolled at Brown University in Rhode Island. Can you imagine the university officials at Brown telling Watson that she would have to make the next two *Harry Potter* films for free, instead of for the $5 million she was offered? Can you imagine Brown University telling Watson that all the revenue from Harry Potter merchandise bearing her likeness would have to be paid directly to the university for the rest of her life? They would if Watson were an athlete instead of an actor.

> Do you think this analogy is effective?

In fact, compared with musicians and actors, student athletes have an even greater need to earn money while they are still in college. Athletes' professional careers are likely to be much shorter than musicians' or actors'. College may be the only time some athletes have the opportunity to capitalize on their success. (Indeed, rather than focusing student athletes on their academic careers, the NCAA policy sometimes forces students to leave college early, so they can earn a living before their peak playing years are over.) Student athletes often leave school with permanent injuries and no medical insurance or job prospects, whereas student musicians and actors rarely suffer career-ending injuries on the job.

Student athletes are prevented from profiting from their name and image. The NCAA says this rule preserves their standing as amateurs and protects them from the celebrity and media frenzy surrounding professional sports stars. The rule hardly protected 2012 Heisman Trophy winner Johnny Manziel, who could not walk across his campus without being mobbed by fans. Search for a "Johnny Manziel jersey" online, and you can buy officially branded shirts bearing either his last name or his nickname, "Johnny Football," ranging in price from $24 to $89, licensed by Texas A&M. Rick Reilly observes that Manziel's school "is making the GNP of Kuwait off him in jersey sales and T-shirt sales."

Conley 4

Nobody is saying exactly how much money these jerseys have made for Nike, or for the NCAA. What we do know for sure is the amount Johnny Manziel has made off the jerseys: nothing.

> The example of Johnny Manziel illustrates how the definition of amateur works against college athletes.

Defenders of the current system argue that student athletes on scholarships are paid with free tuition, free room and board, free books, and tutoring help. The total package can be the equivalent of $120,000 over four years. For those student athletes who are motivated to take advantage of the opportunity, the lifetime benefits can be enormous. Unfortunately, too few student athletes do take advantage of the opportunity. Seldom does a major college football and men's basketball program have graduation rates at or close to that of the overall student body. A study by the University of North Carolina's College Sports Research Institute released in 2010 accuses the NCAA of playing fast and loose with graduation rates by counting part-time students in statistics for the general student body, making graduation rates for athletes look better in a comparison. Student athletes must be full-time students; thus they should be compared to other full-time students. The North Carolina Institute reports that 54.8% of major college (Football Bowl Subdivision) football players at 117 schools graduated within six years, compared with 73.7% of other full-time students. The gap between basketball players was even greater, with 44.6% of athletes graduating compared with 75.7% of the general student body (Zaiger). For the

> Conley gives evidence that undercuts the argument that college athletes are compensated with a college degree.

handful of talented athletes who can play in the National Football League or the National Basketball Association, college sports provide training for their future lucrative, although short-lived, profession. But as the NCAA itself points out in its ads, the great majority of student athletes "go pro in something other than sports." For the 55% of college basketball players who fail to graduate, the supposed $120,000 package is an air ball.

> The clever use of "air ball" reinforces Conley's argument that the NCAA's definition of amateur is outdated and unfair.

The NCAA would be wise to return to the older definition of amateur, which comes from Latin through old French, meaning "lover of." It doesn't necessarily have to have anything to do with money. Whether it's a jazz performer or a dancer or an athlete, an amateur ought to be considered someone in love with an activity— someone who cares deeply about the activity, studies the activity in depth, and practices in order to be highly proficient. NBA players,

> Conley concludes with her main claim. She proposes a new definition of amateur, one that would permit salaries and royalties to go to the college athlete.

Conley 5

Olympians, college athletes, high school players, and even bird watchers, star gazers, and open-source programmers: they're all amateurs. If they are lucky enough to be paid, so be it.

Conley 6

Works Cited

McCann, Michael. "NCAA Faces Unspecified Damages, Changes in Latest Anti-Trust Case." *SI.com*. Time, Inc., 21 July 2009. Web. 3 Nov. 2013.

"Money and March Madness." *Frontline*. PBS, 29 Mar. 2011. Web. 1 Nov. 2013.

National Collegiate Athletic Association. Advertisement. *NCAA.org*. NCAA, 13 Mar. 2007. Web. 3 Nov. 2013.

Reilly, Rick. "Selling Johnny Football." *ESPN.com*. ESPN, 26 Feb. 2013. Web. 2 Nov. 2013.

Smith, Michael, and John Ourand. "ESPN Pays $2.25B for SEC Rights." *SportsBusiness Journal*. Smith and Street, 25 Aug. 2008. Web. 1 Nov. 2013.

Thamel, Pete. "N.C.A.A. Fails to Stop Licensing Lawsuit." *New York Times*. New York Times, 8 Feb. 2010. Web. 1 Nov. 2013.

Van Riper, Thomas. "The Highest-Paid College Basketball Coaches." *Forbes.com*. Forbes, 8 Mar. 2010. Web. 3 Nov. 2013.

"Welcome to the Music Referral Service." *Butler School of Music*. Univ. of Texas at Austin, n.d. Web. 5 Nov. 2013.

Zaiger, Alan Scher. "Study: NCAA Graduation Rate Comparisons Flawed." *ABC News*. ABC News, 20 Apr. 2010. Web. 1 Nov. 2013.

Zimbalist, Andrew. *Unpaid Professionals: Commercialism and Conflict in Big-Time College Sports*. Princeton UP, 2001. Print.

9 | Causal Arguments

Each year, we hear that American students are falling behind their international peers. Different groups argue that the solution lies in investing more in funding for additional teacher training, or smaller classrooms, or more technology in the classroom. Yet America invests billions more in education than some nations whose students surpass American students in achievement rankings. Still others have suggested that America's problem lies in a wide-scale cultural shift that has created an American student who is less motivated than those of the past. How can America's schools become world leaders again?

Understand How Causal Arguments Work

Causal claims can take three basic forms:

1. One cause leads to one or more effects.

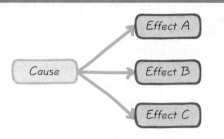

The invention of the telegraph led to the commodities market, the establishment of standard time zones, and news reporting as we know it today.

2. One effect has several causes.

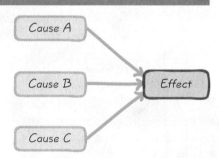

Hurricanes are becoming more financially destructive to the United States because of the greater intensity of recent storms, an increase in the commercial and residential development of coastal areas, and a reluctance to enforce certain construction standards in coastal residential areas.

3. A series of events forms a chain, where one event causes another, which then causes a third, and so on.

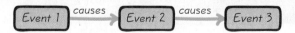

Making the HPV vaccination mandatory for adolescent girls will make unprotected sex seem safer, which will lead to greater promiscuity, and then ultimately to more teenage pregnancies.

Find Causes

The causal claim is at the center of the causal argument. Writing a clear claim about cause and effect can be difficult because if a cause is worth writing about, it is likely to be complex. Obvious cases of cause and effect (staying out in the sun too long without skin protection causes sunburn) usually do not require written arguments because everyone is convinced that the causal relationship exists. Many of the causal claims that most people now accept without question—smoking causes cancer, shifting plates on the Earth's crust cause earthquakes, DDT causes eggshell thinning in bald eagles—were "settled" only after long and complex arguments.

The philosopher John Stuart Mill devised four ways for an investigator to go about finding causes.

- **The Common Factor Method.** Sometimes causes can be identified because two or more similar events share a common factor. The common factor may be the cause. For example, if two people in two different states both develop a rare disease, and both of them recently traveled to Madagascar, they were probably exposed to the illness while there.

- **The Single Difference Method.** Causes can often be identified when two situations or events have different outcomes. If there is a single difference in the two scenarios, that difference may be the cause. At the 1998 Winter Olympics in Nagano, Japan, the speed skating team from the Netherlands introduced a technological innovation to the sport—clap skates, which improve skaters' performance by keeping the skate blade in contact with the ice longer. Racing against the best skaters in the world, the Dutch on their clap skates won eleven of thirty medals, five of which were gold. By the 2002 Winter Olympics, all speed skaters had switched over to the new skates, and the medal count was much more evenly distributed. That year the United States, the Netherlands, and Germany each won three gold medals, and a total of eight medals apiece. Clap skates were the most likely cause of the Netherlands' dominance four years earlier.

- **Concomitant Variation.** Some causes are discovered by observing a shared pattern of variation in a possible cause and possible effect. For example, scientists noticed that peaks in the 11-year sunspot cycle match disruptions in high-frequency radio transmission on Earth, leading them to conclude that the solar activity somehow causes the disruptions.

- **Process of Elimination.** Another way to establish causation is to identify all the possible causes of something, and then test them one by one to eliminate those that can't be the cause. When an electrical appliance stops working, electricians often trace the problem this way, by checking switches one at a time to see if current can flow across them. The switch that doesn't show a continuous flow of current is the one that needs replacing.

A frequent error of people looking for cause and effect is to mistake **correlation** for causation. Just because one event happens after or at the same time as another one, you cannot assume that the first one caused the second. Sometimes it's just a coincidence. For example, you may observe that every time the mail carrier comes to your door, your dog barks at him and then the mail carrier leaves. You might assume that your dog's barking causes the mail carrier to leave (your dog is probably convinced of this). However, the more likely cause is that the carrier has finished delivering your mail, so he goes on to the next house. Using Mills's methods will help you avoid mistaking correlation for causation in your own causal arguments.

To understand how you might use Mills's methods of identifying causes, suppose you want to research the cause of the increase in legalized lotteries in the United States. You research the history of lotteries in order to look for possible causes. You would discover that lotteries go back to colonial times but were controversial because they were run by private companies that sometimes failed to pay the winners. Laws against lotteries were passed in 1840, but after the Civil War, the defeated states of the Confederacy needed money to rebuild bridges, buildings, and schools. Southerners ran lotteries and sold tickets throughout the nation. But once again, these lotteries were run by private companies, and some of them simply took people's money without paying out winnings. Eventually, lotteries were banned again.

In 1964 New Hampshire became the first state to authorize a lottery to fund the state's educational system. Soon other states, realizing that their citizens were spending their money on lottery tickets from New Hampshire, established lotteries of their own. During the 1980s, states began approving other forms of state-run gambling such as keno and video poker. By 1993 only Hawaii and Utah had no legalized gambling of any kind.

Knowing this background, you can begin using Mills's methods to look for the causes of lotteries' recent popularity. Using the common factor method, you consider what current lotteries have in common with earlier lotteries. That factor is easy to identify: It's economic. The early colonies and later the states have turned to lotteries again and again as a way of raising money without raising taxes. But, you wonder, why have lotteries spread so quickly since 1964 and raised so little concern? The single difference method shows you the likely reason: Lotteries in the past were run by private companies, and inevitably someone took off with the money instead of paying it out. Today's lotteries are operated by state agencies or contracted under state control. While they are not immune to scandal, they are much more closely monitored than lotteries in the past.

Mills's other methods might also lead you to potential causes. If you find, for example, that lotteries grow in popularity in the aftermath of wars, this concomitant variation might lead you to suspect that the economic damage of war can be one cause of lotteries' popularity. This in turn might suggest inflation caused by the Vietnam War as a possible contributing cause to the rise of state lotteries in the 1960s and 1970s. The process of elimination could also lead you to some probable causes for lotteries' popularity, although for such a complex topic, it would be time-consuming. You might begin by making a list of all the reasons you could think of: Perhaps people these days are more economically secure and don't mind risking a few dollars on lottery tickets? Or maybe people are more desperate now, and lotteries represent one of the few ways they can accumulate wealth? Each of these possibilities would require research into history, economics, and psychology, but this might lead you to some interesting conclusions about the complex forces contributing to today's extensive lottery system.

Build a Causal Argument

Effective causal arguments move beyond the obvious to get at underlying causes. One great causal mystery today is global warming. Scientists generally agree that the average surface temperature on Earth has gone up by 1.3 degrees Fahrenheit, or 0.7 degrees Celsius, over the last hundred years and that the amount of carbon dioxide in the atmosphere has increased by 25 percent since 1960. But the causes of those phenomena are disputed. Some people argue that the rise in temperature is caused by natural climate variations and that the increase in carbon dioxide has little or nothing to do with it. Others argue that the rise in carbon dioxide traps heat in the atmosphere and has increased the Earth's temperature. They argue further that the increased carbon dioxide is the result of human activity, especially the burning of fossil fuels and the destruction of tropical forests. The debate over global warming continues because the causation at work is not simple or easy to prove.

There are many events that may be caused by global warming, and they are more dramatically evident in arctic and subarctic regions. The decade from January 2000 to December 2009 is the warmest decade since modern temperature records began in the 1880s. Arctic sea ice shrank by 14 percent—an area the size of Texas—from 2004 to 2005, and Greenland's massive ice sheet has been thinning by more than 3 feet a year.

Many scientists consider these phenomena to be effects of global warming. They argue that a single cause—the rise in the Earth's temperature—has led to many dire effects and will lead to more. If you wanted to make an argument along these lines, you would need to construct a causal chain:

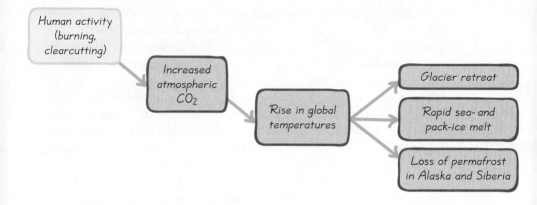

At each step, you would need to show the links between an event and its consequences, and you would need to convince readers that that link is real, not mere coincidence. You might find common factors, single differences, or concomitant variation that supports each causal link. You would also need to use a process of elimination to show that other possible causes are not in fact involved in your causal chain.

Some climate scientists have doubts about all these causal links. While the observable events—the loss of sea ice, glacier retreat, and so on—may be caused by human activity, they may be caused instead by naturally recurring cycles.

Or the effects could be caused partly by natural cycles and partly by humans.

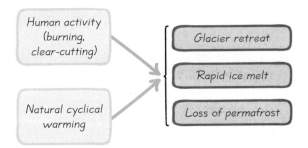

It is difficult to say for certain because much of the detailed data about the great melt in the north goes back only to the early 1990s—not long enough to rule out short-term climate cycles. However, computer models suggest a very low probability that such rapid change could occur naturally. So even if we are in a natural, short-term warming cycle, we still must ask if human activities are contributing to the documented warming and making it even worse.

Identifying the causes of global warming is important because if we do not know the real causes, we cannot make the necessary changes to stop, reduce, or reverse it. If global warming continues unabated, the economic and human costs will be disastrous. But efforts to stop it are expensive and politically risky. Thus correctly establishing the causes of global warming is a crucial first step in solving the problem.

Glaciers in many parts of the world are melting at rates faster than scientists thought possible just a few years ago. Even major oil companies have acknowledged that global warming is real. Yet the American public has taken little notice of world climate change—perhaps because it's difficult to get excited about the mean temperature rising a few degrees and the sea level rising a few feet. What would get Americans thinking seriously about global warming?

Steps to Writing a Causal Argument

Step 1 Make a Claim

Make a causal claim on a controversial trend, event, or phenomenon.

Template

> SOMETHING does (or does not) cause SOMETHING ELSE.

–or–

> SOMETHING causes SOMETHING ELSE, which, in turn, causes SOMETHING ELSE.

Examples

- One-parent families (or television violence, bad diet, and so on) are (or are not) the cause of emotional and behavioral problems in children.
- Firearms control laws (or right-to-carry-handgun laws) reduce (or increase) violent crimes.
- Putting grade school children into competitive sports teaches them how to succeed in later life (or puts undue emphasis on winning and teaches many who are slower to mature to have a negative self-image).

Step 2 What's at Stake in Your Claim?

- If the cause is obvious to everyone, then it probably isn't worth writing about.

Step 3 Think of Possible Causes

- Which are the immediate causes?
- Which are the background causes?
- Which are the hidden causes?
- Which are the causes that most people have not recognized?

Step 4 Analyze Your Potential Readers

- Who are your readers?
- How familiar will they be with the trend, event, or phenomenon that you're writing about?
- What are they likely to know and not know?
- How likely are they to accept your causal explanation?
- What alternative explanation might they argue for?

Step 5 Write a Draft

Introduction

- Describe the controversial trend, event, or phenomenon.
- Give the background that your intended readers will need.

Body

- Explain the cause or chain of causation of a trend, event, or phenomenon that is unfamiliar to your readers.
- Set out the causes that have been offered and reject them one by one. Then you can present the cause that you think is most important.
- Treat a series of causes one by one, analyzing the importance of each.

Conclusion

- Do more than simply summarize. Consider describing additional effects beyond those that have been noted previously.

Step 6 Revise, Edit, Proofread

- For detailed instructions, see Chapter 5.
- For a checklist to use to evaluate your draft, see pages 50–51.

Finding Good Reasons

Why Are Americans Gaining Weight?

Eric Schlosser, author of *Fast Food Nation* (2001), chows down on a grilled cheese sandwich, fries, and a soda. *Fast Food Nation* traces the rise of fast-food restaurants against the background of an American culture based on the automobile. Schlosser claims that one of the effects of fast food is the increase in the number of overweight Americans.

There is no doubt that Americans have grown larger. A 2004 survey of Americans published in *JAMA: The Journal of the American Medical Association* found that nearly one-third (32.5 percent) of adults are obese and two-thirds (66.3 percent) are overweight. An especially disturbing aspect of this trend is that children are increasingly obese. The Center for Disease Control and Prevention reports that the percentage of obese children aged 6 to 11 more than quadrupled from 4 percent in 1974 to 18 percent in 2010, and the percentage of obese children aged 12 to 19 increased from 6 percent in 1974 to 18.4 percent in 2010.

Write about it

To what extent do you think fast food is the cause of the trend toward excess weight? To what extent do you think lifestyle changes and the content of food are causes? In addition to the amount of fast food Americans consume, consider the following.

- More sedentary lifestyle with more driving and less walking
- More time spent watching television, using computers, and playing video games
- Introduction of high-fructose corn syrup in many foods, from ketchup and peanut butter to chocolate milk and yogurt
- Inadequate physical education and reduced outdoor recess periods in schools
- More food advertising directed at children

Emily
Raine

Why Should I Be Nice to You? Coffee Shops and the Politics of Good Service

Emily Raine received a master's degree in communication studies at McGill University in Montreal. She writes about graffiti and street art. This article appeared in the online journal *Bad Subjects* in 2005.

In this article, Raine explains why work in a coffee chain is worse than work in other kinds of service jobs. She also outlines the causes for what she sees as a destructive dynamic in the coffee chain culture and provides a possible alternative.

> "There is no more precious commodity than the relationship of trust and confidence a company has with its employees."
> —*Starbucks Coffee Company chairman Howard Schultz*

I actually like to serve. I'm not sure if this comes from some innate inclination to mother and fuss over strangers, or if it's because the movement and sociability of service work provides a much-needed antidote to the solitude of academic research, but I've always found something about service industry work satisfying. I've done the gamut of service jobs, from fine dining to cocktail waitressing to hip euro-bistro counter work, and the only job where I've ever felt truly whipped was working as a barista at one of the now-ubiquitous specialty coffee chains, those bastions of jazz and public solitude that have spread through urban landscapes over the last ten years or so. The pay was poor, the shifts long and oddly dispersed, the work boring and monotonous, the managers demanding, and the customers regularly displayed that unique spleen that emerges in even the most pleasant people before they've had the morning's first coffee. I often felt like an aproned Coke machine, such was the effect my sparkling personality had on the clientele. And yet, some combination of service professionalism, fear of termination and an imperative to be "nice" allowed me to suck it up, smile and continue to provide that intangible trait that the industry holds above all else, good service.

2   Good service in coffee shops doesn't amount to much. Unlike table service, where interaction with customers spans a minimum of half an hour, the average contact with a café customer lasts less than ten seconds. Consider how specialty cafés are laid

Raine establishes a credible, ethical stance in her introduction.

Even before identifying the effect that she intends to analyze, Raine identifies the cause—an efficient but impersonal assembly-line approach to service.

3 out: the customer service counter is arranged in a long line that clients move along to "use" the café. The linear coffee bar resembles an assembly line, and indeed, café labor is heavily grounded in the rationalism of Fordist manufacturing principles, which had already been tested for use in hospitality services by fast food chains. Each of the café workers is assigned a specific stage in the service process to perform exclusively, such as taking orders, using the cash registers, or handing clients cups of brewed coffee.

4 The specialization of tasks increases the speed of transactions and limits the duration of any one employee's interaction with the clientele. This means that in a given visit a customer might order from one worker, receive food from the next, then brewed coffee or tea from yet another, then pay a cashier before proceeding down the line of the counter, finishing the trip at the espresso machine which is always situated at its end. Ultimately, each of the café's products is processed and served by a different employee, who repeats the same preparation task for hours and attends to each customer only as they receive that one product.

Raine argues that the assembly-line service model precludes real interaction with customers.

Needless to say, the productive work in cafés is dreary and repetitive. Further, this style of service severely curtails interaction with the clientele, and the very brevity of each transaction precludes much chance for authentic friendliness or conversation—even asking about someone's day would slow the entire operation. The one aspect of service work that can be unpredictable—people—becomes redundant, and interaction with customers is reduced to a fatiguing eight-hour-long smile and the repetition of sentiments that allude to good service, such as injunctions to enjoy their purchases or to have a nice day. Rather than friendly exchanges with customers, barista workers' good service is reduced to a quick rictus in the customer's direction between a great deal of friendly interaction with the espresso machine.

Do you agree with this description of a typical coffee shop?

5 As the hospitality industry really took off in the sixties, good service became one of the trademarks of its advertising claims, a way for brands to distinguish themselves from the rest of the pack. One needn't think too hard to come up with a litany of service slogans that holler the good graces of their personnel—at Starbucks where the baristas make the magic, at Pacific Southwest Airlines where smiles aren't just painted on, or at McDonald's where smiles are free. Employee friendliness emerged as one of the chief distinguishing brand features of personal services, which means that the workers themselves become an aspect of the product for sale.

6 Our notions of good service revolve around a series of platitudes about professionalism—we're at your service, with a smile,

where the customer's always right—each bragging the centrality of the customer to everything "we" do. Such claims imply an easy and equal exchange between two parties: the "we" that gladly serves and the "you" that happily receives. There is, however, always a third party involved in the service exchange, and that's whoever has hired the server, the body that ultimately decides just what the dimensions of good service will be.

This "third party"—management, ownership—is the ultimate cause of the phenomenon under discussion.

7   Like most employees, a service worker sells labor to an employer at a set rate, often minimum wage, and the employer sells the product of that labor, the service itself, at market values. In many hospitality services, where gratuities make up the majority of employment revenue, the worker directly benefits from giving good service, which of course translates to good tips. But for the vast majority of service staff, and particularly those employed in venues yielding little or no gratuities—fast food outlets, café chains, cleaning and maintenance operations—this promises many workers little more than a unilateral imperative to be perpetually bright and amenable.

8   The vast majority of service personnel do not spontaneously produce an unaffected display of cheer and good will continuously for the duration of a shift. When a company markets its products on servers' friendliness, they must then monitor and control employees' friendliness, so good service is defined and enforced from above. Particularly in chains, which are premised upon their consistent reproduction of the same experience in numerous locations, organizations are obliged to impose systems to manage employees' interaction with their customers. In some chains, namely the fast food giants such as McDonald's and Burger King, employee banter is scripted into cash registers, so that as soon as a customer orders, workers are cued to offer, "would you like a dessert with that?" (an offer of dubious benefit to the customer) and to wish them a nice day. Ultimately, this has allowed corporations to be able to assimilate "good service"—or, friendly workers—into their overall brand image.

Does your experience as a customer (or worker) at fast food chains match this description?

9   While cafés genuflect toward the notion of good service, their layouts and management styles preclude much possibility of creating the warmth that this would entail. Good service is, of course, important, but not if it interferes with throughput. What's more, these cafés have been at the forefront of a new wave of organizations that not only market themselves on service quality but also describe employees' job satisfaction as the seed from which this flowers.

10   Perhaps the most glaring example of this is Starbucks, where cheerful young workers are displayed behind elevated

counters as they banter back and forth, calling out fancy Italian drink names and creating theatre out of their productive labor. Starbucks' corporate literature gushes not only about the good service its customers will receive, but about the great joy that its "partners" take in providing it, given the company's unique ability to "provide a great work environment and treat each other with respect and dignity," and where its partners are "emotionally and intellectually committed to Starbucks success." In the epigraph to this essay, Starbucks' chairman even describes the company's relationship with its workers as a commodity. Not only does Starbucks offer good service, but it attempts to guarantee something even better: good service provided by employees that are genuinely happy to give it.

The creation of this new kind of worker is in effect a public relations gimmick.

11   Starbucks has branded a new kind of worker, the happy, wholesome, perfume-free barista. The company offers unusual benefits for service workers, including stock options, health insurance, dental plans and other perks such as product discounts and giveaways. Further, they do so very, very publicly, and the company's promotional materials are filled with moving accounts of workers who never dreamed that corporate America could care so much. With the other hand, though, the company has smashed unionization drives in New York, Vancouver and at its Seattle roaster; it schedules workers at oddly timed shifts that never quite add up to full-time hours; the company pays only nominally more than minimum wage, and their staffs are still unable to subsist schlepping lattes alone.

12   Starbucks is not alone in marketing itself as an enlightened employer. When General Motors introduced its Saturn line, the new brand was promoted almost entirely on the company's good relations with its staff. The company's advertising spots often featured pictures of and quotes from the union contract, describing their unique partnership between manufacturer, workers and union, which allowed blue-collar personnel to have a say in everything from automobile designs to what would be served for lunch. The company rightly guessed that this strategy would go over well with liberal consumers concerned about the ethics of their purchases. Better yet, Saturn could market its cars based on workers' happiness whether personnel were satisfied or not, because very few consumers would ever have the chance to interact with them.

13   At the specialty coffee chains, however, consumers have to talk to employees, yet nobody ever really asks. The café service counter runs like a smooth piece of machinery, and I found that most people preferred to pretend that they were interacting with an appliance. In such short transactions, it is exceedingly difficult

for customers to remember the humanity of each of the four to seven people they might interact with to get their coffees. Even fast food counters have one server who processes each customer's order, yet in cafés the workers just become another gadget in the well-oiled café machine. This is a definite downside for the employees—clients are much ruder to café staff than in any other sector of the industry I ever worked in. I found that people were more likely to be annoyed than touched by any reference to my having a personality, and it took no small amount of thought on my part to realize why.

14   Barista workers are hired to represent an abstract category of worker, not to act as individuals. Because of the service system marked by short customer interaction periods and a homogenous staff, the services rendered are linked in the consumer imagination to the company and not to any one individual worker. Workers' assimilation into the company image makes employees in chain service as branded as the products they serve. The chain gang, the workers who hold these eminently collegiate after-school jobs, are proscribed sales scripts and drilled on customer service scenarios to standardize interactions with customers. The company issues protocols for hair length, color and maintenance, visible piercings and tattoos as well as personal hygiene and acceptable odorific products. Workers are made more interchangeable by the use of uniforms, which, of course, serve to make the staff just that. The organization is a constant intermediary in every transaction, interjecting its presence in every detail of the service experience, and this standardization amounts to an absorption of individuals' personalities into the corporate image.

Raine spells out her thesis in this paragraph.

15   Many of the measures that chains take to secure the homogeneity of their employees do not strike us as particularly alarming, likely because similar restrictions have been in place for several hundred years. Good service today has inherited many of the trappings of the good servant of yore, including prohibitions against eating, drinking, sitting or relaxing in front the served, entering and exiting through back doors, and wearing uniforms to visually mark workers' status. These measures almost completely efface the social identities of staff during work hours, providing few clues to workers' status in their free time. Contact between service workers and their customers is thus limited to purely functional relations, so that the public only see them as workers, as makers of quality coffee, and never as possible peers.

16   Maintaining such divisions is integral to good service because this display of class distinctions ultimately underlies our

notions of service quality. Good service means not only serving well, but also allowing customers to feel justified in issuing orders, to feel okay about being served—which, in turn, requires demonstrations of class difference and the smiles that suggest servers' comfort with having a subordinate role in the service exchange.

17   Unlike the penguin-suited household servant staffs whose class status was clearly defined, service industry workers today often have much more in common from a class perspective with those that they serve. This not only creates an imperative for them to wear their class otherness on their sleeves, as it were, but also to accept their subordinate role to those they serve by being unshakably tractable and polite.

18   Faith Popcorn has rather famously referred to the four-dollar latte as a "small indulgence," noting that while this is a lot to pay for a glass of hot milk, it is quite inexpensive for the feeling of luxury that can accompany it. In this service climate, the class status of the server and the served—anyone who can justify spending this much on a coffee—is blurry, indeed. Coffee shops that market themselves on employee satisfaction assert the same happy servant that allows politically conscientious consumers, who are in many cases the workers' own age and class peers, to feel justified in receiving good service. Good service—as both an apparent affirmation of subordinate classes' desire to serve and as an enforced one-sided politeness—reproduces the class distinctions that have historically characterized servant-served relationships so that these are perpetuated within the contemporary service market.

Raine begins to shift attention to the customers' role in coffee shop culture.

19   The specialty coffee companies are large corporations, and for the twenty-somethings who stock their counters, barista work is too temporary to bother fighting the system. Mostly, people simply quit. Dissatisfied workers are stuck with engaging in tactics that will change nothing but allow them to make the best of their lot. These include minor infractions such as taking liberties with the uniforms or grabbing little bits of company time for their own pleasure, what Michel de Certeau calls *la perruque* and the companies themselves call "time theft." As my time in the chain gang wore on, I developed my own tactic, the only one I found that jostled the customers out of their complacency and allowed me to be a barista and a person.

20   There is no easy way to serve without being a servant, and I have always found that the best way to do so is to show my actual emotions rather than affecting a smooth display of interminable patience and good will. For café customers, bettering baristas' lots can be as simple as asking about their day, addressing them

by name—any little gesture to show that you noticed the person behind the service that they can provide. My tactic as a worker is equally simple, but it is simultaneously an assertion of individual identity at work, a refusal of the class distinctions that character-ize the service environment and a rebuttal to the companies that would promote my satisfaction with their system: be rude. Not ar-bitrarily rude, of course—customers are people, too, and nobody gains anything by spreading bad will. But on those occasions when customer or management behavior warranted a zinging comeback, I would give it.

Were you expecting this "solution" to the situation Raine presents?

21   Rudeness, when it is demanded, undermines companies' claims on workers' personal warmth and allows them to retain their individuality by expressing genuine rather than affected feelings in at-work interpersonal exchanges. It is a refusal of the class distinctions that underlie consumers' unilateral pre-rogative of rudeness and servers' unilateral imperative to be nice. It runs contrary to everything that we have been taught, not only about service but about interrelating with others. But this seems to be the only method of asserting one's person-hood in the service environment, where workers' personalities are all too easily reduced to a space-time, conflated with the drinks they serve. Baristas of the world, if you want to avoid becoming a green-aproned coffee dispensary, you're just going to have to tell people off about it.

Raine reveals her specific audience, "baristias of the world," only at the end of her argument.

Sample Student Causal Argument

Tansal 1

Armadi Tansal

Professor Stewart

English 115

29 October 2013

Modern Warfare: Video Games' Link to Real-World Violence

"John" is a nineteen-year-old college student who gets decent grades. He comes from a typical upper-middle-class family and plans to get his MBA after he graduates. John is also my friend, which is why I'm not using his real name.

John has been playing moderately violent video games since he was nine years old. I started playing video and console games around that age too, and I played a lot in junior high, but John plays more than anyone I know. John says that over the past year he has played video games at least four hours every day and "sometimes all day and night on the weekends." I have personally witnessed John play *Call of Duty: Modern Warfare 3* for six hours straight, with breaks only to use the bathroom or eat something.

I've never seen John act violently, and he's never been in trouble with the law. But new research on violent video games suggests that John's gaming habit puts him at risk for violent or aggressive behavior. Dr. Craig Anderson, a psychologist at the University of Iowa, says that "the active role required by video games . . . may make violent video games even more hazardous than violent television or cinema." When people like John play these games, they get used to being rewarded for violent behavior. For example, in the multiplayer version of *Modern Warfare 3*, if the player gets a five-kill streak, he can call in a Predator missile strike. If you kill 25 people in a row, you can call in a tactical nuclear strike. Missile strikes help you advance toward the mission goals more quickly, so the more people you kill, the faster you'll win.

> Armadi Tansal establishes a personal relationship to his subject and audience.

Along with *Modern Warfare 3*, John plays games like *League of Legends, Halo 4,* and versions of *Grand Theft Auto*. All these games are rated M for Mature, which according to the Entertainment Software Rating Board means they "may contain intense violence, blood and gore, sexual content and/

Tansal 2

or strong language." Some M-rated games, like *Grand Theft Auto*, feature random violence, where players can run amok in a city, beat up and kill people, and smash stuff for no reason. In others, like *Modern Warfare 3*, the violence takes place in the context of military action. To do well in all of these games, you have to commit acts of violence. But does acting violently in games make you more violent in real life?

Anderson says studies show that "violent video games are significantly associated with: increased aggressive behavior, thoughts, and affect [feelings]; increased physiological arousal; and decreased prosocial (helping) behavior." He also claims that "high levels of violent video game exposure have been linked to delinquency, fighting at school and during free play periods, and violent criminal behavior (e.g., self-reported assault, robbery)."

Being "associated with" and "linked to" violent behavior doesn't necessarily mean video games cause such behavior. Many people have argued that the links Anderson sees are coincidental, or that any effects video games might have on behavior are so slight that we shouldn't worry about them. Christopher Ferguson and John Kilburn, professors of Criminal Justice at Texas A&M International University, feel that the existing research does not support Anderson's claims. In a report published in the *Journal of Pediatrics*, they point out that in past studies, "the closer aggression measures got to actual violent behavior, the weaker the effects seen" (762).

From what I can tell, John doesn't have any more violent thoughts and feelings than most men his age. When I asked him if he thought the games had made him more violent or aggressive in real life, he said, "I'm actually less violent now. When we were kids we used to play 'war' with fake guns and sticks, chasing each other around the neighborhood and fighting commando-style. We didn't really fight, but sometimes kids got banged up. No one ever gets hurt playing a video game."

Anderson admits that "a healthy, normal, nonviolent child or adolescent who has no other risk factors for high aggression or violence is not going to become a school shooter simply because they play five hours or 10 hours a week of these violent video games" (qtd. in St. George). But just because violent video games don't turn all players into mass murderers, that doesn't mean they have no effect on a player's

---

Tansal identifies the causal question at the heart of his argument.

Direct quotations from published sources build credibility.

Tansal is careful not to accept the easy answer that video games cause everyone to be more violent.

Tansal 3

behavior and personality. For example, my friend John doesn't get into fights or rob people, but he doesn't display a lot of prosocial "helping" behaviors either. He spends most of his free time gaming, so he doesn't get out of his apartment much. Also, the friends he does have mostly play video games with him.

> Here Tansal hints at his thesis, which will be explicitly stated at the end of his argument.

Even though the games restrict his interactions with other humans and condition him to behave violently onscreen, John is probably not at high risk of becoming violent in real life. But according to researchers, this low risk of becoming violent is because none of the dozens of other risk factors associated with violent behavior are present in his life (Anderson et al. 160). If John were a high school dropout, came from a broken home, or abused alcohol and other drugs, his game playing might be more likely to contribute to violent behavior.

> Tansal clarifies his thesis that games can be a contributing cause of violent behavior.

Anderson contends that violent video games are a "causal risk factor" for violence and aggression—not that they cause violent aggression. In other words, the games are a small piece of a much larger problem. People like my friend John are not likely to become violent because of the video games they play. But Anderson's research indicates that some people do. Although there is no simple way to tell who those people are, we should include video games as a possible risk factor when we think about who is likely to become violent.

Even if the risk contributed by violent video games is slight for each individual, the total impact of the games on violence in society could be huge. *Call of Duty: Modern Warfare 3* enjoyed the biggest first day sales of any game ever in 2011 until it was surpassed by its successor, *Black Ops 2*, which brought over $500 million in sales to its publisher Activision on its first day in 2012. Bobby Kotick, the CEO of Activision claims that the *Call of Duty* franchise has exceeded worldwide box office receipts for the *Harry Potter* and *Star Wars* series, the two most popular movie franchises of all time (Sheer). Millions of people play this game, and games like it, and they aren't all as well-adjusted as John. If video games contribute to violent tendencies in only a small fraction of players, they could still have a terrible impact.

> Tansal concludes by arguing that video games may not cause many people to become more violent, but it doesn't take many to be a big problem.

Tansal 4

Works Cited

Anderson, Craig. "Violent Video Games: Myths, Facts, and Unanswered Questions." *Psychological Science Agenda* 16.5 (2003): n. pag. Web. 6 Oct. 2013.

Anderson, Craig, et al. "Violent Video Game Effects on Aggression, Empathy, and Prosocial Behavior in Eastern and Western Countries." *Psychological Bulletin* 136 (2010): 151-73. Print.

Entertainment Software Rating Board. *Game Ratings and Descriptor Guide*. Entertainment Software Association, n.d. Web. 7 Oct. 2013.

Ferguson, Christopher J., and John Kilburn. "The Public Health Risks of Media Violence: A Meta-Analytic Review." *Journal of Pediatrics* 154.5 (2009): 759-63. Print.

John (pseudonym). Personal interview. 4 Oct. 2013.

Sheer, Matthew. "*Black Ops 2* Blasts Past $500 Million in Sales—in 24 Hours." *Christian Science Monitor*. Christian Science Monitor, 16 Nov. 2012. Web. 6 Oct. 2013.

St. George, Donna. "Study Links Violent Video Games, Hostility." *Washington Post*. Washington Post, 3 Nov. 2008. Web. 5 Oct. 2013.

10 | Evaluation Arguments

QUICK TAKE

In this chapter, you will learn to

1. Use evaluation arguments to set out criteria and then judge something to be good or bad according to those criteria (see page 139)
2. Recognize evaluation arguments based on practical, aesthetic, and ethical criteria (see pages 140–141)
3. Analyze an evaluation argument (see pages 142–143)
4. Write an effective evaluation argument (see pages 144–145)

By some estimates, as many as 5 million animals are killed in shelters each year. Are "no-kill" shelters a good idea? Advocates of no-kill shelters argue that alternatives to euthanizing animals can be created by working to increase adoption demand for shelter animals. No-kill shelters also work to promote spaying and neutering to decrease the number of animals sent to shelters in the first place. Others argue that the term "no-kill" is divisive because it implies that some shelters are "kill" shelters and suggests that many shelter workers are cruel or uncaring. Are no-kill shelters an effective solution? What kind of evaluations would support or oppose the concept of the no-kill shelter? How can evaluation arguments be used to support more humane treatment of shelter animals?

People make evaluations all the time. Newspapers, magazines, and television have picked up on this love of evaluation by running "best of" polls. They ask their readers to vote on the best Chinese restaurant, the best pizza, the best local band, the best coffeehouse, the best dance club, the best neighborhood park, the best swimming hole, the best bike ride (scenic or challenging), the best volleyball court, the best place to get married, and so on. If you ask one of your friends who voted in a "best" poll why she picked a particular restaurant as the best of its kind, she might respond by saying simply, "I like it." But if you ask her why she likes it, she might start offering good reasons such as these: The food is tasty, the service prompt, the prices fair, and the atmosphere comfortable. It's really not a mystery why these polls are often quite predictable or why the same restaurants tend to win year after year. Many people think that evaluations are matters of personal taste, but when we begin probing the reasons, we often discover that different people use similar criteria to make evaluations.

The key to convincing other people that your judgment is sound is establishing the criteria you will use to make your evaluation. Sometimes it will be necessary to argue for the validity of the criteria that you think your readers should consider. If your readers accept your criteria, it's likely they will agree with your conclusions.

Understand How Evaluation Arguments Work

Evaluation arguments set out criteria and then judge something to be good or bad (or better, or best) according to those criteria.

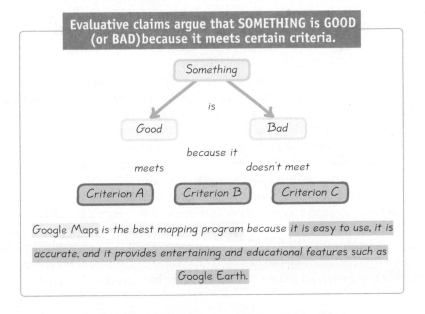

Evaluative claims argue that SOMETHING is GOOD (or BAD) because it meets certain criteria.

Something

is

Good   Bad

because it

meets   doesn't meet

Criterion A   Criterion B   Criterion C

Google Maps is the best mapping program because it is easy to use, it is accurate, and it provides entertaining and educational features such as Google Earth.

Recognize Kinds of Evaluations

Arguments of evaluation are structured much like arguments of definition. Recall that the criteria in arguments of definition are set out in *because* clauses:

SOMETHING is a _____ because it meets certain criteria.

Evaluative claims argue that

SOMETHING is GOOD (or BAD) because it meets certain criteria.

While people often agree about general criteria, they sometimes disagree about the relevance and appropriateness of specific criteria in an evaluation. Take as an example the question of which colleges are good schools. Until twenty years ago, most of the information that people used to evaluate a college came from the college itself. You could find out the price of tuition and what courses were offered, but other information was difficult to find, and it was hard to compare one college with another.

In 1983 the magazine *U.S. News & World Report* began ranking U.S. colleges and universities from a consumer's perspective. These rankings have remained controversial ever since. *U.S. News* evaluates schools using a complex set of criteria. Twenty-five percent of a school's ranking is based on a survey in which officials at each college rate the quality of schools in the same category as their own school. The results of this survey reflect the school's reputation among administrators. The remaining 75 percent is based on six kinds of statistical data. These measure retention of students, faculty resources, student selectivity, financial resources, alumni giving, and, for some schools, graduation rates (the difference between the number of students expected to graduate and the number who actually do).

U.S. News chooses specific types of information to look at in each category. For example, the category "faculty resources" is measured by the size of classes, average faculty pay, the percentage of professors with the highest degree in their field, the overall student-faculty ratio, and the percentage of faculty who are full-time.

Many college officials have criticized the criteria *U.S. News* uses to evaluate colleges. In an August 1998 *U.S. News* article, Gerhard Casper, the president of Stanford University (which is consistently near the top of the rankings), writes, "Much about these rankings—particularly their specious formulas and spurious precision—is utterly misleading." Casper argues that using graduation rates as a criterion rewards schools that pass low-achieving students.

U.S. News replies in its defense that colleges and universities themselves do a lot of ranking, using data and methods that can be questioned. Schools rank students for admission, using SAT or ACT scores, high school GPA, class rank, and other factors, and then grade students and rank them against each other once they are enrolled in college. Schools also evaluate their faculty and take great interest in the national ranking of their departments. They care very much about how they stand in relation to one another. Why, then, *U.S. News* argues, shouldn't people be able to evaluate colleges and universities, since colleges and universities are in the business of evaluating people?

The magazine and the colleges have very different ideas about what constitute fair and relevant criteria for evaluating a college. But the *U.S. News* college rankings generate a tremendous amount of income for the magazine, which suggests that students and their parents agree with the criteria and use them to help make their own decisions about college.

Some evaluation arguments rely more heavily on certain types of criteria than others. For example, a movie review (_____ is a good movie) is likely to focus most closely on aesthetic considerations: engaging characters, an exciting story, beautiful cinematography. Ethical considerations may be relevant—say, if the film is exceptionally violent or celebrates antisocial behavior—but usually don't predominate in a movie review. Practical considerations will probably be least important, since anyone reading a movie review is presumably willing to spend the price of admission to see a film. Use aesthetic, moral, and practical criteria for deciding how good or bad a person, a place, an artifact, or a policy is.

Build an Evaluation Argument

Although evaluation arguments seem very similar to definition arguments, there is a key difference. Definition arguments seek to place something in the correct category by observing its qualities. They hinge on our judgments about similarity and difference. Evaluation arguments focus instead on what we value. Because of this, the criteria you choose when making an evaluation argument are very important. If your criteria do not appeal to the values of your audience, your readers will not feel that your evaluation is accurate.

Suppose that a city task force on downtown revitalization has a plan to demolish the oldest commercial building in your city. Your neighborhood association wants to preserve the building, perhaps by turning it into a museum. To persuade officials to do this, you must show that your plan for preservation is a good one, while the task force's plan for demolition is a bad one. You might argue that a museum would attract visitors to the downtown area, bringing in revenue. You might argue that the elaborately carved stone facade of the building is a rare example of a disappearing craft. Or you might argue that it is only fair to preserve the oldest commercial building in town, since the city's oldest house and other historic buildings have been saved.

Each of these arguments uses different criteria. The argument that a museum will bring in money is based on practical considerations. The argument about the rare and beautiful stonework on the building is based on aesthetic (artistic) considerations. The argument that an old commercial building deserves the same treatment as other old buildings is based on fairness, or ethical concerns. Depending on your audience, you might use all three kinds of criteria, or you might focus more on one or two kinds. If your city is in the middle of a budget crisis, it might be wise to stress the practical, economic benefits of a museum. If several city council members are architects or amateur historians, your argument might focus

Windmills produce energy without pollution and reduce dependence on foreign oil. Do you agree or disagree with people who do not want windmills built near them because they find them ugly?

on the aesthetic criteria. You have to make assumptions about what your audience will value most as they consider your evaluation.

Evaluative arguments can look at just one case in isolation, but often they make comparisons. You could construct an argument about the fate of the old building that only describes your plan and its benefits. Or you might also directly address the demolition proposal, showing how it lacks those benefits. Then your argument might be structured like this:

Finding Good Reasons

What's the Best Alternative Fuel?

Biodiesel is an alternative fuel source that is made from vegetable oil (or animal fats) and alcohol. While biodiesel can be used alone, it is often mixed with petroleum diesel. Blends of up to 20 percent biodiesel can be used in a standard diesel engine without modifications—meaning that many cars on the road today would be capable of using biodiesel if it were to become widely available.

But is biodiesel a realistic solution to the world's dependence on fossil fuels? Many think yes. Proponents point to the reduction in greenhouse gas emissions and the lower dependence on foreign oil that would accompany wide-scale biodiesel adoption. Detractors point to millions of acres of land, which would typically be used for food production, that would be converted to fuel production, inevitably causing shortages and an overall rise in food prices.

Write about it

1. One way to assess a complicated issue like alternative fuel technologies is to evaluate each technology against a set of common criteria. Which of the following criteria are useful for evaluating fuel-efficient cars? Why are they useful?

   - Cost of development and production
   - Sticker price of cars using the technology
   - How long it takes for cars to reach the market
   - Efficiency and reliability of cars using the technology
   - Environmental impact
   - Convenience of refueling and maintenance
   - Driver's aesthetic experience

2. Are any of the above criteria more important than the others? If so, how would you rank them? Why? Are there any criteria you would add?

Steps to Writing an Evaluation Argument

Step 1 Make a Claim

Make an evaluative claim based on criteria.

Template

> SOMETHING is good (bad, the best, the worst) if measured by certain criteria (practicality, aesthetics, ethics).

Examples

- A book or movie review
- An evaluation of a controversial aspect of sports (e.g., the current system of determining who is champion in Division I college football) or a sports event (e.g., this year's WNBA playoffs) or a team
- An evaluation of the effectiveness of a social policy or law such as restrictions on newly licensed drivers, current gun control laws, or environmental regulation

Step 2 Think About What's at Stake

- Does nearly everyone agree with you? Then your claim probably isn't interesting or important. If you can think of people who disagree, then something is at stake.
- Who argues the opposite of your claim?
- Why do they make a different evaluation?

Step 3 List the Criteria

- Which criteria make something either good or bad?
- Which criteria are the most important?
- Which criteria are fairly obvious, and which will you have to argue for?

Step 4 Analyze Your Potential Readers

- Who are your readers?
- How familiar will they be with what you are evaluating?
- Which criteria are they most likely to accept with little explanation, and which will they disagree with?

Step 5 Write a Draft

Introduction

- Introduce the person, group, institution, event, or object that you are going to evaluate. You might want to announce your stance at this point or wait until the concluding section.
- Give the background that your intended readers will need.

Body

- Describe each criterion and then analyze how well what you are evaluating meets that criterion.
- If you are making an evaluation according to the effects someone or something produces, describe each effect in detail.
- Anticipate where readers might question either your criteria or how they apply to your subject.
- Address opposing viewpoints by acknowledging how their evaluations might differ and by showing why your evaluation is better.

Conclusion

- If you have not yet announced your stance, conclude that, on the basis of the criteria you set out or the effects you have analyzed, something is good (bad, the best, the worst).
- If you have made your stance clear from the beginning, end with a compelling example or analogy.

Step 6 Revise, Edit, Proofread

- For detailed instructions, see Chapter 5.
- For a checklist to use to evaluate your draft, see pages 50–51.

**Glenn
Loury**

A Nation of Jailers

Glenn Loury is Merton P. Stoltz Professor of the Social Sciences at Brown University and a guest on many television and radio news programs. He is the author of *One by One, From the Inside Out: Essays and Reviews on Race and Responsibility in America* (1995), *Anatomy of Racial Inequality* (2001), *Ethnicity, Social Mobility and Public Policy: Comparing the US and the UK* (2005), and over two hundred essays and reviews on racial inequality and social policy.

Instead of immediately announcing his thesis, Loury asks what are the criteria for our ideal vision of society?

The most challenging problems of social policy in the modern world are never merely technical. In order properly to decide how we should govern ourselves, we must take up questions of social ethics and human values. What manner of people are we Americans? What vision would we affirm, and what example would we set, before the rest of the world? What kind of society would we bequeath to our children? How shall we live? Inevitably, queries such as these lurk just beneath the surface of the great policy debates of the day. So, those who would enter into public argument about what ails our common life need make no apology for speaking in such terms.

In paragraph 2, Loury narrows the focus to evaluate the massive-scale imprisonment of poor Americans.

2   It is precisely in these terms that I wish to discuss a preeminent moral challenge for our time—that imprisonment on a massive scale has become one of the central aspects of our nation's social policy toward the poor, powerfully impairing the lives of some of the most marginal of our fellow citizens, especially the poorly educated black and Hispanic men who reside in large numbers in our great urban centers.

3   The bare facts of this matter—concerning both the scale of incarceration and its racial disparity—have been much remarked upon of late. Simply put, we have become a nation of jailers and, arguably, racist jailers at that. The past four decades have witnessed a truly historic expansion, and transformation, of penal institutions in the United States—at every level of government, and in all regions of the country. We have, by any measure, become a vastly more punitive society. Measured in constant dollars and taking account of all levels of government, spending on corrections and law enforcement in the United States has more than quadrupled over the last quarter century. As a result, the American prison system has grown into a leviathan unmatched in human history. This development should be deeply troubling to anyone who professes to love liberty.

4   Here, as in other areas of social policy, the United States is a stark international outlier, sitting at the most rightward end of

the political spectrum: We imprison at a far higher rate than the other industrial democracies—higher, indeed, than either Russia or China, and vastly higher than any of the countries of Western Europe. According to the International Centre for Prison Studies in London, there were in 2005 some 9 million prisoners in the world; more than 2 million were being held in the United States. With approximately one twentieth of the world's population, America had nearly one fourth of the world's inmates. At more than 700 per 100,000 residents, the U.S. incarceration rate was far greater than our nearest competitors (the Bahamas, Belarus, and Russia, which each have a rate of about 500 per 100,000.) Other indus-trial societies, some of them with big crime problems of their own, were less punitive than we by an order of magnitude: the United States incarcerated at 6.2 times the rate of Canada, 7.8 times the rate of France, and 12.3 times the rate of Japan.

Comparisons with other na-tions make a strong argument that the United States has an incarceration problem.

5   The demographic profile of the inmate population has also been much discussed. In this, too, the U.S. is an international outlier. African Americans and Hispanics, who taken together are about one fourth of the population, account for about two thirds of state prison inmates. Roughly one third of state prisoners were locked up for committing violent offenses, with the remainder be-ing property and drug offenders. Nine in ten are male, and most are impoverished. Inmates in state institutions average fewer than eleven years of schooling.

6   The extent of racial disparity in imprisonment rates exceeds that to be found in any other arena of American social life: at eight to one, the black to white ratio of male incarceration rates dwarfs the two to one ratio of unemployment rates, the three to one non-marital child bearing ratio, the two to one ratio of infant mortality rates and the one to five ratio of net worth. More black male high school dropouts are in prison than belong to unions or are en-rolled in any state or federal social welfare programs. The brute fact of the matter is that the primary contact between black Ameri-can young adult men and their government is via the police and the penal apparatus. Coercion is the most salient feature of their encounters with the state. According to estimates compiled by so-ciologist Bruce Western, nearly 60% of black male dropouts born between 1965 and 1969 had spent at least one year in prison before reaching the age of 35.

Statistics show the degree to which the prob-lem applies to black men.

7   For these men, and the families and communities with which they are associated, the adverse effects of incarceration will extend beyond their stays behind bars. My point is that this is not merely law enforcement policy. It is social policy writ large. And no other country in the world does it quite like we do.

8   This is far more than a technical issue—entailing more, that is, than the task of finding the most efficient crime control policies. Consider, for instance, that it is not possible to conduct a cost-benefit analysis of our nation's world-historic prison buildup over the past 35 years without implicitly specifying how the costs imposed on the persons imprisoned, and their families, are to be reckoned. Of course, this has not stopped analysts from pronouncing on the purported net benefits to "society" of greater incarceration without addressing that question! Still, how—or, indeed, whether—to weigh the costs born by law-breakers—that is, how (or whether) to acknowledge their humanity—remains a fundamental and difficult question of social ethics. Political discourses in the United States have given insufficient weight to the collateral damage imposed by punishment policies on the offenders themselves, and on those who are knitted together with offenders in networks of social and psychic affiliation.

Loury introduces an ethical criterion that imprisonment policies cause far greater costs than simply keeping criminals in jail.

9   Whether or not one agrees, two things should be clear: social scientists can have no answers for the question of what weight to put on a "thug's," or his family's, well-being; and a morally defensible public policy to deal with criminal offenders cannot be promulgated without addressing that question. To know whether or not our criminal justice policies comport with our deepest values, we must ask how much additional cost borne by the offending class is justifiable per marginal unit of security, or of peace of mind, for the rest of us. This question is barely being asked, let alone answered, in the contemporary debate.

10   Nor is it merely the scope of the mass imprisonment state that has expanded so impressively in the United States. The ideas underlying the doing of criminal justice—the superstructure of justifications and rationalizations—have also undergone a sea change. Rehabilitation is a dead letter; retribution is the thing. The function of imprisonment is not to reform or redirect offenders. Rather, it is to keep *them* away from *us*. "The prison," writes sociologist David Garland, "is used today as a kind of reservation, a quarantine zone in which purportedly dangerous individuals are segregated in the name of public safety." We have elaborated what are, in effect, a "string of work camps and prisons strung across a vast country housing millions of people drawn mainly from classes and racial groups that are seen as politically and economically problematic." We have, in other words, marched quite a long way down the punitive road, in the name of securing public safety and meting out to criminals their just deserts.

11   And we should be ashamed of ourselves for having done so. Consider a striking feature of this policy development, one that is

crucial to this moral assessment: the ways in which we now deal with criminal offenders in the United States have evolved in recent decades in order to serve expressive and not only instrumental ends. We have wanted to "send a message," and have done so with a vengeance. Yet in the process we have also, in effect, provided an answer for the question: who is to blame for the maladies that beset our troubled civilization? That is, we have constructed a narrative, created scapegoats, assuaged our fears, and indulged our need to feel virtuous about ourselves. We have met the enemy and the enemy, in the now familiar caricature, is *them*—a bunch of anomic, menacing, morally deviant "thugs." In the midst of this dramaturgy—unavoidably so in America—lurks a potent racial subplot.

12   This issue is personal for me. As a black American male, a baby-boomer born and raised on Chicago's South Side, I can identify with the plight of the urban poor because I have lived among them. I am related to them by the bonds of social and psychic affiliation. As it happens, I have myself passed through the courtroom, and the jailhouse, on my way along life's journey. I have sat in the visitor's room at a state prison; I have known, personally and intimately, men and women who lived their entire lives with one foot to either side of the law. Whenever I step to a lectern to speak about the growth of imprisonment in our society, I envision voiceless and despairing people who would have me speak on their behalf. Of course, personal biography can carry no authority to compel agreement about public policy. Still, I prefer candor to the false pretense of clinical detachment and scientific objectivity. I am not running for high office; I need not pretend to a cool neutrality that I do not possess. While I recognize that these revelations will discredit me in some quarters, this is a fate I can live with.

Loury introduces personal examples in support of his ethical criteria.

13   So, my racial identity is not irrelevant to my discussion of the subject at hand. But, then, neither is it irrelevant that among the millions now in custody and under state supervision are to be found a vastly disproportionate number of the black and the brown. There is no need to justify injecting race into this discourse, for prisons are the most race-conscious public institutions that we have. No big city police officer is "colorblind" nor, arguably, can any afford to be. Crime and punishment in America have a color—just turn on a television, or open a magazine, or listen carefully to the rhetoric of a political campaign—and you will see what I mean. The fact is that, in this society as in any other, order is maintained by the threat and the use of force. We enjoy our good lives because we are shielded by the forces of law and order upon which we rely to keep the unruly at bay. Yet, in this society to an extent unlike virtually any other, those bearing the heavy

burden of order-enforcement belong, in numbers far exceeding their presence in the population at large, to racially defined and historically marginalized groups. Why should this be so? And how can those charged with the supervision of our penal apparatus sleep well at night knowing that it is so?

14   This punitive turn in the nation's social policy is intimately connected, I would maintain, with public rhetoric about responsibility, dependency, social hygiene, and the reclamation of public order. And such rhetoric, in turn, can be fully grasped only when viewed against the backdrop of America's often ugly and violent racial history: There is a reason why our inclination toward forgiveness and the extension of a second chance to those who have violated our behavioral strictures is so stunted, and why our mainstream political discourses are so bereft of self-examination and searching social criticism. An historical resonance between the stigma of race and the stigma of prison has served to keep alive in our public culture the subordinating social meanings that have always been associated with blackness. Many historians and political scientists—though, of course, not all—agree that the shifting character of race relations over the course of the nineteenth and twentieth centuries helps to explain why the United States is exceptional among democratic industrial societies in the severity of its punitive policy and the paucity of its social-welfare institutions. Put directly and without benefit of euphemism, the racially disparate incidence of punishment in the United States is a morally troubling residual effect of the nation's history of enslavement, disenfranchisement, segregation, and discrimination. It is not merely the accidental accretion of neutral state action, applied to a racially divergent social flux. It is an abhorrent expression of who we Americans are as a people, even now, at the dawn of the twenty-first century.

Loury again emphasizes the ethical dimension of his evaluation.

15   My recitation of the brutal facts about punishment in today's America may sound to some like a primal scream at this monstrous social machine that is grinding poor black communities to dust. And I confess that these facts do at times leave me inclined to cry out in despair. But my argument is intended to be moral, not existential, and its principal thesis is this: we law-abiding, middle-class Americans have made collective decisions on social and incarceration policy questions, and we benefit from those decisions. That is, we benefit from a system of suffering, rooted in state violence, meted out at our behest. Put differently our society—the society we together have made—first tolerates crime-promoting conditions in our sprawling urban ghettos, and then goes on to act out rituals of punishment against them as some awful form of human sacrifice.

After expressing anger Loury returns to a reasoned argument about public policy based on ethical criteria.

16   It is a central reality of our time that a wide racial gap has opened up in cognitive skills, the extent of law-abidingness, stability

of family relations, and attachment to the work force. This is the basis, many would hold, for the racial gap in imprisonment. Yet I maintain that this gap in human development is, as a historical matter, rooted in political, economic, social, and cultural factors peculiar to this society and reflective of its unlovely racial history. That is to say, *it is a societal, not communal or personal, achievement.* At the level of the individual case we must, of course, act as if this were not so. There could be no law, and so no civilization, absent the imputation to persons of responsibility for their wrongful acts. But the sum of a million cases, each one rightly judged fairly on its individual merits, may nevertheless constitute a great historic wrong. This is, in my view, now the case in regards to the race and social class disparities that characterize the very punitive policy that we have directed at lawbreakers. And yet, the state does not only deal with individual cases. It also makes policies in the aggregate, and the consequences of these policies are more or less knowable. It is in the making of such aggregate policy judgments that questions of social responsibility arise.

17   This situation raises a moral problem that we cannot avoid. We cannot pretend that there are more important problems in our society, or that this circumstance is the necessary solution to other, more pressing problems—unless we are also prepared to say that we have turned our backs on the ideal of equality for all citizens and abandoned the principles of justice. We ought to be asking ourselves two questions: Just what manner of people are we Americans? And in light of this, what are our obligations to our fellow citizens—even those who break our laws?

Loury's case is based on logic and evidence, but his strong passion is evident as well. How does he create emotion?

18   Without trying to make a full-fledged philosophical argument here, I nevertheless wish to gesture—in the spirit of the philosopher John Rawls—toward some answers to these questions. I will not set forth a policy manifesto at this time. What I aim to do is suggest, in a general way, how we ought to be thinking differently about this problem. Specifically, given our nation's history and political culture, I think that there are severe limits to the applicability in this circumstance of a pure ethic of personal responsibility, as the basis for distributing the negative good of punishment in contemporary America. I urge that we shift the boundary toward greater acknowledgment of social responsibility in our punishment policy discourse—even for wrongful acts freely chosen by individual persons. In suggesting this, I am not so much making a "root causes" argument—he did the crime, but only because he had no choice— as I am arguing that the society at large is implicated in his choices because we have acquiesced in structural arrangements which work to our benefit and his detriment, and yet which shape his consciousness and sense of identity in such a way that the choices

he makes. We condemn those choices, but they are nevertheless compelling to him. I am interested in the moral implications of what the sociologist Loïc Wacquant has called the "double-sided production of urban marginality." I approach this problem of moral judgment by emphasizing that closed and bounded social structures—like racially homogeneous urban ghettos—create contexts where "pathological" and "dysfunctional" cultural forms emerge, but these forms are not intrinsic to the people caught in these structures. Neither are they independent of the behavior of the people who stand outside of them.

19   Several years ago, I took time to read some of the nonfiction writings of the great nineteenth-century Russian novelist Leo Tolstoy. Toward the end of his life he had become an eccentric pacifist and radical Christian social critic. I was stunned at the force of his arguments. What struck me most was Tolstoy's provocative claim that the core of Christianity lies in Jesus' Sermon on the Mount: You see that fellow over there committing some terrible sin? Well, if you have ever lusted, or allowed jealousy, or envy or hatred to enter your own heart, then you are to be equally condemned! This, Tolstoy claims, is the central teaching of the Christian faith: we're all in the same fix.

20   Now, without invoking any religious authority, I nevertheless want to suggest that there is a grain of truth in this religious sentiment that is relevant to the problem at hand: That is, while the behavioral pathologies and cultural threats that we see in society—the moral erosions "out there"—the crime, drug addiction, sexually transmitted disease, idleness, violence and all manner of deviance—while these are worrisome, nevertheless, our moral crusade against these evils can take on a pathological dimension of its own. We can become self-righteous, legalistic, ungenerous, stiff-necked, and hypocritical. We can fail to see the beam in our own eye. We can neglect to raise questions of social justice. We can blind ourselves to the close relationship that actually exists between, on the one hand, behavioral pathology in the so-called urban underclass of our country and, on the other hand, society-wide factors—like our greed-driven economy, our worship of the self, our endemic culture of materialism, our vacuous political discourses, our declining civic engagement, and our aversion to sacrificing private gain on behalf of much needed social investments. We can fail to see, in other words, that the problems of the so-called underclass—to which we have reacted with a massive, coercive mobilization—are but an expression, at the bottom of the social hierarchy, of a more profound and widespread moral deviance—one involving all of us.

The Rawls, Wacquant, and Tolstoy references build ethos.

Loury returns to the challenge that he set out in the opening paragraph: What is our collective vision of the ideal society?

21   Taking this position does not make me a moral relativist. I merely hold that, when thinking about the lives of the disadvantaged in our society, the fundamental premise that should guide us is that we are all in this together. *Those* people languishing in the corners of our society are *our* people—they are *us*—whatever may be their race, creed, or country of origin, whether they be the crack-addicted, the HIV-infected, the mentally ill homeless, the juvenile drug sellers, or worse. Whatever the malady, and whatever the offense, we're all in the same fix. We're all in this thing together.

Loury anticipates and answers a possible objection.

22   Just look at what we have wrought. We Americans have established what, to many an outside observer, looks like a system of racial caste in the center of our great cities. I refer here to millions of stigmatized, feared, and invisible people. The extent of disparity in the opportunity to achieve their full human potential, as between the children of the middle class and the children of the disadvantaged— a disparity that one takes for granted in America—is virtually unrivaled elsewhere in the industrial, advanced, civilized, free world.

23   Yet too many Americans have concluded, in effect, that those languishing at the margins of our society are simply reaping what they have sown. Their suffering is seen as having nothing to do with us—as not being evidence of systemic failures that can be corrected through collective action. Thus, as I noted, we have given up on the ideal of rehabilitating criminals, and have settled for simply warehousing them. Thus we accept—despite much rhetoric to the contrary—that it is virtually impossible effectively to educate the children of the poor. Despite the best efforts of good people and progressive institutions—despite the encouraging signs of moral engagement with these issues that I have seen in my students over the years, and that give me hope—despite these things, it remains the case that, speaking of the country as a whole, there is no broadly based demand for reform, no sense of moral outrage, no anguished self-criticism, no public reflection in the face of this massive, collective failure.

Loury offers causal explanation for the current policy.

24   The core of the problem is that the socially marginal are not seen as belonging to the same general public body as the rest of us. It therefore becomes impossible to do just about anything with them. At least implicitly, our political community acts as though some are different from the rest and, because of their culture— because of their bad values, their self-destructive behavior, their malfeasance, their criminality, their lack of responsibility, their unwillingness to engage in hard work—they *deserve* their fate.

25   But this is quite wrongheaded. What we Americans fail to recognize—not merely as individuals, I stress, but as a political community—is that these ghetto enclaves and marginal spaces of

our cities, which are the source of most prison inmates, are products of our own making: Precisely because we do not want those people near us, we have structured the space in our urban environment so as to keep *them* away from *us*. Then, when they fester in their isolation and their marginality, we hypocritically point a finger, saying in effect: "Look at those people. They threaten to the civilized body. They must therefore be expelled, imprisoned, controlled." It is not *we* who must take social responsibility to reform our institutions but, rather, it is *they* who need to take personal responsibility for their wrongful acts. It is not we who must set our *collective* affairs aright, but they who must get their *individual* acts together. This posture, I suggest, is inconsistent with the attainment of a just distribution of benefits and burdens in society.

Having evaluated the policy as ineffective and immoral, Loury moves to the conclusion of his essay—which is to suggest a solution: civic inclusion.

26   Civic inclusion has been the historical imperative in Western political life for 150 years. And yet—despite our self-declared status as a light unto the nations, as a beacon of hope to freedom-loving peoples everywhere—despite these lofty proclamations, which were belied by images from the rooftops in flooded New Orleans in September 2005, and are contradicted by our overcrowded prisons—the fact is that this historical project of civic inclusion is woefully incomplete in these United States.

27   At every step of the way, reactionary political forces have declared the futility of pursuing civic inclusion. Yet, in every instance, these forces have been proven wrong. At one time or another, they have derided the inclusion of women, landless peasants, former serfs and slaves, or immigrants more fully in the civic body. Extending to them the franchise, educating their children, providing health and social welfare to them has always been controversial. But this has been the direction in which the self-declared "civilized" and wealthy nations have been steadily moving since Bismarck, since the revolutions of 1848 and 1870, since the American Civil War with its Reconstruction Amendments, since the Progressive Era and through the New Deal on to the Great Society. This is why we have a progressive federal income tax and an estate tax in this country, why we feed, clothe and house the needy, why we (used to) worry about investing in our cities' infrastructure, and in the human capital of our people. What the brutal facts about punishment in today's America show is that *this American project of civic inclusion remains incomplete*. Nowhere is that incompleteness more evident than in the prisons and jails of America. And this as yet unfulfilled promise of American democracy reveals a yawning chasm between an ugly and uniquely American reality, and our nation's exalted image of herself.

Loury concludes that if Americans would embrace the ideals of the United States, the conditions that lead to massive-scale imprisonment would change.

Sample Student Evaluation Argument

Picchi 1

Jenna Picchi

Professor Alameno

English 102

2 December 2013

Organic Foods Should Come Clean

As a kid growing up not far from rural communities, I took for granted the access to local produce and the farm stands that my family frequented. When I moved to a college town, I assumed I would have access to an even wider variety of foods and better choices. I wanted to continue eating organic as I had at home, even though it would be more work than a campus-dining plan. I learned quickly that even in a large college town, it takes determined searching in most supermarkets to find the organic produce, bread, meat, and dairy products that are scattered in less-trafficked corners of the store. Instead of shopping at the farmer's market (which I cannot attend), I choose these supermarket fruits and vegetables from the lackluster and small display of things shipped in from California and Central America. Taking a recent look at these organic departments, I noticed that almost all the products are store or national brands. It never occurred to me that living in the middle of an agricultural state my choices would be so limited. After spending much time and energy seeking out organic products in stores all around town, I wondered whether the effort is worth it. How healthy are these foods in the local supermarket? And are these national brands as good for the environment as they seem?

Many people shop for organic foods in the belief that they are free of pesticides, additives, and other chemicals that can harm people and the environment over time. Visit an average supermarket's organic department and you will see signs and labels confirming this idea. Organic foods are marketed as more wholesome or more humanely raised and harvested than other foods in the store. Packaging suggests organic foods are pure, natural, and simply better. But the big businesses that bring these products to consumers are anything but simple. The reality of the organic foods we find at Walmart, Target, and other major retail chains is that they are produced on a mass scale—the same industrial-sized operations that bring us cheap, "regular" products. And it may

Picchi introduces herself by giving personal background and explaining why she is invested in her subject.

After beginning with a personal narrative to connect with her readers, Picchi introduces her topic.

Picchi 2

be that the policy of producing and selling organic foods on a massive, industrial scale is not as good for the environment or consumers as producing and selling organic foods on a smaller scale. Although industrially produced organic foods are convenient, they present a natural, earth-friendly image that is often not the reality. The industrial organic food industry makes many claims that deserve a closer look.

Consumers willing to pay more for organic foods might be surprised to learn that mass-produced organic foods come from farms that barely resemble the old-fashioned images on their milk carton. The majority of organic food sales come via a very large industry, not an idealistic or environmentalist movement. In fact, organic foods are the fastest-growing category in the food industry, now worth about $11 billion (Pollan 136). The way food is produced has been changing more over the past fifty years than in the previous 10,000 years (Kenner). Many organic foods are grown by big, industrial producers. These companies—often owned by large corporations—use many of the same practices as mainstream factory farms to keep costs low. They can distribute and market their products nationally, and while organic foods cost more overall, these corporations succeed because they have made organic food available to average customers (not just affluent ones). If the goal is to offer healthy choices to consumers who are trained to expect cheap, convenient options, industrial producers of organic foods have made significant contributions. The organic label works wonders in marketing, and the big corporations who produce and deliver the foods in our supermarkets are taking advantage of it.

The history of the organic food movement was originally small, locally based, and in response to the industrialization of food. The evolution away from an organic movement toward an organic food industry is fairly recent. The organic pioneers of the 1970s had "a vision of small farms, whole food, and local distribution" (Fromartz 194). They hoped to help people eat fewer processed foods, produced organically and distributed from local sources. But for some farmers the allure of reaching more consumers and national sales has led to compromises. In *Omnivore's Dilemma*, Michael Pollan traces the pressure some farmers felt in the early 1990s to "sell out" and work with agribusiness (153). Farmers like Gene Kahn, the founder of Cascadian Farm (now owned by food giant General Mills), saw that he

Picchi gives the history of the organic food movement to show how the production of organic foods has changed.

Picchi 3

could change and redefine the way food is grown and still reach a mass market. Even though this meant giving up on two ideals of the organic movement—local distribution and eating more whole foods—organic foods were becoming a large-scale business, bringing more naturally produced choices to more and more consumers.

One concern for Pollan and others is that the organic label is being used by companies who are not invested in organic principles. In fact, chemical farming and big agribusinesses had once been the enemy of the organic movement. Big agribusinesses changed their stance once they realized how profitable organic produce could become (Fromartz 194). As industrial organic operations grow and adopt more and more big agribusiness methods, the worry for consumers is whether the term *organic* is becoming just another marketing gimmick.

Picchi introduces the criteria that she will use in her evaluation.

As organic foods become increasingly industrial, it is important for consumers to be able to verify whether the products they buy are defined and produced using truly organic standards. Organic standards have evolved in recent years and now regulate not just small farms but also large-scale industrial operations. But even as the standards are changing, they must at a minimum guarantee healthy foods that are sustainably produced. Organic agriculture is valuable for the way it protects the environment. Marion Nestle, a scholar on food and public health, describes research that organic farming uses less energy and leaves soils in better condition than traditional farms (213).

Picchi describes how local farming can reduce energy consumption.

In addition to protecting lands from excessive chemical use, another possible benefit of organic, local farming is that it can require less use of fossil fuels. Fossil fuels are spent whenever farm supplies must be shipped or when foods are sent for processing. Foods travel long distances across the country and foods are shipped from across the world, consuming fossil fuels. But Pollan states that organic food can be produced with about one-third less fossil fuel than conventional food (183). Using fewer fossil fuels and chemicals should be a goal for any organic farmer or consumer concerned with pollution and creating a more sustainable food industry.

Picchi examines the health benefits of organic foods.

Less research is available to prove that organic foods are better nutritionally. Officially, Pollan says, the government takes the position that "organic food is no better than conventional food" (178). But he believes current research reveals organic foods grown in more naturally fertile soil to be more nutritious. And Nestle believes organic foods may be safer than conventional foods because people who eat them will have fewer synthetic pesticides and chemicals in their bodies (213). If consumers can rely on organic foods for their health benefits, a larger good would be granted in overall public health. As a society we all benefit when people eat whole foods and organic foods as part of diets that maintain health and fight weight-related disease. Foods with an organic label should be able to guarantee these benefits to individuals and to public health.

Another benefit to taxpayers is that organic farms are far less subsidized and in particular do not receive direct government payments (Pollan 182). Many organic farms do not participate in the complicated system of paying farmers directly that mainstream farmers participate in, though Pollan points out that many industrial organic farms do benefit from less direct subsidies. For example, many states subsidize access to cheaper water and electricity to power farms. However, supporting the less subsidized farmers may bring savings to taxpayers in the end.

> Picchi argues that organic farming can cut government subsidies to farmers and thus lower overall federal spending.

Organic labels and standards are difficult but crucial to police and enforce. Consumers who are willing to pay extra for natural food choices will lose faith if it turns out the organic labels are not honest. Organic farmers traditionally set themselves up as an alternative to big agribusiness. But as Pollan explains, as giant manufacturers and chains sell more and more of the organic foods in supermarkets, organic agriculture has become more and more like the industrial food system it was supposed to challenge (151). As a result, it is more likely that without scrutiny organic standards are not being met.

Organic milk offers one example of a product where organic standards have recently been an issue. A handful of very large companies produce most of the organic milk we buy. Many chain stores have begun successfully competing, selling their own private-label organic milk. These huge private-label organic brands allow consumers to get organic goods at even lower prices. But one recent case of possible organic fraud involves Aurora Dairy, the supplier for many in-house brands of organic milk for stores such as Walmart and Costco. Aurora was discovered to have broken fourteen of the organic standards in 2007. The USDA cited it because its herds included cows that were fed inappropriate feed

> To give a concrete example, Picchi focuses on a specific organic product, milk, with which her audience will be familiar.

Picchi 5

and because some cows had no access to pastures. It took a federal investigation to bring information about these violations to light and yet even then Aurora continued to operate without penalty (Gunther). But when organic standards are vaguely worded and unenforceable or go unmonitored at factory dairy farms, violations of organic principles are bound to happen.

The overwhelming pressure for access to foods that are cheap and convenient is something all consumers feel. But most people interested in buying organic foods do so because they believe they're doing something positive for their health, for the health of their community, and in the best interests of the environment. Often these consumers have a strong sense of the ethical importance of sustainable produced food. Because of their interest in doing what is right, these consumers are likely to be especially upset by news that the goods they're paying extra for are being misrepresented. These consumers expect and welcome organic standards that are meaningfully set and policed. Good organic agriculture policy would help ensure strong standards; without them consumers will become jaded and not trust the organic label.

> Picchi introduces an ethical component to her argument.

Consumers interested in the monitoring of these standards might be concerned to see how standards in the past decade have changed. In crafting these rules, the government consults with some of the biggest businesses involved in organic food production. Many long-time organic farmers believe that the role of these corporations has watered down organic standards. The farmers themselves are voicing concerns that regulations should be tougher. Elizabeth Henderson, an organic farmer and member of the large organic co-op Organic Valley, spoke out in 2004 about the huge growth of organic food as coming "at an awful price, compromising standards, undercutting small farms, diluting healthy food, ignoring social justice—polluting the very ideals embodied in the word *organic*" (qtd in Fromartz 190).

In one recent example, Horizon Organic, the giant milk producer, fought for the development of USDA rules that ensure its factory farms in Idaho would not be required to give all cows a specific amount of time to graze on pasture (Pollan 157). The watered-down USDA standard Horizon helped to craft instead is very vague. The image most consumers have of organic milk coming from cows grazing in pasture is an ideal that many

> Picchi gives an example of how big business has influence on organic standards.

mainstream organic milk producers don't even approach. Many small dairy farmers follow older organic practices on their own, but current "organic" labels do not guarantee this.

Another challenge for consumers looking for sustainably produced organic products is that the industrial-sized producers are more efficient, which makes it hard for smaller farmers to compete. Local small farms, like personal gardens, are both "more expensive but also less efficient than larger operations in terms of transportation, labor, and materials required" (Dubner). Big organic companies can set lower prices, ship foods long distances quickly, and make distribution simpler for the supermarkets (Pollan 168). The growth of industrially produced organic foods has helped bring prices down overall. The competition is good in theory, allowing more people access to organic choices. But faced with these competing choices, perhaps only very informed consumers of organic foods may sympathize with and support their local organic farmers.

Good organic agriculture policy would ideally avoid having a negative impact on small, local producers. I would acknowledge that locally produced food is not necessarily more sustainable or by definition produced with less energy or better for the environment (McWilliams 22). The smaller-scale farm also has to be committed to sustainable practices. Local farms can be held accountable for whether they are meeting organic standards and following sustainable farming practices. A dairy farmer you can talk to at a local farmer's market can, in theory, earn trust and be held accountable to customers.

> Picchi acknowledges limits to her argument, while proposing what small, local farmers must do.

Small, local organic farmers are well positioned to deliver on the organic movement's original ideals of sustainably produced foods. Consumers should have a right to know where their food comes from and how organic standards are defined. In fact, as organic foods become more widely available to most consumers—even college students—it is worth questioning whether organic standards mean what they seem. Labeling foods organic cannot be just a marketing ploy, and the organic industry will continue to reach and inform more consumers if it can ensure this label has real meaning.

> Picchi concludes her essay with a call to arms, inspiring her audience to act.

Picchi 7

Works Cited

Dubner, Stephen J. "Do We Really Need a Few Billion Locavores?" *New York Times*. New York Times, 9 June 2008. Web. 20 Nov. 2013.

Fromartz, Samuel. *Organic, Inc.: Natural Foods and How They Grew*. New York: Houghton, 2006. Print.

Gunther, Marc. "An Organic Milk War Turns Sour." *Cornucopia Institute*. 3 Oct. 2007. Web. 20 Nov. 2013.

Kenner, Robert, dir. *Food Inc.* 2009. Magnolia Pictures. Film.

McWilliams, James E. *Just Food: Where Locavores Get It Wrong and How We Can Truly Eat Responsibly*. New York: Little, 2009. Print.

Nestle, Marion. "Eating Made Simple." *Food Inc.: How Industrial Food Is Making Us Sicker, Fatter, and Poorer—and What You Can Do About It*. Ed. Karl Weber. New York: PublicAffairs, 2009. 209-18. Print.

Pollan, Michael. *Omnivore's Dilemma: A Natural History of Four Meals*. New York: Penguin, 2006. Print.

11 | Narrative Arguments

In this chapter, you will learn to

1. Understand how narrative arguments rely on stories rather than statistics (see page 163)
2. Recognize the kinds of narrative arguments (see pages 163–165)
3. Analyze a narrative argument (see page 165)
4. Write an effective narrative argument (see pages 166–167)

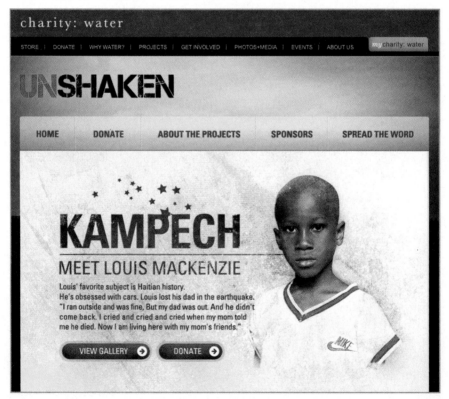

The organization *charity: water* understands the persuasive power of personal stories. Its online campaign features narratives like the story of Louis Mackenzie, a young boy who lost his father in the January 2010 earthquake in Haiti. "I cried and cried and cried when my mom told me he died," the text reads. As many organizations have learned, people often feel more compelled to donate money when they read personal stories like Louis's than when they are barraged with abstract numbers and statistics. Why are such stories effective as arguments? What makes some stories more compelling than others? © 2010 charity: water. Used with permission.

Understand How Narrative Arguments Work

A single, detailed personal story sometimes makes a stronger case than large-scale statistical evidence. The Annenberg Public Policy Center reported that an estimated 1.6 million of 17 million U.S. college students gambled online in 2005, but it was the story of Greg Hogan that made the problem real for many Americans. Hogan, the son of a Baptist minister, was an extraordinarily talented musician, who played onstage twice at Carnegie Hall by age 13. He chose to attend Lehigh University in Pennsylvania, where he was a member of the orchestra and class president. At Lehigh he also acquired an addiction to online poker. He lost $7,500, much of which he borrowed from fraternity brothers. To pay them back, he robbed a bank, only to be arrested a few hours later. Eventually, he received a long prison sentence. Hogan's story helped to influence Congress to pass the Unlawful Internet Gambling Enforcement Act, which requires financial institutions to stop money transfers to gambling sites.

Successful narrative arguments typically don't have a thesis statement but instead tell a compelling story. From the experience of one individual, readers infer a claim and the good reasons that support the claim.

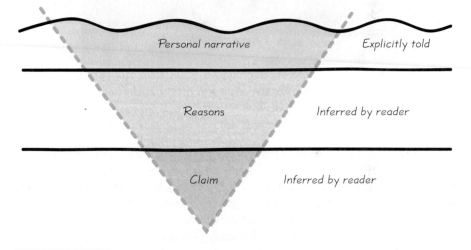

Personal narrative — Explicitly told

Reasons — Inferred by reader

Claim — Inferred by reader

Recognize Kinds of Narrative Arguments

Using narrative to make an argument is part of human nature. As far back as we have records, we find people telling stories and singing songs that argue for change. During periods of history when it is dangerous to make explicit arguments, stories allow people to safely criticize authority or imagine how life could be different. The history of folk music is a continuous recycling of old tunes, phrases, and narratives to engage new political situations. Anti-war ballads popular in Ireland in the 1840s were sung in the 1960s by Americans protesting their country's involvement in Vietnam. All the popular narrative genres—short stories, novels, movies, and theater—have been used as ways to make arguments for change.

Singer/songwriter Shawn Colvin is one of many contemporary folk, blues, rock, and rap artists who continue the tradition of making narrative arguments in their songs. Can you think of a song that makes a narrative argument? How successful is the song in making the argument? Why?

Narrative arguments allow readers to fill in the good reasons and come to their own conclusions. The personal connection readers can feel with the writer of a narrative argument makes this strategy a compelling means of persuasion. Moreover, because the writer usually refrains from making an outright claim, people reading narrative arguments are more likely to feel that they are "making up their own minds" rather than being reluctantly persuaded.

Narrative arguments can be representative anecdotes or they can be longer accounts of particular events that express larger ideas. One such story is George Orwell's account of a hanging in Burma (the country now known as Myanmar) while he was a British colonial administrator in the late 1920s. In "A Hanging," first published in 1931, Orwell narrates the story of an execution of a nameless prisoner who was convicted of a nameless crime. Everyone present quietly and dispassionately performs his job—the prison guards, the hangman, the superintendent, and even the prisoner, who offers no resistance when he is bound and led to the gallows. All is totally routine until a very small incident makes Orwell realize what is happening.

Orwell describes in detail how the prisoner, naked to the waist, walked stiff-legged with a bobbing gait, a lock of hair bouncing up and down. Even though he was being held by men on both sides, he carefully avoided stepping into a puddle on the path. This tiny act of avoiding a puddle made Orwell aware that the prisoner's brain was still thinking and reasoning as he was going to the scaffold. Orwell's sense of what was happening changed instantly. The prisoner was just like the other men at the scene with his organs working, his senses still taking in the world around him, and his mind still capable of remembering, reasoning, and foreseeing the future. Within two minutes, this mind would be removed from the human family.

Orwell writes, "It is curious, but till that moment I had never realized what it means to destroy a healthy, conscious man." Orwell's narrative leads to a dramatic moment of recognition, which gives this story its lasting power. His sudden realization of what execution means to both the prisoner and his executioners is a powerful argument to reconsider the morality of the death penalty.

Build a Narrative Argument

Because storytelling is such a familiar activity, it is easy for writers to get carried away with their narratives, and lose sight of the point they are trying to make. Readers find narrative compelling, but not if the narrative is long-winded and full of unnecessary detail, or has no obvious point. Furthermore, readers are quickly put off if they feel they are being given a lecture.

There are two keys to making effective narrative arguments: establishing that the narrative is truthful, and showing its relevance to a wider problem or question. Writing from personal experience can increase the impact of your argument, but that impact diminishes greatly if readers doubt you are telling the truth. And while the story you tell may be true, it is important that it also be representative—something that has happened to many other people or something that could happen to your readers. Narrative arguments are useful for illustrating how people are affected by particular issues or events, but they are more effective if you have evidence that goes beyond a single incident.

One rule of thumb that you can keep in mind when building a narrative argument is to start out with as much detail and as many events as you can recall, and then revise and edit heavily. It's hard to select the best details and events for your argument until you have written them all down, and often the process of writing and remembering will bring up new details that you had forgotten or hadn't seen the relevance of before. Once you can see the big picture you have painted with your narrative, it is easier to see what your readers do not need, and remove it. This strategy brings your story, and your argument, into sharper focus.

Steps to Writing a Narrative Argument

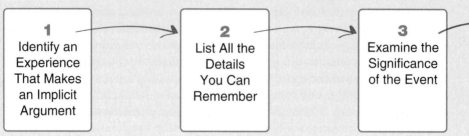

1
Identify an Experience That Makes an Implicit Argument

2
List All the Details You Can Remember

3
Examine the Significance of the Event

Step 1 Identify an Experience That Makes an Implicit Argument

Think about experiences that made you realize that something is wrong or that things need to be changed. The experience does not have to be one that leads to a moral lesson at the end, but it should be one that makes your readers think.

Examples

- Being accused of and perhaps even arrested and hauled to jail for something you didn't do or for standing up for something you believed in
- Moving from a well-financed suburban school to a much poorer rural or urban school in the same state
- Experiencing stereotyping or prejudice in any way—for the way you look, the way you act, your age, your gender, your race, or your sexual orientation

Step 2 List All the Details You Can Remember

- When did it happen?
- How old were you?
- Why were you there?
- Who else was there?
- Where did it happen? If the place is important, describe what it looked like.
- What did it all sound like? smell like? taste like?

Step 3 Examine the Significance of the Event

- How did you feel about the experience when it happened?
- How did it affect you then?
- How do you feel about the experience now?
- What long-term effects has it had on your life?

Step 4 Analyze Your Potential Readers

- Who are your readers?
- How much will your readers know about the background of the experience you are describing?
- Would anything similar ever likely have happened to them?
- How likely are they to agree with your feelings about the experience?

Step 5 Write a Draft

- You might need to give some background first, but if you have a compelling story, often it's best to launch right in.
- You might want to tell the story as it happened (chronological order), or you might want to begin with a striking incident and then go back to tell how it happened (flashback).
- You might want to reflect on your experience at the end, but you want your story to do most of the work. Avoid drawing a simple moral lesson. Your readers should share your feelings if you tell your story well.

Step 6 Revise, Edit, Proofread

- For detailed instructions, see Chapter 5.
- For a checklist to use to evaluate your draft, see pages 50–51.

Finding Good Reasons

Can a Story Make an Argument?

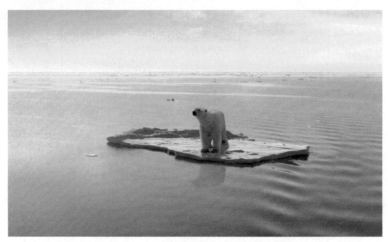

A lone polar bear stands atop a small ice floe in the Arctic Ocean. The National Wildlife Federation describes the plight of the polar bear, struggling to survive in the face of a changing climate.

The National Wildlife Federation has made polar bears its featured species for advocating that nations should limit the impact of climate change. Polar bears are particularly affected by melting sea ice in the Arctic. They depend on seals for food. Because seals are much better swimmers than polar bears, the bears hunt seals from sea ice, grabbing them when they come up to breathe. The best habitat for polar bears is sea ice near land that can be reached with short swims. As sea ice shrinks, bears must either swim further and risk drowning or else find scarce food on land. Increasingly, they have turned to garbage dumps, which leads to fatal encounters with humans. Because of the loss of sea-ice cover, the U.S. Geological Survey estimates the population of polar bears will decline by two-thirds by 2050.

Write about it

1. What argument might the National Wildlife Federation be making about the state of climate change? What details reveal this argument?

2. Why might the National Wildlife Federation have chosen the polar bear to personify the effects of climate change? What other types of animals would have made good choices? poor choices?

3. How does the National Wildlife Federation's account of climate change differ from other accounts that you have heard? What is the other side of this issue? Does this story change your thinking about climate change? Why or why not?

Gregory Kristof

On the Ground with a "Gap Year"

Gregory Kristof, who attends Harvard University, has written op-eds for *The Harvard Crimson* and about education for the *Huffington Post*. In this essay, written at the invitation of his father, Pulitzer Prize–winning columnist Nicholas Kristof, he describes his experiences traveling in China during the time between high school and college. The essay first appeared in the *New York Times*.

Kristof begins with a vivid account of one of his experiences, drawing the reader in with a humorous anecdote that relates to his overall argument.

2   It took place on a frosty peak tucked away in the Tibetan highlands: my friend Rick and I walked in on a group of monks as they were on their knees, groaning.

3   They were performing secret rituals involving yak butter.

Note how Kristof uses language and dialogue to develop his main characters. Phrases like "two white dudes chillin'" and the detail about his ringtone help create a personal connection to his readers.

Peeking out from behind animal fur curtains, Rick and I hoped that they hadn't noticed us yet. They hummed and sat in rows facing a stage of yak butter candles that threw images against the walls like kicked hacky sacks. Back in the shadows, I worried: What would happen if they saw two white dudes chillin' behind the furs?

4   "Pssst," Rick said. "I think we should leave."

5   "Let's make for the door." I said.

6   I flattened myself against the back of the room, inching toward the door. Take it slow, I told myself. Don't drag your feet. Hurry up! I just had a few more feet to go. Two steps to go. Wow, I would make a great spy.

7   One step. And then—right as I was considering tacking on two zeros to the front of my name—ZINGZAMEMEM-BzerrBzerrBzerr …

8   I know, my ringtone sucks. Eyes caved in on me. I sort of just lay there on the dirt floor, not moving much, just looking up sporadically at the curious faces, and feeling sorry that I had disrupted their ritual. And yet I felt warm inside because I was here, getting caught in a mountain temple by Buddhist monks, and not where I shoulda-coulda-woulda been: listening to a PowerPoint lecture in a Boston classroom.

In paragraphs 9–12 Kristof introduces his argument, without explicitly stating it.

9   My decision to defer college for a year wasn't easy. In my New York high school, nearly every kid treads the usual path from graduation to college. Upon hearing that I would hop off the traditional academic bandwagon, some teachers, friends, and other parents would respond with "That sounds great!" while murmuring comforting remarks that I would probably turn out ok.

10   I was extremely excited about college, so it was tough to say "Not this time" to the bounty of friends and general awesomeness that my Freshman year would most assuredly bring me.

Many young people ask themselves the questions in paragraph 11, which suggests that the impetus for Kristof's experience is representative of what others his age might feel.

11   But I remember thinking how most of my great high school memories were localized capsules, like dots on paper waiting to be connected. A great weekend here, a good report card there. It was only when I extracted myself from each individual moment that I would realize that the damn picture still wouldn't come into focus. Where was I going? Where did I want to go?

12   I wanted more. I wanted to see how the other half lived, to learn the things that weren't found in books, to live a phantasmagoria of unforgettable experiences. I wanted to experience a life in which images glided by like kangaroos on rollerblades.

13   So I went to China. So far, I've rock-climbed above Buddhist grottos, showered in underground waterfalls, squeaked my way across 13th-century temples hanging halfway up cliffs, and stayed in earthquake-ravaged villages where everyone still dwells in tents. In a one-street town whose sole cab driver appeared to be blind, Rick and I went deep inside one of the world's most dazzling monasteries to party with monks (the scene was about as bangin' as what you'd expect from a group of pacifists). I've motorcycled across a frozen holy lake in the Himalayas, and I've stared into giant volcano pits on the North Korean border.

Kristof advances his argument by highlighting what he learned on his trip that he would never have learned in an American college. Note the vivid concrete details that authenticate his narrative.

14   Not all of this was safe and rosy. Rick and I spent one night fending off wild dogs with a metal bar and headlamp, after escaping from the clutches of a hawk-nosed Tibetan with a few loose screws. We finally found a place to stay (by barging into a man's tent at 5 a.m. and striking a deal with him to spend the night), but still, the Himalayan winter nearly turned us into popsicles.

15   I even learned the in's and out's of the squat toilet. Do not sink too low when you squat. Trust me.

16   And while we are on the subject of appropriate dinner table conversation, let me warn you never to pee into a strong oncoming Tibetan wind. Unless you are seeking a novel and roundabout face-washing technique. Believe me, it happened.

17   So if you are willing to unrut your wheels, if you enjoy hopscotching through the world of motorcycles and open prairie, or if you're just searching for that extra boost to send yourself hurtling down a road less traveled, then perhaps a year abroad is right for you. Think about it in particular if you're going to study a language in college: why pay expensive tuition to learn Spanish in the States when you can learn it more thoroughly and cheaply in Bolivia?

18   Even a gap year's undesired moments can have a palliative benefit. Setting off for remote mountain villages, only to discover that they have been utterly abandoned; triumphantly finding a town's only bathroom, only to discover that the mud you are now standing in is not actually mud; these are the curve balls that keep you on your toes, that preserve in your life what remains of childhood spontaneity.

19   A gap year is a larky way to mature out of youth. But if you do it right, it's also a way to keep it.

The classroom experience becomes an afterthought when compared with all that Kristof has learned elsewhere.

20   I nearly forgot to mention that the original purpose of traveling to China was to bolster my Chinese at Tsinghua University in Beijing. Thanks to its great program, as well as the superb Ruiwen school in Dalian, I'm now fluent. But talent in Chinese doesn't compare with talent in analyzing terrain for wild dog hangouts, or with kaleidoscopic memories that will refract experiences for a lifetime.

21   So, graduating seniors, now's the time to search the Web for travel abroad programs. Check out Global Citizen Year for a mini peace corps experience. If you're less interested in a formal program, just do what I did: sign up for a foreign language school and book a flight. Because of the dollar's purchasing power, travel in China is very cheap—a rebuttal to those who think gap years are only for rich kids. I hope you choose to defer enrollment for one year, and I hope that your gap year, like mine, goes wrong in all the right ways.

22   When college does roll around, you'll already have gone through your own freshman orientation. After getting lost in a remote village because I was seeking a familiar temple but was approaching it from a completely different direction, I learned that where you are going is not all that matters. Where you are coming from matters, too.

23   It's like this: Spend time huddling for candle warmth on the Tibetan Plateau, and the C in physics ain't gonna seem so harsh.

Kristof returns to his opening to bring closure to his narrative, while driving home the main points of his argument.

24   Eventually the dots begin to connect themselves. That's when I discovered that I got more than what I'd bargained for. I initially wanted simply to get a sense of where I was headed for the next few years. But the poverty I encountered in western China irrevocably challenged me. I felt, on the most profound of levels, the realness of others. I became just one person among very, very many. Especially since I was in China.

25   Speaking of melting into the background, that was exactly my wish that evening when my friend and I got caught in the temple.

26   "I'm just a traveler," I said. After an ungolden silence, a monk stepped forward: "Come eat with us."

After fully establishing his argument through his narrative, Kristof concludes with a pithy statement of one of his main points.

27   Rick and I spent the rest of that evening under a temple rooftop somewhere among the Himalayan foothills—I couldn't find the place now. We and the incredibly hospitable monks traded stories and cheers over yak meat, yak cheese, and yak butter tea well past my bedtime.

28   Who says you need a classroom for an education?

12 | Rebuttal Arguments

QUICK TAKE

In this chapter, you will learn to

1. Understand how rebuttal arguments work (see pages 174–175)
2. Recognize the two basic strategies of rebuttal arguments: refutation and counterargument (see pages 175–178)
3. Analyze a rebuttal argument (see page 178)
4. Write an effective rebuttal argument (see pages 180–181)

Whaling is an ancient form of hunting that greatly expanded in the nineteenth century as the result of worldwide demand for whale oil. By 1986 the worldwide whale populations were so seriously depleted that the International Whaling Committee banned commercial whaling to allow whale populations to replenish. Limited whaling continues for scientific research, but environmental organizations such as Greenpeace insist that "science" is a guise for the continuation of commercial whaling. Greenpeace protests all whaling vigorously—both by peaceful means and by open ocean confrontations with whaling vessels. Could their protests at sea be considered a rebuttal argument?

Understand How Rebuttal Arguments Work

There are two basic approaches to rebutting an argument: you can refute the argument, or you can counterargue. In the first case, **refutation**, you demonstrate the shortcomings of the argument you wish to discredit, and you may or may not offer a positive claim of your own. In the second case, **counterargument**, you focus on the strengths of the position you support and spend little time on the specifics of the argument you are countering. There can be substantial overlap between these two tactics, and good rebuttal arguments often employ both refutation and counterargument.

Because it focuses on the shortcomings in the opposition's argument, a refutation argument often takes much of its structure from the argument being refuted.

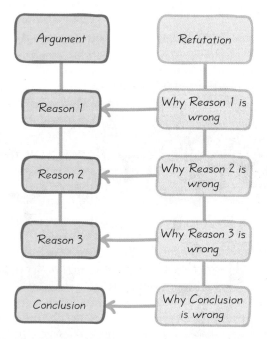

Many college students think that using technology to "multitask" makes them more productive, believing that studying, texting a friend, and listening to music all at once is an efficient use of their time. But research shows that engaging in multiple tasks is distracting, interferes with memory, and makes it difficult to switch from one task to another—all of which causes multitaskers to be less productive than people focusing on one task at a time.

Counterarguments more often take up ideas the opposing claims have not addressed at all, or they take a very different approach to the problem. By largely ignoring the specifics of the argument being countered, they make the implicit claim that the counterargument is superior.

Those who argue for tariffs on goods from China claim that tariffs will protect American manufacturing jobs, but tariffs are a bad idea because they would increase prices on clothing, furniture, toys, and other consumer goods for everyone and would cause the loss of retailing jobs as well.

Recognize Kinds of Rebuttal Arguments

Refutation

A refutation can either challenge the assumptions underlying a claim or question the evidence supporting a claim. Until about five hundred years ago, people believed that the sky, and everything in it, moved, while the Earth remained still. They observed the stars moving from west to east in a regular, circular motion and concluded that all the heavenly bodies orbited around an axis between Earth and Polaris, the northern star. This theory, however, did not explain the movement of the planets. If you watch the path of Mars over several nights, for example, you will notice that it moves, like the stars, from east to west. But occasionally, it will appear to move backward, from west to east, before reversing itself and resuming an east-to-west course. This phenomenon is called retrograde motion, and it is exhibited by all the planets in our solar system. In fact, our word *planet* derives from the Greek term *planetes*, meaning "wanderer." The ancient Greeks assumed that the planets and stars orbited the Earth, but that the planets sometimes wandered from their paths.

In the second century CE, the Greek astronomer Ptolemy made precise and detailed observations of the planets and created a model to predict their retrograde motion. In his treatise, the *Almagest*, he theorized that Mars and the other "wanderers" periodically deviated from their path around the Earth, making small circles, or epicycles, before moving on again. It was a complicated system, but it predicted the movements of the planets very accurately, and so it went unchallenged for over a thousand years.

In the early sixteenth century, the Polish astronomer Nicolaus Copernicus recognized that Ptolemy's observations could be explained more simply if the Earth and other planets circled the Sun. Copernicus's theory, later confirmed by the German astronomer Johannes Kepler, eventually replaced the Ptolemaic model of the solar system as the accepted explanation for observed planetary motion.

Copernicus did not question Ptolemy's evidence—the data he had collected showing where the stars and planets appear in the sky to an Earth-bound observer. Instead, he questioned Ptolemy's central assumption that Earth is the center of the solar system. Because evidence of the planet's retrograde motion had been observed by people over such a long period of time, it was unlikely to be wrong. Instead, it was the theory Ptolemy constructed to explain his data that was incorrect.

But sometimes evidence is wrong. Sometimes, too, evidence is incomplete or not representative, and sometimes counterevidence can be found. People who are bent on persuading others may leave out information that weakens their case or employ evidence in questionable ways to try to bolster their claims. Dermatologists argue that indoor tanning is harmful to people's health because it exposes them to ultraviolet radiation, a known cause of cancer. The tanning industry, not surprisingly, disagrees, arguing that indoor tanning is safer than outdoor tanning because it assures safe levels of UV radiation exposure. While sunbathers often get sunburned, indoor tanners only get safe levels of radiation. This is an intriguing claim, but the AMA has discovered that in fact people who use tanning beds *do* get burned—as many of 50 percent of them. The tanning industry also claims indoor tanning provides people with a "protective" tan that reduces the amount of harmful UV radiation they absorb when they do go out in the sun. Doctors counter this claim by pointing out that a "base tan" provides only as much protection as a sunblock with a sun protection factor, or SPF, of 3, and that the minimum recommended SPF for sunscreen is 15. The protection offered by an indoor tan is minimal at best. Both sides continue to argue over what evidence is valid, and accurate, when assessing the safety of indoor tanning.

Counterargument

Another way to rebut is to counterargue. In a counterargument, you might acknowledge an opposing point of view, but you might not consider it in detail. Rather, you put the main effort into your own argument. A counterarguer, in effect, says, "I hear your argument. But there is more to it than that. Now listen while I explain why another position is stronger." Counterargument is an effective way of persuading audiences, but sometimes it is used as a way to avoid addressing opposing views honestly. People's tendency to be persuaded by counterargument also makes them susceptible to red herrings, when an irrelevant but dramatic detail is put forward as if it were important, and *ad hominem* attacks, where someone makes spurious accusations about an opponent instead of engaging in real debate.

The counterarguer depends on the wisdom of his or her audience members to hear all sides of an issue and make up their own minds about the merits of the case. In the following short poem, Wilfred Owen, a veteran of the horrors of World War I trench warfare, offers a counterargument to those who argue that war is noble, to those who believe along with the poet Horace that "dulce et decorum est pro patria mori"—that it is sweet and fitting to die for one's country. This poem gains in popularity whenever there is an unpopular war, for it rebuts the belief that it is noble to die for one's country in modern warfare.

Dulce et Decorum Est

Bent double, like old beggars under sacks,
Knock-kneed, coughing like hags, we cursed through sludge,
Till on the haunting flares we turned our backs
And towards our distant rest began to trudge.
Men marched asleep. Many had lost their boots
But limped on, blood-shod. All went lame; all blind;
Drunk with fatigue; deaf even to the hoots
Of tired, outstripped Five-Nines that dropped behind.

Gas! Gas! Quick, boys! — An ecstasy of fumbling,
Fitting the clumsy helmets just in time;
But someone still was yelling out and stumbling,
And flound'ring like a man in fire or lime . . .
Dim, through the misty panes and thick green light,
As under a green sea, I saw him drowning.
In all my dreams, before my helpless sight,
He plunges at me, guttering, choking, drowning.

If in some smothering dreams you too could pace
Behind the wagon that we flung him in,
And watch the white eyes writhing in his face,
His hanging face, like a devil's sick of sin;
If you could hear, at every jolt, the blood
Come gargling from the froth-corrupted lungs,
Obscene as cancer, bitter as the cud
Of vile, incurable sores on innocent tongues,
My friend, you would not tell with such high zest
To children ardent for some desperate glory,
The old Lie: Dulce et decorum est
Pro patria mori.

Owen does not summarize the argument in favor of being willing to die for one's country and then refute that argument point by point. Rather, his poem presents an opposing argument, supported by a narrative of the speaker's experience in a poison-gas attack, that he hopes will more than counterbalance what he calls "the old Lie." Owen simply ignores the reasons people give for being willing to die for one's country and argues instead that there are good reasons not to do so. And he hopes that the evidence he summons for his position will outweigh for his audience (addressed as "My friend") the evidence in support of the other side.

Rebuttal arguments frequently offer both refutation and counterargument. Like attorneys engaged in a trial, people writing rebuttals must make their own cases based on good reasons and hard evidence, but they also do what they can to undermine their opponent's case. In the end the jury—the audience—decides.

Build a Rebuttal Argument

As you prepare to rebut an argument, look closely at what your opponent says. What exactly are the claims? What is the evidence? What are the assumptions? What do you disagree with? Are there parts you agree with? Are there assumptions you share? Do you agree that the evidence is accurate?

Knowing where you agree with someone helps you focus your rebuttal on differences. Having points of agreement can also help you build credibility with your audience, if you acknowledge that your opponent makes some logical points, or makes reasonable assumptions.

Consider using counterargument if you generally agree with a claim but do not think it goes far enough, if you feel an argument proposes the wrong solution to a problem, or if you think that, while accurate, it misses the "big picture." Counterargument lets you frame your own, stronger take on the question at hand without spending a lot of time trying to find flaws in the opposing position when there may not be many in it.

If you do have serious objections to an argument, plan to refute it, and start by looking for the most important differences in your respective positions. What are the biggest "red flags" in the argument you disagree with? What are the weakest points of your opponent's argument? What are the strongest points of your own? You will probably want to highlight these differences in your rebuttal. You may find many problems with evidence and logic, in which case you will probably want to prioritize them. You do not necessarily need to point out the flaws in every single element of an argument. Direct your audience to the ones that matter the most.

You can also use counterargument in combination with refutation, first showing why an existing argument is wrong and then offering an alternative. This is one of the more common forms of rebuttal. As you examine your opponent's claims and evidence, look closely for fallacies and faulty logic (see pages 16–19). How do these distort the problem or lead the audience to mistaken conclusions? Pointing them out to your readers will strengthen your position.

Look too at sources. Check your opponent's facts. Scrutinize the experts he or she relies on. And consider the purpose and motivation behind arguments you rebut. Groups funded by major industries, political parties, and special interest groups may have hidden or not-so-hidden agendas driving the arguments they make. Pointing these out to your readers can strengthen your own position.

Finding Good Reasons

Can the Web Be Trusted for Research?

Most Web users are familiar with the huge and immensely popular *Wikipedia*, the online encyclopedia. What makes *Wikipedia* so different from traditional, print encyclopedias is that entries can be contributed or edited by anyone.

In 2007, Jimmy Wales, president of Wikimedia and one of its founders, debated the legitimacy of *Wikipedia* with Dale Hoiberg, editor-in-chief of *Encyclopedia Britannica.* Hoiberg's main criticism of *Wikipedia* is that its structure— an open-source wiki without the formal editorial control that shapes traditional, print encyclopedias—allows for inaccurate entries.

In response, Wales argues that *Britannica* and newspapers also contain errors, but *Wikipedia* has the advantage that they are easily corrected. Furthermore, he asserts that *Wikipedia*'s policy of using volunteer administrators to delete irrelevant entries and requiring authors of entries to cite reliable, published sources ensures quality. Nonetheless, some universities including UCLA and the University of Pennsylvania along with many instructors strongly discourage and even ban students from citing *Wikipedia* in their work. (*Wikipedia* also cautions against using its entries as a primary source for serious research.)

Write about it

1. If your college decided to ban the use of *Wikipedia* as a reference because it lacked the authority of a traditional encyclopedia, would you want to challenge it? Why or why not?

2. If you chose to challenge the college's policy, how would you do so? Would it be effective to refute the college's claims point by point, noting fallacies in logic and reasoning? Would it be effective to build a counterargument in which you examine the assumptions on which the college's claims are based? Which strategy would you choose, and why?

Steps to Writing a Rebuttal Argument

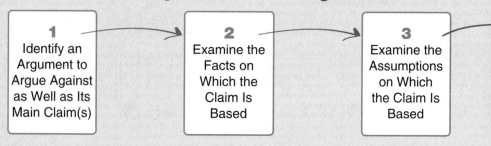

1 Identify an Argument to Argue Against as Well as Its Main Claim(s)

2 Examine the Facts on Which the Claim Is Based

3 Examine the Assumptions on Which the Claim Is Based

Step 1 Identify an Argument to Argue Against as Well as Its Main Claim(s)

- What exactly are you arguing against?
- Are there secondary claims attached to the main claim?
- Include a fair summary of your opponent's position in your finished rebuttal.

Examples

- Arguing against raising taxes for the purpose of building a new sports stadium (examine how proponents claim that a new sports facility will benefit the local economy)
- Arguing for raising the minimum wage (examine how opponents claim that a higher minimum wage isn't necessary and negatively affects small-business owners)

Step 2 Examine the Facts on Which the Claim Is Based

- Are the facts accurate, current, and representative?
- Is there another body of facts that you can present as counterevidence?
- If the author uses statistics, can the statistics be interpreted differently?
- If the author quotes from sources, how reliable are those sources?
- Are the sources treated fairly, or are quotations taken out of context?

Step 3 Examine the Assumptions on Which the Claim Is Based

- What are the primary and secondary assumptions of the claim you are rejecting?
- How are those assumptions flawed?
- Does the author resort to name-calling, use faulty reasoning, or ignore key facts (see pages 16–19)?

Step 4 Analyze Your Potential Readers

- To what extent do your potential readers support the claim that you are rejecting?
- If they strongly support that claim, how might you appeal to them to change their minds?
- What common assumptions and beliefs do you share with them?

Step 5 Write a Draft

Introduction

Identify the issue and the argument you are rejecting.

- Provide background if the issue is unfamiliar to most of your readers.
- Give a quick summary of the competing positions even if the issue is familiar to your readers.
- Make your aim clear in your thesis statement.

Body

Take on the argument that you are rejecting. Consider questioning the evidence that is used to support the argument by doing one or more of the following.

- Challenge the facts and the currency and relevance of examples.
- Present counterevidence and countertestimony.
- Challenge the credibility of sources cited.
- Question the way in which statistical evidence is presented and interpreted.
- Argue that quotations are taken out of context.

Conclusion

- Conclude on a firm note by underscoring your objections.
- Consider closing with a counterargument or counterproposal.

Step 6 Revise, Edit, Proofread

- For detailed instructions, see Chapter 5.
- For a checklist to use to evaluate your draft, see pages 50–51.

Ron Reagan

Speech at the Democratic National Convention, July 27, 2004

Ron Reagan is the son of the fortieth president of the United States. In August 1994, at the age of 83, President Reagan was diagnosed with Alzheimer's disease, an incurable neurological disorder that destroys brain cells, and he died of the disease in June 2004. A few months later, on July 27, Ron Reagan offered the following speech to the delegates to the Democratic National Convention and to the millions of Americans watching on television. It was countered the next day by Richard Doerflinger, whose rebuttal follows this speech.

Good evening, ladies and gentlemen.

2   A few of you may be surprised to see someone with my last name showing up to speak at a Democratic Convention. Apparently some of you are not. Let me assure you, I am not here to make a political speech and the topic at hand should not—must not—have anything to do with partisanship.

3   I am here tonight to talk about the issue of research into what may be the greatest medical breakthrough in our or any lifetime: the use of embryonic stem cells—cells created using the material of our own bodies—to cure a wide range of fatal and debilitating illnesses: Parkinson's disease, multiple sclerosis, diabetes, lymphoma, spinal cord injuries, and much more.

4   Millions are afflicted. And every year, every day, tragedy is visited upon families across the country, around the world. Now, it may be within our power to put an end to this suffering. We only need to try.

5   Some of you already know what I'm talking about when I say embryonic stem cell research. Others of you are probably thinking, that's quite a mouthful. Maybe this is a good time to go for a tall cold one. Well, wait a minute, wait a minute.

6   Let me try and paint as simple a picture as I can while still doing justice to the science, the incredible science involved. Let's say that ten or so years from now you are diagnosed with Parkinson's disease. There is currently no cure, and drug therapy, with its attendant side-effects, can only temporarily relieve the symptoms.

7   Now, imagine going to a doctor who, instead of prescribing drugs, takes a few skin cells from your arm. The nucleus of one of your cells is placed into a donor egg whose own nucleus

In his first three paragraphs, Reagan makes his purpose clear.

Paragraphs 5–10 define stem cell research. Note his simple explanation and the informal tone, appropriate for a speech.

has been removed. A bit of chemical or electrical stimulation will encourage your cell's nucleus to begin dividing, creating new cells which will then be placed into a tissue culture. Those cells will generate embryonic stem cells containing only your DNA, thereby eliminating the risk of tissue rejection. These stem cells are then driven to become the very neural cells that are defective in Parkinson's patients. And finally, those cells—with your DNA—are injected into your brain where they will replace the faulty cells whose failure to produce adequate dopamine led to the Parkinson's disease in the first place.

8   In other words, you're cured.

9   And another thing, these embryonic stem cells, they could continue to replicate indefinitely and, theoretically, can be induced to recreate virtually any tissue in your body.

10   How'd you like to have your own personal biological repair kit standing by at the hospital? Sound like magic? Welcome to the future of medicine.

11   Now by the way, no fetal tissue is involved in this process. No fetuses are created, none destroyed. This all happens in the laboratory at the cellular level.

> Anticipating an objection, he subtly but explicitly distinguishes stem cell research from abortion.

12   Now, there are those who would stand in the way of this remarkable future, who would deny the federal funding so crucial to basic research. They argue that interfering with the development of even the earliest stage embryo, even one that will never be implanted in a womb and will never develop into an actual fetus, is tantamount to murder.

13   A few of these folks, needless to say, are just grinding a political axe and they should be ashamed of themselves. But many are well-meaning and sincere. Their belief is just that, an article of faith, and they are entitled to it. But it does not follow that the theology of a few should be allowed to forestall the health and wellbeing of the many.

14   And how can we affirm life if we abandon those whose own lives are so desperately at risk? It is a hallmark of human intelligence that we are able to make distinctions.

> Reagan uses the language of "life" to acknowledge and refute counterarguments.

15   Yes, these cells could theoretically have the potential, under very different circumstances, to develop into human beings—that potential is where their magic lies. But they are not, in and of themselves, human beings. They have no fingers and toes, no brain or spinal cord. They have no thoughts, no fears. They feel no pain.

16   Surely we can distinguish between these undifferentiated cells multiplying in a tissue culture and a living, breathing person—a parent, a spouse, a child.

The actor Michael J. Fox, who was diagnosed in 1991 with Parkinson's disease, spoke at the Bio International Convention in 2007. Fox appealed to scientists and investors to aggressively translate scientific research into creative treatments for debilitating diseases, including Parkinson's.

Reagan appeals to a single representative example to support his case. Why does he pick this particular example?

17   I know a child—well, she must be 13 now so I guess I'd better call her a young woman. She has fingers and toes. She has a mind. She has memories. She has hopes. She has juvenile diabetes. Like so many kids with this disease, she's adjusted amazingly well. The insulin pump she wears—she's decorated hers with rhinestones. She can handle her own catheter needle. She's learned to sleep through the blood drawings in the wee hours of the morning.

18   She's very brave. She is also quite bright and understands full well the progress of her disease and what that might ultimately mean: blindness, amputation, diabetic coma. Every day, she fights to have a future.

19   What excuse will we offer this young woman should we fail her now? What might we tell her children? Or the millions of others who suffer? That when given an opportunity to help, we turned away? That facing political opposition, we lost our nerve? That even though we knew better, we did nothing?

20   And, should we fail, how will we feel if, a few years from now, a more enlightened generation should fulfill the promise of embryonic stem cell therapy? Imagine what they would say of us who lacked the will.

21   No, we owe this young woman and all those who suffer—we owe ourselves—better than that. We are better than that. We are a wiser people, a finer nation.

22   And for all of us in this fight, let me say: we will prevail. The tide of history is with us. Like all generations who have come before ours, we are motivated by a thirst for knowledge and compelled to see others in need as fellow angels on an often difficult path, deserving of our compassion.

23   In a few months, we will face a choice. Yes, between two candidates and two parties, but more than that. We have a chance to take a giant stride forward for the good of all humanity. We can choose between the future and the past, between reason and ignorance, between true compassion and mere ideology.

Reagan offers his final counter-argument: inevitability. By focusing on the inevitable, he portrays those who disagree with him as stuck in the past and resistant to change.

24   This—this is our moment, and we must not falter.

25   Whatever else you do come November 2, I urge you, please, cast a vote for embryonic stem cell research.

26   Thank you for your time.

Richard M. Doerflinger

Don't Clone Ron Reagan's Agenda

Richard M. Doerflinger is the Associate Director of Pro-Life Activities for the United States Conference of Catholic Bishops. In 2009 Doerflinger was awarded an inaugural Life Prize by the Gerard Health Foundation for his work in "preserving and upholding the sanctity of human life" in areas such as public advocacy, legal action, and outreach. A specialist in bioethics, biotechnology, and public policy, he wrote the essay that follows on July 28, 2004, in response to Ron Reagan's speech, which appears immediately before this essay.

Does Doerflinger offer a fair summary of Reagan's argument?

Ron Reagan's speech at the Democratic convention last night was expected to urge expanded funding for stem cell research using so-called "spare" embryos—and to highlight these cells' potential for treating the Alzheimer's disease that took his father's life.

2   He did neither. He didn't even mention Alzheimer's, perhaps because even strong supporters of embryonic stem cell research say it is unlikely to be of use for that disease. (Reagan himself admitted this on a July 12 segment of MSNBC's *Hardball*.) And he didn't talk about current debates on funding research using existing embryos. Instead he endorsed the more radical agenda of

In paragraphs 2 and 3 he recontextualizes Reagan's argument by using the word *cloning*, which never appears in Reagan's speech. He also describes Reagan's position as "radical," which makes it hard for readers to agree with Reagan.

human cloning—mass-producing one's own identical twins in the laboratory so they can be exploited as (in his words) "your own personal biological repair kit" when disease or injury strikes.

3   Politically this was, to say the least, a gamble. Americans may be tempted to make use of embryos left over from fertility clinics, but most polls show them to be against human cloning for any purpose. Other advanced nations—Canada, Australia, France, Germany, Norway—have banned the practice completely, and the United Nations may approve an international covenant against it this fall. Many groups and individuals who are "pro-choice" on abortion oppose research cloning, not least because it would require the mass exploitation of women to provide what Ron Reagan casually calls "donor eggs." And the potential "therapeutic" benefits of cloning are even more speculative than those of embryonic stem cell research—the worldwide effort even to obtain viable stem cells from cloned embryos has already killed hundreds of embryos and produced exactly one stem cell line in South Korea.

Rather than attacking Reagan, Doerflinger praises him and therefore seems fair-minded.

4   But precisely for these reasons, Ron Reagan should be praised for his candor. The scientists and patient groups promoting embryonic stem cell research know that the current debate on funding is a mere transitional step. For years they have supported the mass manufacture of human embryos through cloning, as the logical and necessary goal of their agenda, but lately they have been coy about this as they fight for the more popular slogan of "stem cell research." With his speech Reagan has removed the mask and allowed us to debate what is really at stake.

5   He claimed in his speech, of course, that what is at stake in this debate is the lives of millions of patients with devastating diseases. But by highlighting Parkinson's disease and juvenile diabetes as two diseases most clearly justifying the move to human cloning, he failed to do his homework. These are two of the diseases that pro-cloning scientists now admit will probably *not* be helped by research cloning.

He rebuts Reagan's argument by citing authorities to add credibility to his claims.

6   Scottish cloning expert Ian Wilmut, for example, wrote in the *British Medical Journal* in February that producing genetically matched stem cells through cloning is probably quite unnecessary for treating any neurological disease. Recent findings suggest that the nervous system is "immune privileged," and will not generally reject stem cells from a human who is genetically different. He added that cloning is probably useless for auto-immune diseases like juvenile diabetes, where the body mistakenly rejects its own insulin-producing cells as though they were foreign. "In such cases," he wrote, "transfer of immunologically identical cells to a patient is expected to induce the same rejection."

7   Wilmut's observations cut the ground out from under Ron Reagan's simple-minded claim that cloning is needed to avoid tissue

rejection. For some diseases, genetically matched cells are unnecessary; for others, they are useless, because they only replicate the genetic profile that is part of the problem. (Ironically, for Alzheimer's both may be true—cloning may be unnecessary to avoid tissue rejection in the brain, and useless because the cloned cells would have the same genetic defect that may lead to Alzheimer's.) Reagan declared that this debate requires us to "choose between . . . reason and ignorance," but he did not realize which side has the monopoly on ignorance.

8   That ignorance poses an obstacle to real advances that are right before our eyes. Two weeks before Ron Reagan declared that a treatment for Parkinson's may arrive "ten or so years from now," using "the material of our own bodies," a Parkinson's patient and his doctor quietly appeared before Congress to point out that this has already been done. Dennis Turner was treated in 1999 by Dr. Michel Levesque of Cedars-Sinai Medical Center in Los Angeles, using his own adult neural stem cells. Dr. Levesque did not use the Rube Goldberg method of trying to turn those cells into a cloned embryo and then killing the embryo to get stem cells—he just grew Turner's own adult stem cells in the lab, and turned them directly into dopamine-producing cells. And with just one injection, on one side of Turner's brain, he produced an almost complete reversal of Parkinson's symptoms over four years.

9   Turner stopped shaking, could eat without difficulty, could put in his own contact lenses again, and resumed his avocation of big-game photography—on one occasion scrambling up a tree in Africa to escape a charging rhinoceros.

10   Amazingly, while this advance has been presented at national and international scientific conferences and featured on ABC-TV in Chicago, the scientific establishment supporting embryonic stem cell research has almost completely ignored it, and most news media have obediently imposed a virtual news blackout on it. That did not change even after the results were presented to the Senate Commerce Subcommittee on Science, Technology and Space this month. Pro-cloning Senators on the panel actually seemed angry at the witnesses, for trying to distract them from their fixation on destroying embryos.

11   Turner also testified that his symptoms have begun to return, especially arising from the side of his brain that was left untreated, and he would like to get a second treatment. For that he will have to wait. Dr. Levesque has received insufficient appreciation and funding for his technique, and is still trying to put together the funds for broader clinical trials—as most Parkinson's foundations and NIH peer reviewers look into the starry distance of Ron Reagan's dreams about embryonic stem cells.

12   But hey, who cares about real Parkinson's patients when there's a Brave New World to sell?

Marginal notes:

Doerflinger takes a very different tone than Reagan. Which do you find more effective?

To contrast Reagan's hypothetical example, Doerflinger provides a real example of treating Parkinson's.

Compare how Doerflinger and Reagan characterize those who disagree with them. Which approach do you find more persuasive?

Sample Student Rebuttal Argument

Ramos 1

Marta Ramos
Professor Jacobs
English 1010
30 April 2013

Oversimplifying the Locavore Ethic

James McWilliams's argument in his book *Just Food* is based on an overly simplistic understanding of the locavore ethic. His claim, that eating locally is an unrealistic goal, fails to take into account the flexibility of locavorism, the ways consumer food preferences drive the free market system, and the realities of food processing infrastructure.

> Ramos identifies the source that she will refute and the source's claim in the first paragraph.

McWilliams's criticism of locavorism would make sense if, as he implies, locavores were a single-minded group of people demanding the complete conversion of the agricultural systems to uniform, regimented local production and consumption. In fact, there is no reason that locavorism has to completely replace the existing agricultural system, and hardly any locavores advocate this. Locavorism, the practice of eating food that is grown locally and in season, is not an all-or-nothing policy. It is a direction in which individuals and communities can move. *Locavores.com*, a Web site run by the chef Jessica Prentice, who coined the term "locavore," spells out local-eating strategies:

> Ramos defines the term "locavore" and asserts that McWilliams misunderstands the movement.

> If not LOCALLY PRODUCED, then ORGANIC.
>
> If not ORGANIC, then FAMILY FARM.
>
> If not FAMILY FARM, then LOCAL BUSINESS.
>
> If not LOCAL BUSINESS, then TERROIR—foods famous for the region they are grown in. ("Guidelines")

This hierarchy of food sources prefers local sources over distant ones and prioritizes local farms and businesses to receive local food dollars. Eating locally, according to Locavores, represents "A step toward regional food self-reliance" ("Top"). Given the political instability of many areas of the world that grow our food and the way energy costs can drastically affect food prices, it makes sense to reduce our dependence on distant food sources. As Jennifer Maiser, one of the founders of the locavore movement, puts it,

> Ramos uses a direct quotation from a respected voice in the locavore community to build credibility.

Ramos 2

Locavores are people who pay attention to where their food comes
from and commit to eating local food as much as possible. The
great thing about eating local is that it's not an all-or-nothing
venture. Any small step you take helps the environment, protects
your family's health and supports small farmers in your area.

The goal is not to end completely our importation of food.

McWilliams cites Phoenix as an example of why locavorism won't
work. Certainly cities like Phoenix, which lacks the water to grow much
food, will always rely on external supply chains to feed their populations.
But the obstacles to local eating in Phoenix should not prevent residents
of San Francisco, Sarasota, or Charleston from eating locally grown foods.
Locavorism doesn't have to work everywhere to be beneficial.

In addition to misrepresenting locavorism's goals, McWilliams
illogically claims that it cannot meet people's food needs. "At current
levels of fruit production," he warns, "apples are the only crop that
could currently feed New Yorkers at a level that meets the U.S.
Recommended Dietary Allowances" (44). McWilliams is wrong when he
claims that if New Yorkers ate locally grown fruits, they could "rarely
indulge in a pear, peach, or basket of strawberries" (44). That might
be the case if New York farmers continued to grow nothing but apples
and grapes. But if some of those crops were replaced with other fruits,
New York could have a very diverse supply of produce that would come
reasonably close to meeting the nutritional needs of its citizens. In fact,
if committed locavores seek out locally grown strawberries, peaches,
and pears, and are willing to pay more money for them than they do
for apples, local farmers will have sound economic reasons for replacing
some of their aging apple trees with peach and pear trees. McWilliams
makes locavorism sound impractical because he tries to imagine it
working within current agricultural realities. In fact, locavores seek to
change the way food is produced and consumed. Moreover, locavorism
works toward this change not, as McWilliams suggests, by advocating
laws that restrict food producers but by encouraging consumers to vote
with their wallets.

McWilliams's argument about New York also rests on the peculiar
assumption that every person in the state has to eat the same fruits in

In her refutation Ramos addresses McWilliams's argument point by point.

Ramos quotes McWilliams and then disproves the quoted claim.

Ramos 3

the same amounts in order for locavorism to work. He points out that except for apples and grapes, "every other fruit the state produces is not being harvested at a level to provide all New Yorkers with an adequate supply" (44). McWilliams implies that if you can't grow enough of a crop to supply every single person in the state, there is no point in growing it; however, the goal of locavorism is choice, not total local supply of all food, a fact McWilliams seems to willfully ignore.

> Ramos questions McWilliams's assumptions and finds them lacking.

Finally, McWilliams claims that the cost and inconvenience of processing food locally will prevent communities from moving toward local eating. He notes that "whereas the conventional system of production and distribution has in place a series of large-scale processing centers capable of handling these tasks in a handful of isolated locations," smaller communities do not (45). There are two problems with this argument. First, many of the "processing centers" McWilliams is thinking of *aren't* capable of handling the task of food production. The National Resources Defense Council reports that "from 1995 to 1998, 1,000 spills or pollution incidents occurred at livestock feedlots in ten states and 200 manure-related fish kills resulted in the death of 13 million fish" ("Facts"). In 2009, Fairbank Farms recalled over half a million pounds of ground beef after nineteen people were hospitalized and two died from E. coli bacteria in the meat (United States). Also in 2009, the King Nut Companies of Solon, Ohio, sickened over four hundred people, including three who died, by producing and distributing peanut butter infected with salmonella ("Virginia"). Large-scale processing plants are not a solution to our food security needs. They are part of the problem.

> Ramos addresses the claim that she takes greatest issue with last. She then gives it further emphasis by providing two distinct counterarguments.

Second, the cost of changing the country's food-processing system from large-scale to small-scale is not as prohibitive as McWilliams makes it sound. Factories age. Machines wear out and have to be replaced. Food production facilities are replaced all the time. Newer facilities could easily be built on a smaller, more regional scale. In fact, given the cost of recalls and lawsuits when tainted food is distributed over a large area, food producers have good reason to think about smaller, more localized production and distribution.

McWilliams either does not understand locavorism or understands it and prefers to misrepresent its goals and methods. His arguments in favor of our current food production system ignore both the very real benefits of local eating, and the considerable cost of the existing system.

> Ramos closes with an appeal to the benefits of locavorism.

Ramos 4

Works Cited

"Facts about Pollution from Livestock Farms." *Natural Resources Defense Council*. Natural Resources Defense Council, 15 July 2005. Web. 7 Apr. 2013.

"Guidelines for Eating Well." *Locavores*. Locavores, 3 June 2009. Web. 9 Apr. 2013.

Maiser, Jennifer. "10 Steps to Becoming a Locavore." *PBS: NOW*. Jump Start Productions, 2 Nov. 2007. Web. 8 Apr. 2013.

McWilliams, James E. *Just Food: Where Locavores Get It Wrong and How We Can Truly Eat Responsibly*. New York: Little, Brown, 2009.

"Top Twelve Reasons to Eat Locally." *Locavores*. Locavores, 3 June 2009. Web. 9 Apr. 2013.

United States. Dept. of Health and Human Services. "Multistate Outbreak of E. coli 0157:H7 Infections Associated with Beef from Fairbanks Farms." *Centers for Disease Control and Prevention*. Dept. of Health and Human Services, 24 Nov. 2009. Web. 8 Apr. 2013.

"Virginia, Minnesota Confirms Salmonella Deaths Related to Tainted Peanut Butter." *Fox News*. Fox News Network, 13 Jan. 2009. Web. 10 Apr. 2013.

13 | Proposal Arguments

QUICK TAKE

In this chapter, you will learn to

1. Understand how proposal arguments work (see page 193)
2. Recognize how a proposal argument identifies a problem and states a solution that readers find fair, effective, and practical (see pages 193–194)
3. Analyze a proposal argument (see pages 194–195)
4. Write an effective proposal argument (see pages 196–197)

The San Francisco Bicycle Coalition, "dedicated to creating safer streets and more livable communities," is an organization whose primary goal is to build a citywide bike network in San Francisco. The success of the coalition's efforts to increase bicycle ridership for commuters created its own problem: Caltrain commuter trains ran out of room for bicycles, and riders were "bumped" because the trains' bike storage cars were filled to capacity. The coalition crafted a new proposal called Bikes On Board to persuade Caltrain to add more bike storage capacity on its trains. The coalition's proposal encourages riders to report "bumps" in order to document exactly how many times cyclists are denied rides on trains because of limited bike storage. This well-defined proposal forms part of a larger campaign and organizational mission encompassing environmental, economic, and personal fitness issues. What local issues inspire you to propose action? How would you go about crafting a proposal argument to promote interest in a cause or solution?

Understand How Proposal Arguments Work

Proposal arguments make the case that someone should do something: "The federal government should raise grazing fees on public lands." "The student union should renovate the old swimming pool in Butler Gymnasium." "All parents should secure their children in booster seats when driving, even for short distances." Proposals can also argue that something should *not* be done, or that people should stop doing something: "The plan to extend Highway 45 is a waste of tax dollars and citizens should not vote for it." "Don't drink and drive."

The challenge for writers of proposal arguments is to convince readers to take action. It's easy for readers to agree that something should be done, as long as they don't have to do it. It's much harder to get readers involved with the situation or convince them to spend their time or money trying to carry out the proposal. A successful proposal argument conveys a sense of urgency to motivate readers and describes definite actions they should take.

The key to a successful proposal is using good reasons to convince readers that if they act, something positive will happen (or something negative will be avoided). If your readers believe that taking action will benefit them, they are more likely to help bring about what you propose.

Proposal arguments take the form shown here.

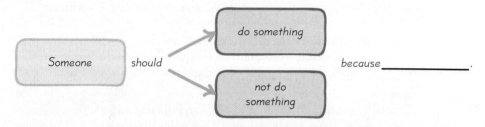

We should convert existing train tracks in the downtown areas to a light-rail system and build a new freight track around the city because we need to relieve traffic and parking congestion downtown.

Recognize Components of Proposal Arguments

Most successful proposals have four major components.

- **Identifying and defining the problem.** Sometimes, your audience is already fully aware of the problem you want to solve. If your city frequently tears up streets and then leaves them for months without fixing them, you shouldn't have to spend much time convincing citizens that streets should be repaired more quickly. But if you raise a problem unfamiliar to your readers, first you will have to convince them that the problem is real. Citizens will not see the need to replace miles of plumbing lines running under the streets, for example, unless you convince them that the pipes are old and corroded and are a risk to everyone's safety. You will also need to define the scope of the problem—does every single pipe need to be replaced, or only those more than forty years old? Is this a job for the city, or do federal clean water regulations mean that other government officials must be involved? The clearer you are about what must be done, and by whom, the stronger your argument will be.

- **Stating a proposed solution.** A strong proposal offers a clear, definite statement of exactly what you are proposing. Vague statements that "Something must be done!" may get readers stirred up about the issue, but are unlikely to lead to constructive action. A detailed proposal also adds credibility to your argument, showing that you are concerned enough to think through the nuts and bolts of the changes to be made. You can state your proposed solution near the beginning of your argument (it's in effect your thesis statement) or introduce it later—for example, after you have considered and rejected other possible solutions.

- **Convincing readers that the proposed solution is well considered and fair.** Once your readers agree that a problem exists and a solution should be found, you have to convince them that your solution is the best one. You have to supply good reasons to favor your proposal. Perhaps you want your city to fire the planning committee members who are responsible for street repair. You will need to show that those officials are indeed responsible for the delays and that, once they are fired, the city will be able to quickly hire new, more effective planners.

- **Demonstrating that the solution is feasible.** Your solution not only has to work; it must be feasible, or practical, to implement. You might be able to raise money for street repairs by billing property owners for repairs to the streets in front of their houses, but opposition to such a proposal would be fierce. Most Americans will object to making individuals responsible for road repair costs when roads are used by all drivers.

You may also have to show how your proposal is better than other possible actions that could be taken. Perhaps others believe your city should hire private contractors to repair the streets more quickly, or reward work crews who finish quickly with extra pay or days off. If there are multiple proposed solutions, all perceived as equally good, then there is no clear course of action for your audience to work for. Very often, that means nothing will happen. Take a clear stand.

Build a Proposal Argument

At this moment, you might not think that you feel strongly enough about anything to write a proposal argument. But if you write a list of things that make you mad or at least a little annoyed, then you have a start toward writing a proposal argument.

Some things on your list are not going to produce proposal arguments that many people would want to read. If your roommate is a slob, you might be able to write a proposal for that person to start cleaning up more, but who else would be interested? Similarly, it might be annoying to you that where you live is too far from the ocean, but it is hard to imagine making a serious proposal to move your city closer to the coast. Short of those extremes, however, are many things that might make you think "Why hasn't someone done something about this?" If you believe that others have something to gain if a problem is solved, or at least that the situation can be made a little better, then you might be able to develop a good proposal argument.

For instance, suppose you are living off campus and you buy a student parking sticker when you register for courses so that you can park in the student lot. However, you quickly find out that there are too many cars and trucks for the number of available spaces, and unless you get to campus by 8:00 A.M., you aren't going to find a place to park in your assigned lot. The situation makes you angry because you believe that if you pay for a sticker, you should have a reasonable chance of finding a place to park. You see that there are unfilled lots reserved for faculty and staff next to the student parking lot, and you wonder why more spaces aren't allotted to students. You decide to write to the president of your college. You want her to direct parking and traffic services to give more spaces to students or else to build a parking garage that will accommodate more vehicles.

When you start talking to other students on campus, however, you begin to realize that the problem may be more complex than your first view of it. Your college has taken the position that if fewer students drive to campus, there will be less traffic on and around your campus. The administration wants more students to ride shuttle buses, to form car pools, or to bicycle to campus instead of driving alone. You also find out that faculty and staff members pay ten times as much as students for their parking permits, so they pay a very high premium for a guaranteed space—much too high for most students. If the president of your college is your primary audience, you first have to argue that a problem really exists. You have to convince the president that many students have no choice but to drive if they are to attend classes. You, for example, are willing to ride the shuttle buses, but they don't run often enough for you to make your classes, get back to your car that you left at home, and then drive to your job.

Next, you have to argue that your solution will solve the problem. An 8-story parking garage might be adequate to park all the cars of students who want to drive, but parking garages are very expensive to build. Even if a parking garage is the best solution, the question remains: who is going to pay for it? Many problems in life could be solved if you had access to unlimited resources, but very few people—or organizations—have such resources at their command. It's not enough to propose a solution that can resolve the problem. You have to be able to argue for the feasibility of your solution. If you want to argue that a parking garage is the solution to the parking problem on your campus, then you must also propose how to finance the garage.

Steps to Writing a Proposal Argument

Step 1 Make a Claim

Make a proposal claim advocating a specific change or course of action.

Template

We should (or should not) do SOMETHING.

Examples

- Redesigning the process of registering for courses, getting e-mail, or making appointments to be more efficient
- Creating bicycle lanes to make cycling safer and to reduce traffic
- Streamlining the rules for recycling newspapers, bottles, and cans to encourage increased participation

Step 2 Identify the Problem

- What exactly is the problem, what causes it, and who is most affected?
- Has anyone tried to do anything about it? If so, why haven't they succeeded?
- What is likely to happen in the future if the problem isn't solved?

Step 3 Propose Your Solution

State your solution as specifically as you can, and support it with good reasons.

- What exactly do you want to achieve?
- What good consequences will follow if your proposal is adopted?
- How exactly will your solution work? Can it be accomplished quickly, or will it have to be phased in over a few years?
- Has anything like it been tried elsewhere? If so, what happened?
- If your solution costs money, how do you propose to pay for it?

Step 4 Consider Other Solutions

- What other solutions have been or might be proposed for this problem, including doing nothing?
- Why is your solution better?

Step 5 Write a Draft

Introduction

- Set out the issue or problem, perhaps by telling about your experience or the experience of someone you know.
- Argue for the seriousness of the problem.
- Give some background about the problem if necessary.
- State your proposal as your thesis.

Body

- Present your solution. Consider setting out your solution first, explaining how it will work, discussing other possible solutions, and arguing that yours is better. Or consider discussing other possible solutions first, arguing that they don't solve the problem or are not feasible, and then presenting your solution.
- Make clear the goals of your solution. Many solutions cannot solve problems completely.
- Describe in detail the steps in implementing your solution and how they will solve the problem you have identified.
- Explain the positive consequences that will follow from your proposal. What good things will happen, and what bad things will be avoided, if your advice is taken?

Conclusion

- Issue a call to action—if your readers agree with you, they will want to take action.
- Restate and emphasize exactly what readers need to do to solve the problem.

Step 6 Revise, Edit, Proofread

- For detailed instructions, see Chapter 5.
- For a checklist to use to evaluate your draft, see pages 50–51.

Finding Good Reasons

Who Should Make Decisions About Economic Development?

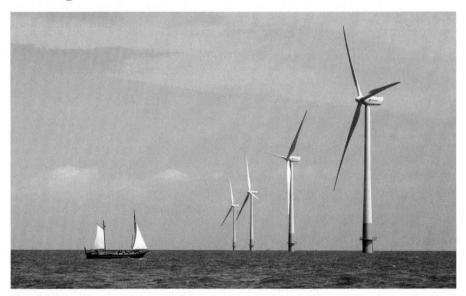

Cape Cod, Massachusetts, is a peninsula that extends from the southern portion of Massachusetts into the Atlantic Ocean. Famous for its beautiful shoreline, Cape Cod is a popular destination for summer vacationers. The Cape Wind project is a proposed 24-square-mile offshore wind farm that would be built beginning a little less than 5 miles off the Cape's southern coast. Proponents of the plan cite the benefits of clean energy. Strong opposition, however, has been voiced by the Alliance to Protect Nantucket Sound, which claims that the proposed wind farm will not only destroy property values, but also irrevocably damage the Cape's priceless views, threaten the vital tourist industry, dislocate necessary shipping lanes, disrupt fish populations, and pose a hazard to birds. Cape Wind has brought a prolonged battle in Massachusetts courts that no doubt will continue with a series of appeals.

Write about it

1. If you were the spokesperson for Cape Wind, what reasons would you give to the Massachusetts courts to persuade them to begin construction of the wind farm?

2. If you were the spokesperson for the Alliance to Protect Nantucket Sound, what reasons would you give to the Massachusetts courts to persuade them to block the construction of the wind farm?

3. If you were a judge on the Massachusetts Bench, what reasons might you expect to hear from these two groups? Draft a proposal that would win your vote.

Adam Gopnik

The Simple Truth About Gun Control*

Adam Gopnik (born 1956) is most commonly associated with the *New Yorker* magazine, where he has written art criticism and social commentary since 1986. His most recent book, *Through the Children's Gate: A Home in New York*, (2006), reflects on his experiences living in New York with his spouse and two children. The following essay appeared in the *New Yorker* in December, 2012, shortly after twenty children and six adult staff were massacred at Sandy Hook Elementary School in Newtown, Connecticut.

Note how Gopnik begins with an extended analogy, one that creates a need for action.

We live, let's imagine, in a city where children are dying of a ravaging infection. The good news is that its cause is well understood and its cure, an antibiotic, easily at hand. The bad news is that our city council has been taken over by a faith-healing cult that will go to any lengths to keep the antibiotic from the kids. Some citizens would doubtless point out meekly that faith healing has an ancient history in our city, and we must regard the faith healers with respect—to do otherwise would show a lack of respect for their freedom to faith-heal. (The faith healers' proposition is that if there were a faith healer praying in every kindergarten the kids wouldn't get infections in the first place.) A few Tartuffes would see the children writhe and heave in pain and then wring their hands in self-congratulatory piety and wonder why a good God would send such a terrible affliction on the innocent—surely he must have a plan! Most of us—every sane person in the city, actually—would tell the faith healers to go to hell, put off worrying about the Problem of Evil till Friday or Saturday or Sunday, and do everything we could to get as much penicillin to the kids as quickly we could.

References to Engel and Lewis establish that this proposal for stiffer gun laws was offered just after the Sandy Hook massacre in a Connecticut elementary school.

2   We do live in such a city. Five thousand seven hundred and forty children and teens died from gunfire in the United States, just in 2008 and 2009. Twenty more, including Olivia Engel, who was seven, and Jesse Lewis, who was six, were killed just last week. Some reports say their bodies weren't shown to their grief-stricken parents to identify them; just their pictures. The overwhelming majority of those children would have been saved with effective gun control. We know that this is so, because, in societies that *have* effective gun control, children rarely, rarely, rarely die of gunshots. Let's worry tomorrow about the problem of Evil. Let's worry more about making sure that when the Problem of Evil appears in a first-grade classroom, it is armed with a penknife.

Gopnik's
proposal is
supported by
consequences
in the form of
reduced gun
violence. He
states that "we
know that this is
so" because of
the experience
of other nations,
but will everyone
accept that as
evidence for the
United States?

3   There are complex, hand-wringing-worthy problems in our social life: deficits and debts and climate change. Gun violence, and the work of eliminating gun massacres in schools and movie houses and the like, is not one of them. Gun control works on gun violence as surely as antibiotics do on bacterial infections. In Scotland, after Dunblane, in Australia, after Tasmania, in Canada, after the Montreal massacre—in each case the necessary laws were passed to make gun-owning hard, and in each case . . . well, you will note the absence of massacre-condolence speeches made by the Prime Ministers of Canada and Australia, in comparison with our own President.

4   The laws differ from place to place. In some jurisdictions, like Scotland, it is essentially impossible to own a gun; in others, like Canada, it is merely very, very difficult. The precise legislation that makes gun-owning hard in a certain sense doesn't really matter—and that should give hope to all of those who feel that, with several hundred million guns in private hands, there's no point in trying to make America a gun-sane country.

More argument
by consequence
and by analogy:
If we could take
effective action
to curb crime in
New York City,
why should
we not be able
to take steps
to curb gun
violence?

5   The central insight of the modern study of criminal violence is that all crime—even the horrific violent crimes of assault and rape—is at some level opportunistic. Building a low annoying wall against them is almost as effective as building a high impenetrable one. This is the key concept of Franklin Zimring's amazing work on crime in New York; everyone said that, given the social pressures, the slum pathologies, the profits to be made in drug dealing, the ascending levels of despair, that there was no hope of changing the ever-growing cycle of violence. The right wing insisted that this generation of predators would give way to a new generation of super-predators.

6   What the New York Police Department found out, through empirical experience and better organization, was that making crime even a little bit harder made it much, much rarer. This is undeniably true of property crime, and common sense and evidence tells you that this is also true even of crimes committed by crazy people (to use the plain English the subject deserves). Those who hold themselves together enough to be capable of killing anyone are subject to the same rules of opportunity as sane people. Even madmen need opportunities to display their madness, and behave in different ways depending on the possibilities at hand. Demand an extraordinary degree of determination and organization from someone intent on committing a violent act, and the odds that the violent act will take place are radically reduced, in many cases to zero.

Gopnik uses
an authority
to support his
case.

7   Look at Harvard social scientist David Hemenway's work on gun violence: the phrase "more guns = more homicide" tolls through it like a grim bell. The more guns there are in a country, the more gun murders and massacres of children there will be.

Even within this gun-crazy country, states with strong gun laws have fewer gun murders (and suicides and accidental killings) than states without them. (Hemenway is also the scientist who has shown that the inflated figure of guns used in self-defense every year, running even to a million or two million, is a pure fantasy, even though it's still cited by pro-gun enthusiasts. Those hundreds of thousands intruders shot by gun owners left no records in emergency wards or morgues; indeed, left no evidentiary trace behind. This is because they did not exist.) Hemenway has discovered, as he explained in an interview with *Harvard Magazine*, that what is usually presented as a case of self-defense with guns is, in the real world, almost invariably a story about an escalating quarrel. "How often might you appropriately use a gun in self-defense?" Hemenway asks rhetorically. "Answer: zero to once in a lifetime. How about inappropriately—because you were tired, afraid, or drunk in a confrontational situation? There are lots and lots of chances."

8   So don't listen to those who, seeing twenty dead six- and seven-year-olds in ten minutes, their bodies riddled with bullets designed to rip apart bone and organ, say that this is impossibly hard, or even particularly complex, problem. It's a very easy one. Summoning the political will to make it happen may be hard. But there's no doubt or ambiguity about what needs to be done, nor that, if it is done, it will work. One would have to believe that Americans are somehow uniquely evil or depraved to think that the same forces that work on the rest of the planet won't work here. It's always hard to summon up political will for change, no matter how beneficial the change may obviously be. Summoning the political will to make automobiles safe was difficult; so was summoning the political will to limit and then effectively ban cigarettes from public places. At some point, we will become a gun-safe, and then a gun-sane, and finally a gun-free society. It's closer than you think. (I'm grateful to my *New Yorker* colleague Jeffrey Toobin for showing so well that the idea that the Second Amendment assures individual possession of guns, so far from being deeply rooted in American law, is in truth a new and bizarre reading, one that would have shocked even Warren Burger.)

Gopnik shows consistent awareness of the arguments against his position.

9   Gun control is not a panacea, any more than penicillin was. Some violence will always go on. What gun control is good at is controlling guns. Gun control will eliminate gun massacres in America as surely as antibiotics eliminate bacterial infections. Those who oppose it have made a moral choice: that they would rather have gun massacres of children continue rather than surrender whatever idea of freedom or pleasure they find wrapped up in owning guns or seeing guns owned—just as the faith

More argument by analogy

healers would rather watch the children die than accept the reality of scientific medicine. This is a moral choice; many faith healers make it to this day, and not just in thought experiments. But it is absurd to shake our heads sapiently and say we can't possibly know what would have saved the lives of Olivia and Jesse.

10   On gun violence and how to end it, the facts are all in, the evidence is clear, the truth there for all who care to know it—indeed, a global consensus is in place, which, in disbelief and now in disgust, the planet waits for us to us to join. Those who fight against gun control, actively or passively, with a shrug of helplessness, are dooming more kids to horrible deaths and more parents to unspeakable grief just as surely as are those who fight against pediatric medicine or childhood vaccination. It's really, and inarguably, just as simple as that.

Gopnik's argument is a stereotypical proposal: A problem is dramatized; a solution is proposed; good consequences are demonstrated; opposing viewpoints are addressed.

Sample Student Proposal Argument

Lee 1

Kim Lee

Professor Patel

RHE 306

31 March 2013

Let's Make It a Real Melting Pot with Presidential Hopes for All

The image the United States likes to advertise is one of a country that embraces diversity and creates a land of equal opportunity for all. As the Statue of Liberty cries out, "give me your tired, your poor, your huddled masses yearning to breathe free," American politicians gleefully evoke such images to frame the United States as a bastion for all things good, fair, and equal. As a proud American, however, I must nonetheless highlight one of the cracks in this façade of equality. Imagine that an infertile couple decides to adopt an orphaned child from China. The couple follows all of the legal processes deemed necessary by both countries. They fly abroad and bring home their (once parentless) 6-month-old baby boy. They raise and nurture him, and while teaching him to embrace his ethnicity, they also teach him to love Captain Crunch, baseball, and *The Three Stooges*. He grows and eventually attends an ethnically diverse American public school.

One day his fifth-grade teacher tells the class that anyone can grow up to be president. To clarify her point, she turns to the boy, knowing his background, and states, "No, you could not be president, Stu, but you could still be a senator. That's something to aspire to!" How do Stu's parents explain this rule to this American-raised child? This scenario will become increasingly common, yet as the Constitution currently reads, only "natural-born" citizens may run for the offices of president and vice president. Neither these children nor the thousands of hardworking Americans who chose to make America their official homeland may aspire to the highest political position in the land. While the huddled masses may enter, it appears they must retain a second-class citizen ranking.

The issue arose most recently when bloggers, media personalities, and some elected officials alleged that Barack Obama was born in Kenya, not Hawaii, and that his birth certificate is a forgery. The release of a certified copy of Obama's Certificate of Live Birth (the "long form")

Lee sets out the problem with a concrete scenario.

Lee 2

and other evidence including birth announcements in two Hawaii
newspapers in August 1961 answered Donald Trump and other prominent
"birthers" (Shear). Lost in the controversy was this question: Should it
matter where Obama or any other candidate was born? In a land where
all citizens but American Indians are immigrants or descendants of
immigrants, why should being born in the United States be considered an
essential qualification for election as president?

The provision arose from circumstances very different from those
of today. The "natural-born" stipulation regarding the presidency stems
from the selfsame meeting of minds that brought the American people
the Electoral College. During the Constitutional Convention of 1787, the
Congress formulated the regulatory measures associated with the office of
the president. A letter sent from John Jay to George Washington during
this period reads as follows:

> Permit me to hint whether it would not be wise and seasonable
> to provide a strong check to the admission of foreigners into
> the administration of our national government; and to declare
> expressly that the Commander in Chief of the American army
> shall not be given to, nor devolve on, any but a natural-born
> citizen. (Mathews A1)

Shortly thereafter, Article II, Section I, Clause V, of the Constitution
declared that "No Person except a natural born Citizen, or a Citizen of
the United States at the time of the Adoption of this Constitution, shall
be eligible to the Office of President." Jill A. Pryor states in the *Yale Law
Journal* that "some writers have suggested that Jay was responding to
rumors that foreign princes might be asked to assume the presidency"
(881). Many cite disastrous examples of foreign rule in the eighteenth
century as the impetus for the "natural-born" clause. For example, in
1772—only fifteen years prior to the adoption of the statute—Poland
had been divided up by Prussia, Russia, and Austria (Kasindorf). Perhaps
an element of self-preservation and not ethnocentrism led to the
questionable stipulation. Nonetheless, in the twenty-first century this
clause reeks of xenophobia.

Lee gives
the historical
background of
the "natural-
born" restriction.

The Fourteenth Amendment clarified the difference between
"natural-born" and "native-born" citizens by spelling out the citizenship

Lee 3

status of children born to American parents outside of the United States (Ginsberg 929). This clause qualifies individuals such as Senator John McCain—born in Panama—for presidency. This change, however, is not adequate. I propose that the United States abolish the natural-born clause and replace it with a stipulation that allows naturalized citizens to run for president. This amendment would state that a candidate must have been naturalized and must have lived in residence in the United States for a period of at least twenty-five years. The present time is ideal for this change. This amendment could simultaneously honor the spirit of the Constitution, protect and ensure the interests of the United States, promote an international image of inclusiveness, and grant heretofore-withheld rights to thousands of legal and loyal United States citizens.

> Lee states her proposal in this paragraph.

In our push for change, we must make clear the importance of this amendment. It would not provide special rights for would-be terrorists. To the contrary, it would fulfill the longtime promises of the nation. Naturalized citizens have been contributing to the United States for centuries. Many nameless Mexican, Irish, and Asian Americans sweated and toiled to build the American railroads. Americans have welcomed naturalized citizens such as Bob Hope, Albert Pujols, and Peter Jennings into their hearts and living rooms. Individuals such as German-born Henry Kissinger and Czechoslovakian-born Madeleine Albright have held high posts in the American government and have served as respected aides to its presidents. The amendment must make clear that it is not about one person's celebrity. Approximately seven hundred foreign-born Americans have won the Medal of Honor and over sixty thousand proudly serve in the United States military today (Siskind 5). The "natural-born" clause must be removed to provide each of these people—over half a million naturalized in 2003 alone—equal footing with those who were born into citizenship rather than having to work for it (United States).

> Lee gives examples of people who are qualified to become president yet are ineligible.

Since the passing of the Bill of Rights, only seventeen amendments have been ratified. This process takes time and overwhelming congressional and statewide support. To alter the Constitution, a proposed amendment must pass with a two-thirds "super-majority" in both the House of Representatives and the Senate. In addition, the proposal must find favor in two-thirds (38) of state legislatures. In short,

Lee 4

this task will not be easy. In order for this change to occur, a grassroots campaign must work to dispel misinformation regarding naturalized citizens and to force the hands of senators and representatives wishing to retain their congressional seats. We must take this proposal to ethnicity-specific political groups from both sides of the aisle, business organizations, and community activist groups. We must convince representatives that this issue matters. Only through raising voices and casting votes can the people enact change. Only then can every American child see the possibility for limitless achievement and equality. Only then can everyone find the same sense of pride in the possibility for true American diversity in the highest office in the land.

> Lee explains the process of amending the Constitution and ends with a call for action.

Lee 5

Works Cited

Ginsberg, Gordon. "Citizenship: Expatriation: Distinction between Natu-
    ralized and Natural Born Citizens." *Michigan Law Review* 50 (1952):
    926-29. *JSTOR*. Web. 6 Mar. 2013.

Kasindorf, Martin. "Should the Constitution Be Amended for Arnold?"
    USA Today 2 Dec. 2004. *LexisNexis Academic*. Web. 8 Mar. 2013.

Mathews, Joe. "Maybe Anyone Can Be President." *Los Angeles Times* 2
    Feb. 2005: A1. *LexisNexis Academic*. Web. 6 Mar. 2013.

Pryor, Jill A. "The Natural Born Citizen Clause and Presidential Eligibil-
    ity: An Approach for Resolving Two Hundred Years of Uncertainty."
    Yale Law Journal 97.5 (1988): 881-99. Print.

Shear, Michael D. "With Document, Obama Seeks to End 'Birther' Issue."
    New York Times. New York Times, 27 Apr. 2011. Web. 28 Apr. 2013.

Siskind, Lawrence J. "Why Shouldn't Arnold Run?" *Recorder* 10 Dec.
    2004: 5. *LexisNexis Academic*. Web. 10 Mar. 2013.

United States. Dept. of Commerce. Census Bureau. "The Fourth of July
    2005." *Facts for Features*. US Dept. of Commerce, 27 June 2005.
    Web. 17 Mar. 2013.

Designing and Presenting Arguments

PART

4

14 | Designing Multimedia Arguments

QUICK TAKE

In this chapter, you will learn to

1. Identify the advantages and disadvantages of different media for reaching your audience (see below)
2. Analyze how an image or a graphic communicates to an audience (see page 210)
3. Describe the argument made by an image or a graphic (see pages 210–211)
4. List the elements important to designing a print page (see pages 211–212)
5. Create effective multimedia projects involving images, Web site production, audio, and video (see pages 212–213)

Arguments do not communicate with words alone. Even written arguments that do not contain graphics or images have a look and feel that also communicate meaning. Many arguments depend on presenting information visually, in multimedia, or in images, in addition to using written language. Using effective design strategies will make your arguments more engaging and compelling.

Think About Which Media Will Reach Your Audience

Before you graduate from college, it's likely you will find occasions when you want to persuade an audience beyond your instructor, classmates, and friends—possibly for your work, possibly for an organization you belong to, or possibly because an issue concerns you. You may have a clear sense of your message and the good reasons to support that message. But no matter how good your argument, nothing will happen unless you can command the scarcest commodity in our multitasking world—the attention of your audience.

Most college assignments specify the medium, which is typically a printed paper that you submit to the instructor. In the workplace and in life outside college, the choice of medium often isn't immediately evident. For example, if you want to address a neighborhood issue, would a brochure or a Web site be more effective?

Think about your options.

PRINTED TEXT

- Advantages: Low technological requirements to produce; complex, in-depth arguments are possible.
- Disadvantages: Unless published in an established forum like a newspaper, it can be difficult to get people to read the argument.

WEB SITE

- Advantages: Inexpensive to create and allows images, video, audio, and animations to be embedded.
- Disadvantages: How do people find your Web site among the millions of other sites?

BLOG

- Advantages: Inexpensive to create and many sites host blogs.
- Disadvantages: Requires frequent, interesting content to keep readers coming back.

AUDIO PODCAST

- Advantages: Inexpensive to create and can be downloaded from a Web site.
- Disadvantages: Requires some audio editing skills. Like other Web-based media, you have to have a strategy for getting people to listen.

VIDEO

- Advantages: Can be uploaded to sites like *YouTube* and *Vimeo*.
- Disadvantages: Producing quality original video takes time, equipment, and editing skills.

Know When to Use Visual Evidence

Personal computers, digital cameras, scanners, printers, and the Web have made it easy to include images and graphics in writing and to link to audio and video. But these technologies don't tell you if, when, or how images and graphics should be used.

Think about what an image or graphic communicates

- **What are your readers' expectations for the medium you are using?** Most essays don't include images; most Web sites and brochures do.
- **What is the purpose for an image or graphic?** Does it illustrate a concept? Does it highlight an important point? Does it show something that is hard to explain with words alone? If you don't know the purpose, you may not need the image.
- **Where should an image or graphic be placed in your text?** Images should be as close as possible to the relevant point in your text.
- **What will readers focus on when they see the image?** Will they focus on the part that matters? If not, you may need to crop the image.
- **What explanation do readers need in order to understand the image?** Provide informative captions for the images and graphics you use, and refer to the images in your text.

Think About the Argument an Image Makes

Images don't speak for themselves, but if they are referenced in your text and captioned, they can make supporting arguments. Think strategically when you include arguments.

Say, for example, you are making a proposal argument for more students to become involved in feeding homeless people in your city. Students are aware that there are homeless people, but many students are not aware of organizations that deliver food to hungry people. You might want to photograph the volunteers instead of homeless people.

Volunteers work to make sandwiches that will be distributed by a food truck to homeless people.

Think about the argument a chart or graph makes

Charts and graphs are useful for visually representing statistical trends and for making comparisons. For example, the U.S. Department of Education uses a bar chart to show how a college or career school education increases your chances of making more money and having more job opportunities. This bar chart offers a direct comparison of earnings and unemployment rates for each level of education.

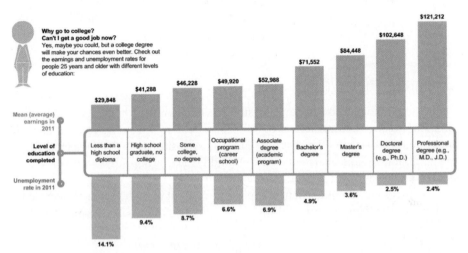

Source: Bureau of Labor Statistics, Current Population Survey, unpublished tables, 2012.

Bar chart comparing mean earnings and unemployment rates for levels of education

Design Arguments for Print

Writing on a computer gives you a range of options for designing a page that is appropriate to your assignment. Thinking about design will lead to a more effective presentation of your argument.

- **Choose the orientation, size of your page, and number of columns.** You can usually use the defaults on your computer for academic essays (remember to select double-spacing for line spacing if the default is single-spaced). For other kinds of texts you may want a horizontal rather than a vertical orientation, a size other than a standard sheet of paper, and two or more columns rather than one.
- **Divide your text into units.** The paragraph is the basic unit of extended writing, but also think about when to use lists. This list is a bulleted list. You can also use a numbered list.
- **Use left-aligned text with a ragged-right margin.** Fully justified text aligns the right margin, which gives a more formal look but can also leave unsightly rivers of extra white space running through the middle of your text. Ragged-right text is easier to read.

- **Be conscious of white space.** White space can make your text more readable and set off more important elements. Headings stand out more with white space surrounding them. Leave room around graphics. Don't crowd words too close to graphics because both the words and the visuals will become hard to read.
- **Be aware of MLA and APA design specifications.** MLA and APA styles have specifications for margins, indentions, reference lists, and other aspects of paper formatting. See the sample paper on pages 277–283 for guidelines on designing a paper using MLA style.

Design Multimedia Arguments

Digital technologies now make it possible to create on your home computer multimedia projects that formerly required entire production staffs. You can publish multimedia projects on the Internet (either as Web sites or as downloadable files), as stand-alone media distributed on CDs and DVDs, or in print with posters, brochures, and essays with images.

College viewers and listeners expect the content of multimedia projects to be high in quality. They expect

- your project to be well organized and free of errors,
- your claims to be supported with evidence,
- your analysis to be insightful,
- your sources to be documented, and
- your work to be clearly distinguished from the work of others.

Creating multimedia projects

If you decide to create a multimedia project, find out what resources are available for students on your campus. Many colleges and universities have digital media labs, which offer workshops and can provide video and audio studios, technical assistance, equipment, and software. Look for links to digital media services on your college's Web site.

Oral presentation with visuals (see Chapter 15)
Essay with images

- **Example project**: Evaluation argument concerning the poor condition of parks in your city
- Plan: Visit several parks, make notes, and take photographs.
- Produce: Write the project. Edit your images with an image editor and insert them in your project with captions.
- Edit: Revise with the comments of classmates and your instructor.

Web site production

- **Example project**: Web site making a definition argument that censorship of the Internet is a violation of the right to free speech
- Plan: Collect all the materials you will need for your site including text; digital images; graphics; and audio, video, and animation files.
- Produce: If you don't have a Web editor on your computer, find a campus lab that has Dreamweaver or similar software. Upload your site to a server. Many colleges offer server space to host student Web sites.
- Edit: Test your site to ensure that all links are working and all images and other files are showing up correctly. Edit with a Web editor.

Audio production

- **Example project**: Oral history of neighborhood residents making a causal argument about why a neighborhood declined after a freeway was built through the middle of it
- Plan: Arrange and record interviews and write a script.
- Produce: Reserve a campus audio production lab or record on your computer. Create an audio file by combining the interviews with your narration.
- Edit: Edit with an audio editor. Export the video into a format such as WAV or MP3 that you can put on the Web or share as a downloadable file.

Video production

- **Example project**: Proposal to create bike lanes on a busy street near your campus
- Plan: Identify locations, get permission to film if necessary, and write a script.
- Produce: Shoot video of the street with cars and bikes competing. Interview cyclists, drivers, and local business owners about their sense of urgency of the problem and the effects of creating bike lanes.
- Edit: Edit with a video editor. Export the video into a format such as QuickTime that you can put on the Web or share as a downloadable file.

15 | Presenting Arguments

QUICK TAKE

In this chapter, you will learn to

1. Plan an effective presentation—state a goal, identify your audience, organize your material, and assemble evidence (see below)
2. Design visuals for a presentation and use audio and video clips strategically (see pages 216–218)
3. Deliver an effective presentation (see pages 218–219)

Plan a Presentation

If you are assigned to give a presentation, look carefully at the assignment for guidance on finding a topic. Finding a topic for a presentation is similar to finding a topic for a written assignment (see Chapter 3). If your assignment requires research, you will need to document the sources of information just as you do for a research paper (see Chapters 16–19).

Start with your goal in mind

What is the real purpose of your presentation? Are you informing, persuading, or motivating? Take the elevator test. Imagine you are in an elevator with the key people who can approve or reject your ideas. Their schedule is very tight. You have only thirty seconds to convince them. Can you make your case?

This scenario is not far-fetched. One executive demanded that every new idea had to be written in one sentence on the back of a business card. What's your sentence?

It's all about your audience

Who is your audience? In college your audience is often your instructor and fellow students—an audience you know well. Many times you will not have this advantage.

Take a few minutes to answer these questions.

- Will my audience be interested in the topic?
- Why does it matter to them?
- What are they likely to know and believe about the topic?
- What are they likely not to know?
- Where are they likely to disagree?
- What do I want them to do?
- How much time do I have?
- If they remember only one thing, what should it be?

Get organized

Start with pen and paper before you begin creating slides. Post-it notes are another useful planning tool.

- **Make a list of key points.** Think about the best order for your major points.
- **Plan your introduction.** Your success depends on your introduction. You must gain the attention of your audience, introduce your topic, indicate why it's important, and give a sense of where you are headed. That's a tall order, but if you don't engage your audience in the first two minutes, you will lose them.
- **Plan your conclusion.** You want to end on a strong note. Stopping abruptly or rambling on only to tail off leaves your audience with a bad impression. Give your audience something to take away, a compelling example or an idea that captures the gist of your presentation.

Build content

Content alone does not make a presentation successful, but you cannot succeed without solid content. Support your major points with relevant evidence.

- **Facts.** Speakers who know their facts build credibility.
- **Statistics.** Effective use of statistics can tell the audience that you have done your homework. Statistics can also indicate that a particular example is representative.
- **Statements by authorities.** Quotations from credible experts can support key points.
- **Narratives.** Narratives are brief stories that illustrate key points. Narratives can hold the attention of the audience—but keep them short or they will become a distraction.

Design Visuals for a Presentation

Less is more with slides. One text-filled slide after another is mind-numbingly dull. Presentations using slides don't have to be this bad.

Keep it simple

Imagine you are making an argument that fewer animals would be euthanized at animal shelters if more people in your city knew that they could save a pet's life by adopting it. You could fill your slides with statistics alone. Or you tell your audience the facts while showing them slides that give emotional impact to your numbers.

Simple design rules! Keep in mind these principles.

- One point per slide
- Very few fonts
- Quality photos, not clipart
- Less text, more images
- Easy on the special effects

Compare the following examples.

Pet Overpopulation in the United States

- Estimated number of animals that enter shelters each year: 6–8 million

- Estimated number of animals euthanized at shelters each year: 3–4 million

- Estimated number of animals adopted at shelters each year: 3–4 million

Source: "HSUS Pet Overpopulation Estimates." *Humane Society of the U.S.* Humane Society of the U.S., 9 Nov. 2009. Web. 18 Oct. 2013.

Pet Overpopulation in the United States

- Estimated number of animals entering shelters each year: 6–8 million
- Estimated number of animals euthanized at shelters each year: 3–4 million
- Estimated number of animals adopted at shelters: 3–4 million

Source: "HSUS Pet Overpopulation Estimates." *Humane Society of the U.S.* Humane Society of the U.S., 9 Nov. 2009. Web. 18 Oct. 2013.

Save a pet

Which slide makes the point most effectively?

But what if you have a lot of data to show? Make a handout that the audience can study later. They can make notes on your handout, which gives them a personal investment. Keep your slides simple and emphasize the main points in the presentation.

Use audio and video clips strategically

Short audio and video clips can offer concrete examples and add some variety to your presentation. An audience appreciates hearing and even seeing the people you interview. PowerPoint, Prezi, Keynote, and other presentation software make it simple to embed the files within a presentation. Be careful, however, in using built-in sound effects such as canned applause. Most sound effects are annoying and make you come off as inexperienced.

Deliver an Effective Presentation

If you are not passionate about your subject, you will never get your audience committed to your subject, no matter how handsome your slides. Believe in what you say; enthusiasm is contagious.

It's all about you

The audience didn't come to see the back of your head in front of slides. Move away from the podium and connect with them. Make strong eye contact with individuals. You will make everyone feel as if you were having a conversation instead of giving a speech.

Prepare in advance

Practice your presentation, even if you have to speak to an empty chair. Check out the room and equipment in advance. If you are using your laptop with a projector installed in the room, make sure it connects. If the room has a computer connected to the projector, bring your presentation on a flash drive and download it to the computer.

Be professional

Pay attention to the little things.

- **Proofread carefully.** A glaring spelling error can destroy your credibility.
- **Be consistent.** If you randomly capitalize words or insert punctuation, your audience will be distracted.

■ **Pay attention to the timing of your slides.** Stay in sync with your slides. Don't leave a slide up when you are talking about something else.

■ **Use the "B" key.** If you get sidetracked, press the "B" key, which makes the screen go blank so the audience can focus on you. When you are ready to resume, press the "B" key again and the slide reappears.

■ **Involve your audience.** Invite response during your presentation where appropriate, and leave time for questions at the end.

■ **Add a bit of humor.** Humor can be tricky, especially if you don't know your audience well. But if you can get people to laugh, they will be on your side.

■ **Slow down.** When you are nervous, you tend to go too fast. Stop and breathe. Let your audience take in what's on your slides.

■ **Finish on time or earlier.** Your audience will be grateful.

■ **Be courteous and gracious.** Remember to thank anyone who helped you and the audience for their comments. Eventually you will run into someone who challenges you, sometimes politely, sometimes not. If you remain cool and in control, the audience will remember your behavior long after the words are forgotten.

Convert a Written Text into a Presentation

The temptation when converting a written text into a presentation is to dump sentences and paragraphs onto the slides. Indeed, it's simple enough to cut and paste big chunks of text, but you risk losing your audience.

Make a list of the main points in your written text, and then decide which ones you need to show on slides and which you can tell the audience. Your voice supplies most of the information; your slides help your audience to remember and organize your presentation.

People learn better when your oral presentation is accompanied by engaging images and graphics. Slides can also add emotional involvement.

Unwanted dogs

Carlos

a playful mixed-breed pup who was recently adopted

Arrange your slides so they tell a story. For example, if you are arguing that fewer dogs would be euthanized if your city were more active in promoting adoption, you can show slides that give statistics, or you can report statistics in your presentation while letting your audience identify with individual dogs.

Researching Arguments

PART

5

16 | Planning Research

QUICK TAKE

In this chapter, you will learn to
1. Analyze an assignment or research task (see below)
2. Find a subject and develop a research question (see pages 223–224)
3. Gather information through field research, including interviews, surveys, and observations (see pages 224–227)
4. Draft a working thesis to guide you through further research and the development of your argument (see page 227)

Analyze the Research Task

Research is a creative process, which is another way of saying it is a messy process. However, your results will improve if you keep the big picture in mind while you are immersed in research. When you get a research assignment, look at it closely.

Look for key words
Often the assignment will tell you what is expected.

- An assignment that asks you, for example, how the usual *definition* of intellectual property applies to *YouTube* invites you to write a definition argument (see Chapter 8).
- An *analysis of causes* requires you to write a causal argument (see Chapter 9).
- An *evaluation* requires you to make critical judgments based on criteria (see Chapter 10).
- A *proposal* requires you to assemble evidence in support of a solution to a problem or a call for the audience to do something (see Chapter 13).

Identify your potential readers
- How familiar are your readers with your subject?
- What background information will you need to supply?

- If your subject is controversial, what opinions or beliefs are your readers likely to hold?
- If some readers are likely to disagree with you, how can you convince them?

Assess the project's length, scope, and requirements

- What kind of research are you being asked to do?
- What is the length of the project?
- What kinds and number of sources or field research are required?
- Which documentation style is required such as MLA (see Chapter 20) or APA (see Chapter 21)?

Set a schedule

- Note the due dates on the assignment for drafts and final versions.
- Set dates for yourself on finding and evaluating sources, drafting your thesis, creating a working bibliography, and writing a first draft.
- Give yourself enough time to do a thorough job.

Find a Subject

One good way to begin is by browsing, which may also show you the breadth of possibilities in a topic and lead you to new topics (see Chapter 3).

You might begin browsing by doing one or more of the following.

- **Visit "Research by Subject" on your library's Web site.** Clicking on a subject such as "African and African American Studies" will take you to a list of online resources.
- **Look for topics in your courses.** Browse your course notes and readings. Are there topics you might explore in greater depth?
- **Browse a Web subject directory.** Web subject directories, including *Yahoo Directory*, are useful when you want to narrow a topic or learn what subcategories a topic might contain. In addition to the Web subject directories, your library's Web site may have a link to the *Opposing Viewpoints* database.
- **Look for topics as you read.** When you read actively, you ask questions and respond to ideas in the text. Review what you wrote in the margins or the notes you have made about something you read that interested you. You may find a potential topic.

Ask a Research Question

Often you'll be surprised by the amount of information your initial browsing uncovers. Your next task will be to identify a question for your research project within that mass of information. This **researchable question** will be the focus of the remainder of your research and ultimately of your research project or paper. Browsing on the subject of organic foods, for example, might lead you to one of the following researchable questions.

- How do farmers benefit from growing organic produce?
- Why are organic products more expensive than nonorganic products?
- Are Americans being persuaded to buy more organic products?

Once you have formulated a research question, you should begin thinking about what kind of research you will need to do to address the question.

Gather Information About the Subject

Most researchers rely partly or exclusively on the work of others as sources of information. Research based on the work of others is called **secondary research**. In the past this information was contained almost exclusively in collections of print materials housed in libraries, but today enormous amounts of information are available through library databases and on the Web (see Chapter 17).

Much research done at a university creates new data through **primary research**—experiments, examination of historical documents—and **field research**, including data-gathering surveys, interviews, and detailed observations.

Conducting field research

Sometimes you may be researching a question that requires you to gather firsthand information with field research. For example, if you are researching a campus issue such as the impact of a new fee on students' budgets, you may need to conduct interviews, make observations, and give a survey.

Interviews

College campuses are a rich source of experts in many areas, including people on the faculty and in the surrounding community. Interviewing experts on your research subject can help build your knowledge base. You can use interviews to discover what the people most affected by a particular issue are thinking, such as why students object to some fees and not others.

Arrange interviews

Before you contact anyone, think carefully about your goals. Knowing what you want to find out will help you determine whom you need to interview and what questions you need to ask. Use these guidelines to prepare for an interview.

- Decide what you want or need to know and who best can provide that information for you.
- Schedule each interview in advance, and let the person know why you are conducting the interview. Estimate how long your interview will take, and tell your subject how much time you will need.
- Choose a location that is convenient for your subject but not too chaotic or loud. An office or study room is better than a noisy cafeteria.
- Plan in advance. Write down a few questions and have a few more in mind. Background reading helps avoid unnecessary questions.
- If you want to make an audio recording, ask for permission in advance.

Conduct interviews

- Come prepared with your questions and a tablet, laptop, or paper notebook.
- Listen carefully so you can follow up on key points. Make notes when important questions are raised or answered, but don't attempt to transcribe every word the person is saying.
- When you are finished, thank your subject, and ask his or her permission to get in touch again if you have additional questions.

Surveys

Extensive surveys that can be projected to large populations, like the ones used in political polls, require the effort of many people. Small surveys, however, often can provide insight on local issues, such as what percentage of students might be affected if library hours were reduced.

Plan surveys

What information do you need for your research question? Decide what exactly you want to know, and design a survey that will provide that information. Probably you will want both close-ended questions (multiple choice, yes or no, rating scale) and open-ended questions that allow detailed responses.

- Write a few specific, unambiguous questions. People will fill out your survey quickly. If the questions are confusing, the results will be meaningless.

- Include one or two open-ended questions, such as "What do you like about X?" or "What don't you like about X?" These can be difficult to interpret, but they turn up information you had not anticipated.
- Test the questions on a few people before you conduct the survey.
- Think about how you will interpret your survey. Multiple-choice formats make data easy to tabulate, but often they miss key information. Open-ended questions will require you to figure out a way to sort responses into categories.

Administer surveys

- Decide on whom you need to survey and how many respondents your survey will require. For example, if you want to claim that the results of your survey represent the views of residents of your dormitory, your method of selecting respondents should give all residents an equal chance to be selected. Don't select only your friends.
- Decide how you will contact participants in your survey. If you are conducting your survey in person on private property, you will need permission from the property owner.
- If you e-mail your survey, include a statement about what the survey is for.

Observations

Observing can be a valuable source of data. For example, if you are researching why a particular office on your campus does not operate efficiently, observe what happens when students enter and how the staff responds to their presence.

Make observations

- Choose a place where you can observe with the least intrusion. The less people wonder about what you are doing, the better.
- Carry a tablet, laptop, or paper notebook and write extensive field notes. Record as much information as you can, and worry about analyzing it later.
- Record the date, exactly where you were, exactly when you arrived and left, and important details like the number of people present.

Analyze observations

You must interpret your observations so they make sense in the context of your argument. Ask yourself the following questions.

- What patterns of behavior did you observe?
- How was the situation you observed unique? How might it be similar to other locations?

- What constituted "normal" activity during the time when you were observing? Did anything out of the ordinary happen?
- Why were the people there? What can you determine about the purposes of the activities you observed?

Draft a Working Thesis

Once you have done some preliminary research into your question, you can begin to craft a working thesis. Let's take one topic as an example—the increasing popularity of organic products, including meat, dairy products, and produce. If you research this topic, you will discover that because of this trend, large corporations such as Walmart are beginning to offer organic products in their stores. However, the enormous demand for organic products is actually endangering smaller organic farmers and producers. As you research the question of why small farmers and producers in the United States are endangered and what small farmers and producers in other countries have done to protect themselves, a working thesis begins to emerge.

Write down your subject, research question, and working thesis, and refer to them frequently. You may need to revise your working thesis several times until the wording is precise. As you research, ask yourself, does this information tend to support my thesis? Information that does not support your thesis is still important! It may lead you to adjust your thesis or even to abandon it altogether. You may need to find another source or reason that shows your thesis is still valid.

Example

SUBJECT: Increased demand for organic products endangering smaller farmers and producers.

RESEARCH QUESTION: How can successful smaller organic farmers and producers protect themselves from becoming extinct?

WORKING THESIS: In order to meet the increasing demand for organic products that has been created by larger corporations such as Walmart, smaller organic farmers and producers should form regional co-ops. These co-ops will work together to supply regional chains, much as co-ops of small farmers and dairies in Europe work together, thereby cutting transportation and labor costs and ensuring their survival in a much-expanded market.

17 | Finding Sources

Develop Strategies for Finding Sources

The Internet makes available vast quantities of searchable facts and data. Nevertheless, libraries still contain many resources not available on the Web. Even more important, libraries have professional research librarians who can help you locate sources quickly.

Determine where to start looking

Searches using *Google* or *Yahoo!* turn up thousands of items, many of which are often not useful for research. Considering where to start is the first step.

Scholarly books and articles in scholarly journals often are the highest-quality sources, but the lag in publication time makes them less useful for very current topics. Newspapers cover current issues, but often not in the depth of books and scholarly journals. Government Web sites and publications are often the best for finding statistics and are also valuable for researching science and medicine.

Learn the art of effective keyword searches

Keyword searches take you to the sources you need. Start with your working thesis and generate a list of possible keywords for researching your thesis.

First, think of keywords that make your search more specific. For example, a search for sources related to Internet privacy issues might focus more specifically on privacy *and*

Internet

cookies

data retention

social media

photographs

You should also think about more general ways to describe what you are doing. What synonyms can you think of for your existing terms? Other people may have discussed the topic using those terms instead. Instead of relying on "privacy," you can also try keywords like

identity theft

data protection

electronic records

You can even search using terms that refer to related people, events, or movements that you are familiar with.

Facebook

Google

phishing

Many databases have a thesaurus that can help you find more keywords.

Find Sources in Databases

Sources found through library **databases** have already been filtered for you by professional librarians. They will include some common sources like popular magazines and newspapers, but the greatest value of database sources are the many journals, abstracts, studies, e-books, and other writing produced by specialists whose work has been scrutinized and commented on by other experts. When you read a source from a library database, chances are you are hearing an informed voice in an important debate.

Locate databases

You can find databases on your library's Web site. Sometimes you will find a list of databases. Sometimes you select a subject, and then you are directed to databases. Sometimes you select the name of a database vendor such as *EBSCOhost* or *ProQuest*. The vendor is the company that provides databases to the library.

Use databases

Your library has a list of databases and indexes by subject. If you can't find this list on your library's Web site, ask a **reference librarian** for help. Follow these steps to find articles.

1. Select a database appropriate to your subject or a comprehensive database like *Academic Search Complete, Academic Search Premier,* or *LexisNexis Academic.*
2. Search the database using your list of keywords.
3. Once you have chosen an article, print or e-mail to yourself the complete citation to the article. Look for the e-mail link after you click on the item you want.
4. Print or e-mail to yourself the full text if it is available. The full text is better than cutting and pasting because you might lose track of which words are yours, which could lead to unintended plagiarism.
5. If the full text is not available, check the online library catalog to see if your library has the journal.

Your library will probably have printed handouts or online information that tells you which database to use for a particular subject. Ask a librarian who works at the reference or information desk to help you.

If you wish to get only full-text articles, you can filter your search by checking that option. Full-text documents give you the same text you would find in print. Sometimes the images are not reproduced in the HTML versions, but the PDF versions show the actual printed copy. Get the PDF version if it is available. Articles in HTML format usually do not contain the page numbers.

Common Databases

Academic OneFile	Indexes periodicals from the arts, humanities, sciences, social sciences, and general news, with full-text articles and images. (Formerly *Expanded Academic ASAP)*
Academic Search Premier and Complete	Provides full-text articles for thousands of scholarly publications, including social sciences, humanities, education, computer sciences, engineering, language and linguistics, literature, medical sciences, and ethnic-studies journals.

(*Continued*)

Common Databases

ArticleFirst	Indexes journals in business, the humanities, medicine, science, and social sciences.
EBSCOhost Research Databases	Gateway to a large collection of EBSCO databases, including *Academic Search Premier* and *Complete, Business Source Premier* and *Complete, ERIC,* and *Medline.*
Factiva	Provides full-text articles on business topics, including articles from the *Wall Street Journal.*
Google Books	Allows you to search within books and gives you snippets surrounding search terms for copyrighted books. Many books out of copyright have the full text. Available for everyone.
Google Scholar	Searches scholarly literature according to criteria of relevance. Available for everyone.
General OneFile	Contains millions of full-text articles about a wide range of academic and general-interest topics.
LexisNexis Academic	Provides full text of a wide range of newspapers, magazines, government and legal documents, and company profiles from around the world.
Opposing Viewpoints Resource Center	Provides full-text articles representing differing points of view on current issues.
ProQuest Databases	Like *EBSCOhost, ProQuest* is a gateway to a large collection of databases with over 100 billion pages, including the best archives of doctoral dissertations and historical newspapers.

Find Sources on the Web

Because anyone can publish on the Web, there is no overall quality control and there is no system of organization—two strengths we take for granted in libraries. Nevertheless, the Web offers you some resources for current topics that would be difficult or impossible to find in a library. The key to success is knowing where you are most likely to find current and accurate information about the particular question you are researching and knowing how to access that information.

Use search engines wisely

Search engines designed for the Web work in ways similar to library databases and your library's online catalog but with one major difference. Databases typically do some screening of the items they list, but search engines potentially take you to everything on the Web—millions of pages in all. Consequently, you have to work harder to limit searches on the Web or you can be deluged with tens of thousands of items.

Kinds of search engines

A search engine is a set of programs that sort through millions of items at incredible speed. There are four basic kinds of search engines.

1. **Keyword search engines** (e.g., *Bing, Google, Yahoo!*). Keyword search engines give different results because they assign different weights to the information they find.
2. **Meta-search engines** (e.g., *Dogpile, MetaCrawler, Surfwax*). Meta-search engines allow you to use several search engines simultaneously. While the concept is sound, metasearch agents are limited because many do not access *Google* or *Yahoo!*
3. **Web directories** (e.g., Britannica.com, *Yahoo! Directory*). Web directories classify Web sites into categories and are the closest equivalent to the cataloging system used by libraries. On most directories professional editors decide how to index a particular Web site. Web directories also allow keyword searches.
4. **Specialized search engines** are designed for specific purposes:

   - regional search engines (e.g., *Baidu* for China)
   - medical search engines (e.g., *WebMD*)
   - legal search engines (e.g., *Lexis*)
   - job search engines (e.g., Monster.com)
   - property search engines (e.g., *Zillow*)

Advanced searches

Search engines often produce too many hits and are therefore not always useful. If you look only at the first few items, you may miss what is most valuable. The alternative is to refine your search. Most search engines offer you the option of an advanced search, which gives you the opportunity to limit numbers.

Google searches can be focused by using the "Search tools" option. You can specify the time range from the past hour to the past year to a custom date range. You can also specify that *Google* finds the exact phrase you type in with the Verbatim option under "All results." Another useful way of limiting searches is to specify the domain, e.g., **site:.gov**.

The "Search tools" option on *Google* allows you to specify a date range.

The **OR** operator is useful if you don't know exactly which term will get the results you want, especially if you are searching within a specific site. For example, you could try this search: "face-to-face OR f2f site:webworkerdaily.com."

You can also exclude terms by putting a minus sign before the term. If you want to search for social network privacy, but not *Facebook*, try "social network privacy–Facebook."

Find online government sources

The federal government has made many of its publications available on the Web. Also, many state governments now publish important documents on the Web. Often the most current and most reliable statistics are government statistics. Among the more important government resources are the following.

- **Bureau of Labor Statistics** (www.bls.gov/). Source for official U.S. government statistics on employment, wages, and consumer prices
- **Census Bureau** (www.census.gov/). Contains a wealth of links to sites for population, social, economic, and political statistics, including the *Statistical Abstract of the United States* (www.census.gov/compendia/statab/)
- **Centers for Disease Control** (www.cdc.gov/). Authoritative and trustworthy source for health statistics
- **CIA World Factbook** (www.cia.gov/library/publications/the-world-factbook/). Resource for geographic, economic, demographic, and political information on the nations of the world
- **Library of Congress** (www.loc.gov/). Access to many of the resources of the largest library in the world
- **NASA** (www.nasa.gov/). A rich site with much information and images concerning space exploration and scientific discovery
- **National Institutes of Health** (www.nih.gov/). Extensive health information including *MedlinePlus* searches
- **Thomas** (thomas.loc.gov/). The major source of legislative information, including bills, committee reports, and voting records of individual members of Congress
- **USA.gov** (www.usa.gov/). The place to start when you are not sure where to look for government information

Find online reference sources

Your library's Web site has a link to reference sites, either on the main page or under another heading like "research tools."

Reference sites are usually organized by subject, and you can find resources under the subject heading.

- **Business information** (links to business databases and sites like *Hoover's* that profiles companies)
- **Dictionaries** (including the *Oxford English Dictionary* and various subject dictionaries and language dictionaries)
- **Education** (including *The College Blue Book* and others)
- **Encyclopedias** (including *Britannica* and others)
- **Government information** (links to federal, state, and local Web sites)
- **Reference books** (commonly used books like atlases, almanacs, biographies, handbooks, and histories)
- **Statistics and demographics** (links to federal, state, and local government sites; *FedStats* [www.fedstats.gov/] is a good place to start)

Search interactive media

The Internet allows you to access other people's opinions on thousands of topics. Millions of people post messages on discussion lists and groups, *Facebook* groups, blogs, RSS feeds, *Twitter*, and so on. Much of what you read on interactive media sites is undocumented and highly opinionated, but you can still gather important information about people's attitudes and get tips about other sources, which you can verify later.

Several search engines have been developed for interactive media. *Facebook* and *Twitter* also have search engines for their sites.

Discussion list search engines

- **Big Boards** (www.big-boards.com). Tracks over two thousand of the most active discussion forums
- **Google Groups** (groups.google.com). Archives discussion forums dating back to 1981
- **Yahoo! Groups** (groups.yahoo.com). A directory of groups by subject

Blog search engines

- **Bloglines** (www.bloglines.com). Web-based aggregator that delivers RSS feeds
- **Google Blog Search** (blogsearch.google.com). Searches blogs in several languages besides English
- **IceRocket** (blogs.icerocket.com). Searches blogs, *MySpace*, and *Twitter*
- **Technorati** (www.technorati.com). Searches blogs and other user-generated content

Know the limitations of *Wikipedia*

Wikipedia is a valuable resource for current information and for popular culture topics that are not covered in traditional encyclopedias. You can find out, for example, that SpongeBob SquarePants's original name was "SpongeBoy," but the name had already been copyrighted.

Nevertheless, many instructors and the scholarly community in general do not consider *Wikipedia* a reliable source of information for a research paper. The fundamental problem with *Wikipedia* is stability, not whether the information is correct or incorrect. *Wikipedia* and other wikis constantly change. The underlying idea of documenting sources is that readers can consult the same sources that you consulted. Consult other sources to confirm what you find on *Wikipedia* and cite those sources. Often the *Wikipedia* entry includes a list of references that you can use as a starting point for your own research.

Find Multimedia Sources

Massive collections of images; audio files including music, speeches, and podcasts; videos; maps, charts, and graphs; and other resources are now available on the Web.

Find images

The major search engines for images include the following.

- **Bing Images** (www.bing.com/images/)
- **Google Image Search** (images.google.com/)
- **Picsearch** (www.picsearch.com/)
- **Yahoo! Image Search** (images.search.yahoo.com)

Libraries and museums also offer large collections of images that may help you in your research. For example, the *American Memory* collection in the Library of Congress offers an important visual record of the history of the United States (memory.loc.gov/ammem/).

Find videos

- **Bing Videos** (www.bing.com/videos/)
- **blinkx** (www.blinkx.com/)
- **Google Videos** (video.google.com/)
- **Vimeo** (vimeo.com)
- **Yahoo! Video Search** (video.search.yahoo.com)
- **YouTube** (www.youtube.com)

Find podcasts

- **iTunes Podcast Resources** (www.apple.com/itunes/podcasts/)
- **PodcastDirectory.com** (www.podcastdirectory.com/)

Find charts, graphs, and maps

You can find statistical data represented in charts and graphs on many government Web sites.

- **Statistical Abstract of the United States** (www.census.gov/compendia/statab/)
- **Google Earth** (earth.google.com/)

- **National Geographic Map Machine**
  (mapmachine.nationalgeographic.com/)
- **Perry Casteñada Map Collection, University of Texas**
  (www.lib.utexas.edu/maps/map_sites/map_sites.html)

Respect copyright

Just because images, videos, and other multimedia files are easy to download from the Web does not mean that everything is available for you to use. Look for the creator's copyright notice and suggested credit line. This notice will tell you if you can reproduce the multimedia file. Include properly formatted citations for each electronic resource you include in your paper.

Find Print Sources

Print sources may seem "old fashioned" if you grew up with the Internet. You might even feel a little bit intimidated by them. But they are the starting point for much of the research done by experts. In college and beyond, they are indispensable. No matter how current the topic you are researching, you will likely find information in print sources that is simply not available online.

Print sources have other advantages as well.

- Books are shelved according to subject, which allows for easy browsing.
- Books often have bibliographies, directing you to other research on the subject.
- You can search for books in multiple ways: author, title, subject, or call letter.
- The majority of print sources have been evaluated by scholars, editors, and publishers, who decided whether they merited publication.

Find books

Nearly all libraries now shelve books according to the Library of Congress Classification System, which uses a combination of letters and numbers to give you the book's unique location in the library. The Library of Congress call number begins with a letter or letters that represent the broad subject area into which the book is classified.

Locating books in your library

The floors of your library where books are shelved are referred to as the stacks. The call number will enable you to find the item in the stacks. You will need to consult the locations guide for your library, which gives the level and section where an item is shelved.

Locating e-books

Use your library's online catalog to find e-books the same way you find printed books. You'll see on the record "e-book" or "electronic resource." Click on the link and you can read the book and often download a few pages or the entire book.

Find journal articles

Like books, **scholarly journals** provide in-depth examinations of subjects. The articles in scholarly journals are written by experts, and they usually contain lists of references that can guide you to other research on a subject.

Popular journals are useful for gaining general information. Articles in popular magazines are usually short with few, if any, source references and are typically written by journalists. Some instructors frown on using popular magazines, but these journals can be valuable for researching current opinion on a particular topic.

Many scholarly journals and popular magazines are available on your library's Web site. Find them the same way you look for books, using your library's online catalog. Databases increasingly contain the full text of articles, allowing you to read and copy the contents onto your computer. If the article you are looking for isn't available online, the paper copy will be shelved with the books in your library.

18 Evaluating and Recording Sources

QUICK TAKE

In this chapter, you will learn to
1. Use the working thesis to decide a source's relevance (see below)
2. Distinguish among sources: anonymous versus edited, popular versus scholarly, and primary versus secondary sources (see pages 240–241)
3. Evaluate library database and print sources (see page 242)
4. Evaluate the quality of Web sources (see pages 243–244)
5. Keep track of sources, including recording all the information you need to cite a source (see pages 245–247)

Determine the Relevance of Sources

Whether you use print or online sources, a successful search will turn up many more items than you can expect to use in your final product. You have to make a series of decisions as you evaluate your material. Use your research question and working thesis to create guidelines for yourself about importance and relevance.

If you ask a research question about contemporary events such as the NCAA's policy on compensating student athletes (see pages 155–161), you will need to find both background information and current information. You will need to know, for example, the most recent statistics on how many scholarship athletes actually graduate because the NCAA's main defense of not paying scholarship athletes is that they get a free education.

Use these guidelines to determine the importance and relevance of your sources to your research question.

- Does your research question require you to consult primary or secondary sources?
- Does a source you have found address your question?
- Does a source support or disagree with your working thesis? (You should not throw out work that challenges your views. Representing opposing views accurately enhances your credibility.)
- Does a source add significant information?

- Is the source current? (For most topics try to find the most up-to-date information.)
- What indications of possible bias do you note in the source?

Determine the Quality of Sources

In the digital era, we don't lack for information, but we do lack filters for finding quality information. Two criteria will help you to make a beginning assessment of quality: individual vs. edited sources and popular vs. scholarly sources.

Distinguish individual and anonymous sources from edited sources

Anyone with a computer and Internet access can put up a Web site. Furthermore, people can put up sites anonymously or under an assumed name. It's no wonder that so many Web sites contain misinformation or are intentionally deceptive.

In general, sources that have been edited and published in scholarly journals, scholarly books, major newspapers, major online and print magazines, and government Web sites are considered of higher quality than what an individual might put on a personal Web site, on a *Facebook* page, in a user review, or in a blog.

Edited sources can have biases, and indeed some are quite open about their perspectives. *National Review* offers a conservative perspective, the *Wall Street Journal* is pro-business, and the *Nation* is a liberal voice. The difference from individual and anonymous sites is that we know the editorial perspectives of these journals, and we expect the editors to check the facts. On self-published Web sites and in self-published books, anything goes.

Distinguish popular sources from scholarly sources

Scholarly books and **scholarly journals** are published by and for experts. Scholarly books and articles published in scholarly journals undergo a **peer review** process in which a group of experts in a field reviews them for their scholarly soundness and academic value. Scholarly books and articles in scholarly journals include

- author's name and academic credentials and
- a list of works cited.

Newspapers, **popular books**, and **popular magazines** vary widely in quality. Newspapers and popular magazines range from highly respected publications such as the *Los Angeles Times, Scientific American,* and the *Atlantic Monthly* to the sensational tabloids at grocery-store checkouts. Popular sources are not peer reviewed and require more work on your part to determine their quality. *EBSCOhost* databases allow you to limit searches to scholarly journals.

Distinguish primary sources from secondary sources

Another key distinction for researchers is primary versus secondary sources. In the humanities and fine arts, **primary sources** are original, creative works and original accounts of events written close to the time they occurred. **Secondary sources** interpret creative works and primary sources of events.

In the sciences, primary sources are the factual results of experiments, observations, and clinical trials, and other factual data. Secondary sources analyze and interpret those results.

Read sources critically

Evaluating sources requires you to read critically, which includes the following.

- Identifying the source, which is not always easy on the Web
- Identifying the author and assessing the author's credentials
- Understanding the content—what the text says
- Recognizing the author's purpose—whether the author is attempting to reflect, inform, or persuade
- Recognizing biases in the choices of words, examples, and structure
- Recognizing what the author does not include or address
- Developing an overall evaluation that takes into account all of the above

Evaluate the quality of visual sources

Evaluating the quality of visual sources involves skills similar to critical reading skills. As in critical reading, you should

- identify and assess the source,
- identify the creator,
- identify the date of creation,
- describe the content,
- assess the purpose, and
- recognize how the purpose influences the image, graphic, or video.

For visuals including charts and graphs, pay attention to the source of any data presented and see that the data are presented fairly.

Evaluate Database and Print Sources

Books are expensive to print and distribute, so book publishers generally protect their investment by providing some level of editorial oversight. Printed and online materials in your library undergo another review by professional librarians who select them for their collections.

This initial screening doesn't free you, however, from the responsibility of evaluating the quality of the sources. Many printed and database sources contain their share of inaccurate, misleading, and biased information. Also, all sources carry the risk of becoming outdated if you are looking for current information.

Checklist for evaluating database and print sources

Over the years librarians have developed a set of criteria for evaluating sources, and you should apply them in your research.

1. **Source.** Who published the book or article? Enter the publisher's name on *Google* or another search engine to learn about the publisher. Scholarly books and articles in scholarly journals are generally more reliable than popular magazines and books, which tend to emphasize what is sensational or entertaining at the expense of accuracy and comprehensiveness.

2. **Author.** Who wrote the book or article? Enter the author's name on *Google* or another search engine to learn more about him or her. What are the author's qualifications? Does the author represent an organization?

3. **Timeliness.** How current is the source? If you are researching a fast-developing subject such as treating ADHD, then currency is very important, but even historical topics are subject to controversy or revision.

4. **Evidence.** Where does the evidence come from—facts, interviews, observations, surveys, or experiments? Is the evidence adequate to support the author's claims?

5. **Biases.** Can you detect particular biases of the author? How do the author's biases affect the interpretation offered?

6. **Advertising.** For print sources, is advertising a prominent part of the journal or newspaper? How might the ads affect the credibility or the biases of the information that gets printed?

Evaluate Web Sources

Researching on the Web has been compared to drinking from a fire hose. The key to success is not only getting the torrent down to the size of a glass, but also making sure the water in the glass is pure enough to drink.

Pay attention to domain names

Domain names can give you clues about the quality of a Web site.

- **.com** Commercial site. The information on a .com site is generally about a product or company. While the information may be accurate, keep in mind that the purpose of the site may be to sell a product or service.
- **.edu** Educational institution. The suffix tells you the site is on a school server, ranging from kindergarten to higher education. If the information is from a department or research center, it is generally credible, but if the site is an individual's, treat it as you would other kinds of self-published information.
- **.gov** Government. If you see this suffix, you're viewing a federal or state government site. Most government sites are considered credible sources.
- **.org** Nonprofit organization. Initially, nonpartisan organizations like the Red Cross used this domain, but increasingly partisan political groups and commercial interests have taken the .org suffix. Evaluate these sites carefully.
- **.mil** Military. This domain suffix is owned by the various branches of the armed forces.
- **.net** Network. Anyone can use this domain. Seek out information about the site's origin.

Be alert for biased Web sites

Nearly every large company and political and advocacy organization has a Web site. We expect these sites to represent the company or the point of view of the organization. Many sites on the Web, however, are not so clearly labeled.

For example, if you do a search for "Sudden Infant Death Syndrome (SIDS)" and "vaccines," you'll find near the top of the list an article titled "Vaccines and Sudden Infant Death Syndrome: Is There a Link?" The article concludes that vaccines cause SIDS. If you look at the home page, you'll find that the site's sponsor, Global Vaccine Institute, opposes all vaccinations of children.

Always look for other objective sources for verification of your information. The U.S. Centers for Disease Control and Prevention publishes fact sheets with the latest information about diseases and their prevention (www.cdc.gov/vaccinesafety/

Concerns/sids_faq.html). The fact sheet on SIDS and vaccines reports that people associate sudden infant death syndrome with vaccinations because babies are given vaccinations when they are between 2 and 4 months old, the same age babies die of SIDS. There is no scientific evidence that vaccines cause SIDS.

Checklist for evaluating Web sources

Web sources present special challenges for evaluation. When you find a Web page by using a search engine, you will often go deep into a complex site without having any sense of the context for that page. To evaluate the credibility of the site, you would need to examine the home page, not just the specific page you get to first. Use the following criteria for evaluating Web sites.

1. **Source.** What organization sponsors the Web site? Look for the site's owner at the top or bottom of the home page or in the Web address. Enter the owner's name on *Google* or another search engine to learn about the organization. If a Web site doesn't indicate ownership, then you have to make judgments about who put it up and why.

2. **Author.** Is the author identified? Look for an "About Us" link if you see no author listed. Enter the author's name on *Google* or another search engine to learn more about the author. Often Web sites give no information about their authors other than an e-mail address, if that. In such cases, it is difficult or impossible to determine the author's qualifications. Be cautious about information on an anonymous site.

3. **Purpose.** Is the Web site trying to sell you something? Many Web sites are infomercials that might contain useful information, but they are no more trustworthy than other forms of advertising. Is the purpose to entertain? to inform? to persuade?

4. **Timeliness.** When was the Web site last updated? Look for a date on the home page. Many Web pages do not list when they were last updated; thus you cannot determine their currency.

5. **Evidence.** Are sources of information listed? Any factual information should be supported by indicating where the information came from. Reliable Web sites that offer information will list their sources.

6. **Biases.** Does the Web site offer a balanced point of view? Many Web sites conceal their attitude with a reasonable tone and seemingly factual evidence such as statistics. Citations and bibliographies do not ensure that a site is reliable. Look carefully at the links and sources cited, and peruse the "About Us" link if one is available.

Keep Track of Sources

As you begin to collect your sources, make sure you get full bibliographic information for everything you might want to use in your project. Your instructor likely will tell you which documentation style you will use. (Two major documentation styles—MLA and APA—are explained in detail in Chapters 20 and 21.)

Locate elements of a citation in database sources

For any sources you find on databases, MLA style requires you to provide the full print information, the name of the database in italics, the medium of publication (Web), and the date you accessed the database. If page numbers are not included, use "n. page." Do not include the URL of the database.

See pages 263–264 for detailed coverage.

Author's name	Shaughnessy, Dan
Title of article	"They've Had Some Chief Concerns"
Publication information	
Name of periodical	*Boston Globe*
Date of publication	12 Oct. 2007
Section and page number	C5
Database information	
Name of database	*LexisNexis Academic*
Medium of publication	Web
Date you accessed the site	19 Apr. 2013

Citation in MLA-style list of works cited

Shaughnessy, Dan. "They've Had Some Chief Concerns." *Boston Globe* 12 Oct. 2007: C5. *LexisNexis Academic*. Web. 19 Apr. 2013.

Many databases include a feature that shows you how to cite the source; some have a built-in citation generator. Double-check the format before you include the citation in your paper to ensure accuracy.

Locate elements of a citation in online sources

As you conduct your online research, make sure you collect the necessary bibliographic information for everything you might want to use as a source. Because of the potential volatility of online sources (they can and do disappear overnight), their citations require extra information. Depending on the citation format you use, you'll arrange this information in different ways.

See page 264 for detailed coverage.

Author's name	Zaiger, Alan Scher
Title of work	"Study: NCAA Graduation Rate Comparisons Flawed"
Title of the overall Web site	*ABC News*
Publication information	
Publisher or sponsor	ABC News
Date of publication	20 Apr. 2010
Medium of publication	Web
Date you accessed the site	1 Nov. 2013

Citation in MLA-style list of works cited

Zaiger, Alan Scher. "Study: NCAA Graduation Rate Comparisons Flawed." *ABC News*. ABC News, 20 Apr. 2010. Web. 1 Nov. 2013.

Locate elements of a citation in print sources

For books you will need, at minimum, the following information, which can typically be found on the front and back of the title page.

See pages 262–263 for detailed coverage.

Author's name	Fleitz, David L.
Title of the book	Louis Sockalexis: The First Cleveland Indian
Publication information	
Place of publication	Jefferson
Name of publisher	McFarland
Date of publication	2002
Medium of publication	Print

Citation in MLA-style list of works cited

Fleitz, David L. *Louis Sockalexis: The First Cleveland Indian*. Jefferson: McFarland, 2002. Print.

19 | Writing the Research Project

QUICK TAKE

In this chapter, you will learn to

1. Assess the thesis for your research project and determine your contribution and main points (see below)
2. Understand what is considered plagiarism in college writing (see pages 249–251)
3. Avoid plagiarism in quoting sources (see pages 252–253)
4. Avoid plagiarism in summarizing and paraphrasing (see pages 254–255)
5. Decide when to quote and when to paraphrase (see page 256)
6. Integrate quotations into your text, including using signal phrases and block quotations (see pages 257–258)

Review Your Goals and Plan Your Organization

If you have chosen a subject you're interested in, asked questions about it, and researched it thoroughly, you have a wealth of ideas and information to communicate to your audience.

Review your assignment and thesis

Before you begin writing a research project, review the assignment to remind yourself of the purpose of your argument, your potential readers, and the requested length of the finished paper.

By now you should have formulated a **working thesis**, which will be the focus of your project. You also should have located, read, evaluated, and taken notes on enough source material to write your project, and perhaps have conducted field research. At this stage in the writing process, your working thesis may be rough and may change as you write your draft, but having a working thesis will help keep your project focused.

Determine your contribution

A convincing and compelling source-based argument does not make claims based solely on the word of you, the writer. To be persuasive, it must draw on the expertise and reputations of others as well. However, you must also demonstrate that you have thought about and synthesized the evidence you have gathered from your sources, and you must show your readers which elements of your project represent your original thinking.

Determine exactly what you are adding to the larger conversation about your subject by answering these questions.

- Whom do you agree with?
- Whom do you disagree with?
- Which positions do you agree with but can add an additional point or example to?
- What original analysis or theorizing do you have to offer?

See pages 32–34 for examples of how to identify your contribution in relation to your sources.

Determine your main points

Look back over your notes on your sources and determine how to group the ideas you researched. Decide what your major points will be and how those points support your thesis. Group your research findings so that they match up with your major points.

Now it is time to create a working outline. Always include your thesis at the top of your outline as a guiding light. Some writers create formal outlines with roman numerals and the like; others compose the headings for the paragraphs of their project and use them to guide their draft; still others may start writing and then determine how they will organize their draft when they have a few paragraphs written. Experiment and decide which method works best for you.

Avoid Plagiarism

Plagiarism means claiming credit for someone else's intellectual work no matter whether it's to make money or get a better grade. Intentional or not, plagiarism has dire consequences. Reputable authors have gotten into trouble through carelessness by copying passages from published sources without acknowledging those sources. A number of famous people have had their reputations tarnished by accusations of plagiarism, and several prominent journalists have lost their jobs and careers for copying the work of other writers and passing it off as their own.

Deliberate plagiarism

If you buy a paper on the Web, copy someone else's paper word for word, or take an article off the Web and turn it in as yours, it's plain stealing, and people who take that risk should know that the punishment can be severe—usually failure for the course and sometimes expulsion. Deliberate plagiarism is easy for your instructors to spot because they recognize shifts in style, and it is easy for them to use search engines to find the sources of work stolen from the Web.

Patch plagiarism

The use of the Web has increased instances of plagiarism in college. Some students view the Internet as a big free buffet where they can grab anything, paste it in a file, and submit it as their own work. Other students intend to submit work that is their own, but they commit patch plagiarism because they aren't careful in taking notes to distinguish the words of others from their own words.

What you are not required to acknowledge

Fortunately, common sense governs issues of academic plagiarism. The standards of documentation are not so strict that the source of every fact you cite must be acknowledged. You do not have to document the following.

- **Facts available from many sources.** For example, many reference sources report that the death toll of the sinking of the *Titanic* on April 15, 1912, was around 1,500.
- **Results of your own field research.** If you take a survey and report the results, you don't have to cite yourself. You do need to cite interviews that you conduct.

What you are required to acknowledge

The following sources should be acknowledged with an in-text citation and an entry in the list of works cited (MLA style) or the list of references (APA style).

- **Quotations.** Short quotations should be enclosed within quotation marks, and long quotations should be indented as a block. See page 257 for how to integrate quotations with signal phrases.
- **Summaries and paraphrases.** Summaries represent the author's argument in miniature as accurately as possible. Paraphrases restate the author's argument in your own words.
- **Facts that are not common knowledge.** For facts that are not easily found in general reference works, cite the source.
- **Ideas that are not common knowledge**. The sources of theories, analyses, statements of opinion, and arguable claims should be cited.
- **Statistics, research findings, examples, graphs, charts, and illustrations.** As a reader you should be skeptical about statistics and research findings when the source is not mentioned. When a writer does not cite the sources of statistics and research findings, there is no way of knowing how reliable the sources are or whether the writer is making them up.

Plagiarism in college writing

If you find any of the following problems in your academic writing, you may be guilty of plagiarizing someone else's work. Because plagiarism is usually inadvertent, it is especially important that you understand what constitutes using sources responsibly. Avoid these pitfalls.

- **Missing attribution.** Make sure the author of a quotation has been identified. Include a lead-in or signal phrase that provides attribution to the source, and identify the author in the citation.

- **Missing quotation marks.** You must put quotation marks around material quoted directly from a source.

- **Inadequate citation.** Give a page number to show where in the source the quotation appears or where a paraphrase or summary is drawn from.

- **Paraphrase that relies too heavily on the source.** Be careful that the wording or sentence structure of a paraphrase does not follow the source too closely.

- **Distortion of meaning.** Don't allow your paraphrase or summary to distort the meaning of the source, and don't take a quotation out of context so that the result is a change of meaning.

- **Missing works-cited entry.** The Works Cited page must include all the works cited in the project.

- **Inadequate citation of images.** A figure or photo must appear with a caption and a citation to indicate the source of the image. If material includes a summary of data from a visual source, an attribution or citation must be given for the graphic being summarized.

Avoid plagiarism when taking notes

The best way to avoid unintentional plagiarism is to take care to distinguish source words from your own words. Don't mix words from the source with your own words.

- **Create a working bibliography and make separate files for content notes.** Create a file for each source and label it clearly with the author's name. If you work on paper, use a separate page for each source. At the top of each page, write down all the information you need for a list of works cited or a list of references in your working bibliography.

- **If you copy anything from a source when taking notes, place those words in quotation marks and note the page number(s) where those words appear.** If you copy words from an online source, take special care to note the source. You could easily copy online material and later not be able to find where it came from.

- **Print out the entire source or e-mail it to yourself so you can refer to it later.** Having a complete copy allows you to double-check later that you haven't used words from the source by mistake and that any words you quote are accurate.

Avoid Plagiarism When Quoting Sources

Effective research writing builds on the work of others. You can summarize or paraphrase the work of others, but often it is best to let the authors speak in your text by quoting their exact words. Indicate the words of others by placing them inside quotation marks.

Most people who get into plagiarism trouble lift words from a source and use them without quotation marks. Look carefully at this example to see where the line is drawn. In the following passage, Steven Johnson takes sharp issue with the metaphor of surfing applied to the Web:

> The concept of "surfing" does a terrible injustice to what it means to navigate around the Web. . . .What makes the idea of cybersurf so infuriating is the implicit connection drawn to television. Web surfing, after all, is a derivation of channel surfing—the term thrust upon the world by the rise of remote controls and cable panoply in the mid-eighties. . . . Applied to the boob tube, of course, the term was not altogether inappropriate. Surfing at least implied that channel-hopping was more dynamic, more involved, than the old routine of passive consumption. Just as a real-world surfer's enjoyment depended on the waves delivered up by the ocean, the channel surfer was at the mercy of the programmers and network executives. The analogy took off because it worked well in the one-to-many system of cable TV, where your navigational options were limited to the available channels.
>
> But when the term crossed over to the bustling new world of the Web, it lost a great deal of precision. . . . Web surfing and channel surfing are genuinely different pursuits; to imagine them as equivalents is to ignore the defining characteristics of each medium. Or at least that's what happens in theory. In practice, the Web takes on the greater burden. The television imagery casts the online surfer in the random, anesthetic shadow of TV programming, roaming from site to site like a CD player set on shuffle play. But what makes the online world so revolutionary is the fact that there *are* connections between each stop on a Web itinerant's journey. The links that join those various destinations are links of association, not randomness. A channel surfer hops back and forth between different channels because she's bored. A Web surfer clicks on a link because she's interested.

> —Steven Johnson, *Interface Culture: How New Technology
> Transforms the Way We Create and Communicate*
> (New York: Harper, 1997), 107–109.

If you were writing a paper or creating a Web site that concerns Web surfing, you might want to mention the distinction that Johnson makes between channel surfing and surfing on the Web.

Quoting directly

If you quote directly, you must place quotation marks around all words you take from the original.

> One observer marks this contrast: "A channel surfer hops back and forth between different channels because she's bored. A Web surfer clicks on a link because she's interested" (Johnson 109).

Notice that the quotation is introduced and not just dropped in. This example follows MLA style, where the citation—(Johnson 109)—goes outside the quotation marks but before the final period. In MLA style, source references are made according to the author's last name, which refers you to the full citation in the list of works cited at the end. Following the author's name is the page number where the quotation can be located. (Notice that there is no comma after the name.)

Attributing every quotation

If the author's name appears in the sentence, cite only the page number, in parentheses.

> According to Steven Johnson, "A channel surfer hops back and forth between different channels because she's bored. A Web surfer clicks on a link because she's interested" (109).

Quoting words that are quoted in your source

Use single quotation marks to quote material that is already quoted in your source.

> Steven Johnson uses the metaphor of a Gothic cathedral to describe a computer interface: "'The principle of the Gothic architecture,' Coleridge once said, 'is infinity made imaginable.' The same could be said for the modern interface" (42).

Avoid Plagiarism When Summarizing and Paraphrasing

Summarizing

When you summarize, you state the major ideas of an entire source or part of a source in a paragraph or perhaps even a sentence. The key is to put the summary in your own words. If you use words from the source, you must put those words within quotation marks.

Plagiarized

> Steven Johnson argues in *Interface Culture* that the concept of "surfing" is misapplied to the Internet because channel surfers hop back and forth between different channels because they're bored, but Web surfers click on links because they're interested.

[Most of the words are lifted directly from the original; see page 252.]

Acceptable summary

> Steven Johnson argues in *Interface Culture* that the concept of "surfing" is misapplied to the Internet because users of the Web consciously choose to link to other sites while television viewers mindlessly flip through the channels until something catches their attention.

Paraphrasing

When you paraphrase, you present the idea of the source in your own words at about the same length as the original. You still need to include the reference to the source of the idea. The following example illustrates an unacceptable paraphrase.

Plagiarized

> Steven Johnson argues that the concept of "surfing" does a terrible injustice to what it means to navigate around the Web. What makes the idea of Web surfing infuriating is the association with television. Surfing is not a bad metaphor for channel hopping, but it doesn't fit what people do on the Web. Web surfing and channel surfing are truly different activities; to imagine them as the same is to ignore their defining characteristics. A channel surfer skips around because she's bored while a Web surfer clicks on a link because she's interested (107-09).

Even though the source is listed, this paraphrase is unacceptable. Too many of the words in the original are used directly here, including much or all of entire sentences. When a string of words is lifted from a source and inserted without quotation marks, the passage is plagiarized. Changing a few words in a sentence is not a paraphrase. Compare these two sentences.

Source

Web surfing and channel surfing are genuinely different pursuits; to imagine them as equivalents is to ignore the defining characteristics of each medium.

Unacceptable paraphrase

Web surfing and channel surfing are truly different activities; to imagine them as the same is to ignore their defining characteristics.

The paraphrase takes the structure of the original sentence and substitutes a few words. It is much too similar to the original.

A true paraphrase represents an entire rewriting of the idea from the source.

Acceptable paraphrase

Steven Johnson argues that "surfing" is a misleading term for describing how people navigate on the Web. He allows that "surfing" is appropriate for clicking across television channels because the viewer has to interact with what the networks and cable companies provide, just as the surfer has to interact with what the ocean provides. Web surfing, according to Johnson, operates at much greater depth and with much more consciousness of purpose. Web surfers actively follow links to make connections (107-09).

Even though this paraphrase contains a few words from the original, such as *navigate* and *connections*, these sentences are original in structure and wording while accurately conveying the meaning of the source.

Decide When to Quote and When to Paraphrase

The general rule in deciding when to include direct quotations and when to paraphrase lies in the importance of the original wording.

- If you want to refer to an idea or fact and the original wording is not critical, make the point in your own words.
- Save direct quotations for language that is memorable or conveys the character of the source.

Use quotations effectively

Quotations are a frequent problem area in research projects. Review every quotation to ensure that each is used effectively and correctly.

- **Limit the use of long quotations.** If you have more than one block quotation on a page, look closely to see if one or more can be paraphrased or summarized. Use direct quotations only if the original wording is important.
- **Check that each quotation is supporting your major points rather than making major points for you.** If the ideas rather than the original wording are what's important, paraphrase the quotation and cite the source.
- **Check that each quotation is introduced and attributed.** Each quotation should be introduced and the author or title named. Check for signal phrases, which point to a quotation: Smith *claims*, Jones *argues*, Brown *states*.
- **Check that each quotation is properly formatted and punctuated.** Prose quotations longer than four lines (MLA) or forty words (APA) should be indented 1 inch in MLA style or 1/2 inch in APA style. Shorter quotations should be enclosed within quotation marks.
- **Check that you cite the source for each quotation.** You are required to cite the sources of all direct quotations, paraphrases, and summaries.
- **Check the accuracy of each quotation.** It's easy to leave out words or mistype a quotation. Compare what is in your project to the original source. If you need to add words to make the quotation grammatical, make sure the added words are in brackets. Use ellipses to indicate omitted words.
- **Read your project aloud to a classmate or a friend.** Each quotation should flow smoothly when you read your project aloud. Put a check beside rough spots as you read aloud so you can revise later.

Use signal phrases

Signal verbs often indicate your stance toward a quotation. Introducing a quotation with "X says" or "X believes" tells your readers nothing. Find a livelier verb that suggests how you are using the source. For example, if you write "X contends," your reader is alerted that you likely will disagree with the source. Be as precise as possible.

Signal phrases that report information or a claim

X argues that . . .

X asserts that . . .

X claims that . . .

X observes that . . .

As X puts it, . . .

X reports that . . .

As X sums it up, . . .

Signal phrases when you agree with the source

X affirms that . . .

X has the insight that . . .

X points out insightfully that . . .

X theorizes that . . .

X verifies that . . .

Signal phrases when you disagree with the source

X complains that . . .

X contends that . . .

X denies that . . .

X disputes that . . .

X overlooks that . . .

X rejects that . . .

X repudiates that . . .

Signal phrases in the sciences

Signal phrases in the sciences often use the past tense, especially for interpretations and commentary.

X described . . .

X found . . .

X has suggested . . .

Introduce block quotations

Long direct quotations, called **block quotations**, are indented from the margin instead of being placed in quotation marks. In MLA style, a quotation longer than four lines should be indented 1 inch. A quotation of forty words or longer is indented 1/2 inch in APA style. In both MLA and APA styles, long quotations are double-spaced. You still need to integrate a block quotation into the text of your project by mentioning who wrote or said it.

- No quotation marks appear around the block quotation.
- Words quoted in the original retain the double quotation marks.
- The page number appears in parentheses after the period at the end of the block quotation.

It is a good idea to include at least one or two sentences following the quotation to describe its significance to your thesis.

Double-check quotations

Whether they are long or short, you should double-check all quotations you use to be sure they are accurate and that all words belonging to the original are set off with quotation marks or placed in a block quotation. If you wish to leave out words from a quotation, indicate the omitted words with ellipses (. . .), but make sure you do not alter the meaning of the original quotation. If you need to add words of your own to a quotation to make the meaning clear, place your words in square brackets.

Write a Draft

Some writers begin by writing the title, first paragraph, and concluding paragraph.

Write a specific title

A bland, generic title says to readers that you are likely to be boring.

Generic

Good and Bad Fats

Specific titles are like tasty appetizers; if you like the appetizer, you'll probably like the main course.

Specific

> The Secret Killer: Hydrogenated Fats

Write an engaging introduction

Get off to a fast start. If, for example, you want to alert readers to the dangers of partially hydrogenated oils in the food we eat, you could begin by explaining the difference in molecular structure between natural unsaturated fatty acids and trans-fatty acids. And you would probably lose your readers by the end of the first paragraph.

Instead, let readers know what is at stake along with giving some background and context; consider dramatizing a problem that your paper will address. State your thesis early on. Then go into the details in the body of your project.

Write a strong conclusion

The challenge in writing ending paragraphs is to leave the reader with something provocative, something beyond pure summary of the previous paragraphs. Connect back to your thesis, and use a strong concluding image, example, question, or call to action to leave your readers with something to remember and think about.

Review and Revise

After you've gone through the peer editing process or assessed your own draft, sit down with your project and consider the changes you need to make. Start from the highest level, reorganizing paragraphs and possibly even cutting large parts of your project and adding new sections. If you make significant revisions, likely you will want to repeat the overall evaluation of your revised draft when you finish (see Chapter 5).

When you feel your draft is complete, begin the editing phase. Use the guidelines on pages 55–56 to revise style and grammatical errors. Finally, proofread your project, word by word, checking for mistakes.

20 | Documenting Sources in MLA Style

In this chapter, you will learn to

1. Describe the elements of MLA documentation, including in-text references and the works-cited list (see below)
2. Identify the basic patterns for MLA in-text citations (see pages 265–268)
3. Identify the basic patterns for MLA works-cited entries, including entries for books, periodicals, databases, online sources, and nonprint sources (see pages 268–276)
4. Format research papers using MLA style (see pages 277–283)

The two styles of documentation used most frequently are APA style and MLA style. APA stands for American Psychological Association, which publishes a style manual used widely in the social sciences and education (see Chapter 21). MLA stands for the Modern Language Association, and its style is the norm for the humanities and fine arts, including English and rhetoric and composition. If you have questions that this chapter does not address, consult the *MLA Handbook for Writers of Research Papers*, Seventh Edition (2009), and the *MLA Style Manual and Guide to Scholarly Publishing*, Third Edition (2008).

Elements of MLA Documentation

Citing a source in your paper

Citing sources is a two-part process. When readers find a reference to a source (called an in-text or parenthetical citation) in the body of your paper, they can turn to the works-cited list at the end and find the full publication information. Place the author's last name and the page number inside parentheses at the end of the sentence.

Anticipating the impact of *Google*'s project of digitally scanning books in major research libraries, one observer predicts that "the real magic will come in the second act, as each word in each book is cross-linked, clustered, cited, extracted, indexed, analyzed, annotated, remixed, reassembled and woven deeper into the culture than ever before" (Kelly 43).

Author not mentioned in text

If you mention the author's name in the sentence, you do not have to put the name in the parenthetical reference at the end. Just cite the page number.

> Anticipating the impact of *Google*'s project of digitally scanning books in major research libraries, Kevin Kelly predicts that "the real magic will come in the second act, as each word in each book is cross-linked, clustered, cited, extracted, indexed, analyzed, annotated, remixed, reassembled and woven deeper into the culture than ever before" (43).

Author mentioned in text

The corresponding entry in the works-cited list at the end of your paper would be as follows.

Works Cited

> Kelly, Kevin. "Scan This Book!" *New York Times* 14 May 2006, late ed., sec. 6: 43+. Print.

Entry in the works-cited list

Citing an entire work, a Web site, or another electronic source

If you wish to cite an entire work (a book, a film, a performance, and so on), a Web site, or an electronic source that has no page numbers or paragraph numbers, MLA style instructs that you mention the name of the person (for example, the author or director) in the text with a corresponding entry in the works-cited list. You do not need to include the author's name in parentheses. If you cannot identify the author, mention the title in your text.

> Joel Waldfogel discusses the implications of a study of alumni donations to colleges and universities, observing that parents give generously to top-rated colleges in the hope that their children's chances for admission will improve.

Author mentioned in text

Works Cited

> Waldfogel, Joel. "The Old College Try." *Slate*. Washington Post Newsweek Interactive, 6 July 2007. Web. 27 Jan. 2014.

MLA style requires the medium of publication (print, Web, performance, etc.) to be included in each citation.

Creating an MLA-style works-cited list

To create your works-cited list, go through your paper and find every reference to the sources you consulted during your research. Each in-text reference must have an entry in your works-cited list. Do not include any sources on your works-cited list that you do not refer to in your paper.

Organize your works-cited list alphabetically by authors' last names or, if no author is listed, by the first word in the title other than *a*, *an*, or *the*. (See pages 282–283 for a sample works-cited list.) MLA style uses four basic forms for entries in the works-cited list: books, periodicals (scholarly journals, newspapers, magazines), online library database sources, and other online sources (Web sites, discussion forums, blogs, online newspapers, online magazines, online government documents, and e-mail messages). There are also specific formats for citation of interviews, images, music, and film.

Works-cited entries for books

Entries for books have three main elements.

> Pollan, Michael. *In Defense of Food: An Eater's Manifesto*. New York: Penguin, 2008. Print.

1. Author's name.
- List the author's name with the last name first, followed by a period.

2. *Title of book*.
- Find the exact title on the title page, not the cover.
- Separate the title and subtitle with a colon.
- Italicize the title and put a period at the end.

3. Publication information.
- Give the city of publication and a colon.
- Give the name of the publisher, using accepted abbreviations, and a comma.
- Give the date of publication, followed by a period.
- Give the medium of publication (Print), followed by a period.

Works-cited entries for periodicals

Entries for periodicals (scholarly journals, newspapers, magazines) have three main elements.

Pilgrim, Sarah, David Smith, and Jules Pretty. "A Cross-Regional Assessment of the Factors Affecting Ecoliteracy: Implications for Policy and Practice." *Ecological Applications* 17.6 (2007): 1742-51. Print.

1. Author's name.
- List the author's name with the last name first, followed by a period.

2. "Title of article."
- Place the title of the article inside quotation marks.
- Insert a period before the closing quotation mark.

3. Publication information.
- Italicize the title of the journal.
- Give the volume number and, if there is one, the issue number.
- List the date of publication, in parentheses, followed by a colon.
- List the page numbers, followed by a period. (Note: MLA uses hyphens in page spans and does not use full numbers.)
- Give the medium of publication (Print), followed by a period.

Works-cited entries for library database sources

Basic entries for library database sources have four main elements.

Damiano, Jessica. "Growing Vegetables in Small Spaces: Train Them up Trellises and Plant Crops in Succession." *Newsday* 2 May 2010: G107. *LexisNexis Academic*. Web. 8 Apr. 2013.

1. Author's name.
- List the author's name with the last name first, followed by a period.

2. "Title of article."
- Place the title of the article inside quotation marks.
- Insert a period before the closing quotation mark.

3. Print publication information
- Give the print publication information in standard format, in this case for a periodical (see pages 271–273).

4. Database information
- Italicize the name of the database, followed by a period.
- List the medium of publication, followed by a period. For all database sources, the medium of publication is Web.
- List the date you accessed the source (day, month, and year), followed by a period.

Works-cited entries for other online sources

Basic entries for online sources (Web sites, discussion forums, blogs, online newspapers, online magazines, online government documents, and e-mail messages) have three main elements. Sometimes information such as the author's name or the date of publication is missing from the online source. Include the information you are able to locate.

There are many formats for the different kinds of electronic publications. Here is the format of an entry for an online article.

Jacobs, Ruth. "Organic Garden Gives Back." *Colby Magazine* 99.1 (2013): n. pag. Web. 2 Apr. 2013.

1. Author's name.
- List the author's name with the last name first, followed by a period.

2. "Title of work"; Title of the overall Web site
- Place the title of the work inside quotation marks if it is part of a larger Web site.
- Italicize the name of the overall site if it is different from the title of the work.
- Some Web sites are updated periodically, so list the version if you find it (e.g., 2014 edition).

3. Publication information.
- List the publisher or sponsor of the site, followed by a comma. If not available, use N.p. (for "no publisher").
- List the date of publication if available; if not, use n.d. (for "no date")
- List the medium of publication (Web).
- List the date you accessed the source (day, month, and year).

MLA In-Text Citations

1. Author named in your text

Put the author's name in a signal phrase in your sentence. Put the page number in parentheses at the end of the sentence.

> Sociologist Daniel Bell called this emerging U.S. economy the "postindustrial society" (3).

2. Author not named in your text

Put the author's last name and the page number inside parentheses at the end of the sentence.

> In 2012, the Gallup poll reported that 56% of adults in the United States think secondhand smoke is "very harmful," compared with only 36% in 1994 (Saad 4).

3. Work by a single author

The author's last name comes first, followed by the page number. There is no comma.

> (Bell 3)

4. Work by two or three authors

The authors' last names follow the order of the title page. If there are two authors, join the names with *and*. If there are three authors, use a comma between the first two names and a comma with *and* before the last name.

> (Francisco, Vaughn, and Lynn 7)

5. Work by four or more authors

You may use the phrase *et al.* (meaning "and others") for all names but the first, or you may write out all the names. Make sure you use the same method for both the in-text citations and the works-cited list.

> (Abrams et al. 1653)

6. Work by an unnamed author

Use a shortened version of the title that includes at least the first important word. Your reader will use the shortened title to find the full title in the works-cited list.

> A review in the *New Yorker* of Ryan Adams's new album focuses on the artist's age ("Pure" 25).

Notice that "Pure" is in quotation marks because it is the shortened title of an article. If it were a book, the short title would be in italics.

7. Work by a group or organization
Treat the group or organization as the author, but try to identify the group author in the text and place only the page number in parentheses.

> According to the *Irish Free State Handbook*, published by the Ministry for Industry and Finance, the population of Ireland in 1929 was approximately 4,192,000 (23).

8. Quotations longer than four lines
When using indented (block) quotations of more than four lines, place the period *before* the parentheses enclosing the page number.

> In her article "Art for Everybody," Susan Orlean attempts to explain the popularity of painter Thomas Kinkade:
>> People like to own things they think are valuable. ...
>> The high price of limited editions is part of their appeal:
>> it implies that they are choice and exclusive, and that
>> only a certain class of people will be able to afford
>> them. (128)
> This same statement could possibly also explain the popularity of phenomena like PBS's *Antiques Road Show*.

If the source is longer than one page, provide the page number for each quotation, paraphrase, and summary.

9. Online sources including Web pages, blogs, podcasts, tweets, social media, wikis, videos, and other multimedia sources
Give the author's name in the text instead of in parentheses.

> Andrew Keen ironically used his own blog to claim that "blogs are boring to write (yawn), boring to read (yawn) and boring to discuss (yawn)."

If you cannot identify the author, mention the title in your text.

> The podcast "Catalina's Cubs" describes the excitement on Catalina Island when the Chicago Cubs went there for spring training in the 1940s.

10. Work in an anthology

Cite the name of the author of the work within an anthology, not the name of the editor of the collection. Alphabetize the entry in the list of works cited by the author, not the editor.

> In "Beard," Melissa Jane Hardie explores the role assumed by Elizabeth Taylor as the celebrity companion of gay actors including Rock Hudson and Montgomery Clift (278-79).

11. Two or more works by the same author

When an author has two or more items in the works-cited list, distinguish which work you are citing by using the author's last name and then a shortened version of the title of each source.

> The majority of books written about coauthorship focus on partners of the same sex (Laird, *Women* 351).

Note that *Women* is italicized because it is the name of a book; if an article were named, quotation marks would be used.

12. Different authors with the same last name

If your list of works cited contains items by two or more different authors with the same last name, include the initial of the first name in the parenthetical reference.

> Web surfing requires more mental involvement than channel surfing (S. Johnson 107).

Note that a period follows the initial.

13. Two or more sources within the same sentence

Place each citation directly after the statement it supports.

> In the 1990s, many sweeping pronouncements were made that the Internet is the best opportunity to improve education since the printing press (Ellsworth xxii) or even in the history of the world (Dyrli and Kinnaman 79).

14. Two or more sources within the same citation

If two sources support a single point, separate them with a semicolon.

> (McKibbin 39; Gore 92)

15. Work quoted in another source

When you do not have access to the original source of the material you wish to use, put the abbreviation *qtd. in* ("quoted in") before the information about the indirect source.

> National governments have become increasingly what Ulrich Beck, in a 1999 interview, calls "zombie institutions"—institutions that are "dead and still alive" (qtd. in Bauman 6).

16. Literary works

To supply a reference to a literary work, you sometimes need more than a page number from a specific edition. Readers should be able to locate a quotation in any edition of the book. Give the page number from the edition that you are using, then a semicolon and other identifying information.

> "Marriage is a house" is one of the most memorable lines in *Don Quixote* (546; pt. 2, bk. 3, ch. 19).

MLA Works-Cited List: Books

One author

17. Book by one author

The author's last name comes first, followed by a comma, the first name, and a period.

> Doctorow, E. L. *The March*. New York: Random, 2005. Print.

18. Two or more books by the same author

In the entry for the first book, include the author's name. In the second entry, substitute three hyphens and a period for the author's name. List the titles of books by the same author in alphabetical order.

> Grimsley, Jim. *Boulevard*. Chapel Hill: Algonquin, 2002. Print.
> ---. *Dream Boy*. New York: Simon, 1995. Print.

Multiple authors

19. Book by two or three authors

Second and subsequent authors' names appear first name first. A comma separates the authors' names.

Chapkis, Wendy, and Richard J. Webb. *Dying to Get High: Marijuana as Medicine*. New York: New York UP, 2008. Print.

20. Book by four or more authors

You may use the phrase *et al.* (meaning "and others") for all authors but the first, or you may write out all the names. Use the same method in the in-text citation as you do in the works-cited list.

Zukin, Cliff, et al. *A New Engagement? Political Participation, Civic Life, and the Changing American Citizen*. New York: Oxford UP, 2006. Print.

Anonymous and group authors

21. Book by an unknown author

Begin the entry with the title.

Encyclopedia of Americana. New York: Somerset, 2001. Print.

22. Book by a group or organization

Treat the group as the author of the work.

United Nations. *The Charter of the United Nations: A Commentary*. New York: Oxford UP, 2000. Print.

23. Religious texts

Do not italicize the title of a sacred text, including the Bible, unless you are citing a specific edition.

King James Text: Modern Phrased Version. New York: Oxford UP, 1980. Print.

Imprints, reprints, and undated books

24. Book with no publication date

If no year of publication is given but can be approximated, put a *c.* ("circa") and the approximate date in brackets: [c. 2009]. Otherwise, put *n.d.* ("no date"). For works before 1900, you do not need to list the publisher.

O'Sullivan, Colin. *Traditions and Novelties of the Irish Country Folk*. Dublin, [c. 1793]. Print.

James, Franklin. *In the Valley of the King*. Cambridge: Harvard UP, n.d. Print.

25. Reprinted works

For works of fiction that have been printed in many different editions or reprints, give the original publication date after the title.

> Wilde, Oscar. *The Picture of Dorian Gray*. 1890. New York: Norton, 2001. Print.

Parts of books

26. Introduction, foreword, preface, or afterword

Give the author and then the name of the specific part being cited. Next, name the book. Then, if the author for the whole work is different, put that author's name after the word *By*. Place inclusive page numbers at the end.

> Benstock, Sheri. Introduction. *The House of Mirth*. By Edith Wharton. Boston: Bedford-St. Martin's, 2002. 3-24. Print.

27. Single chapter written by same author as the book

> Ardis, Ann L. "Mapping the Middlebrow in Edwardian England." *Modernism and Cultural Conflict: 1880-1922*. Cambridge: Cambridge UP, 2002. 114-42. Print.

28. Selection from an anthology or edited collection

> Sedaris, David. "Full House." *The Best American Nonrequired Reading 2004*. Ed. Dave Eggers. Boston: Houghton, 2004. 350-58. Print.

29. Article in a reference work

You can omit the names of editors and most publishing information for an article from a familiar reference work. Identify the edition by date. There is no need to give the page numbers when a work is arranged alphabetically. Give the author's name, if known.

> "Utilitarianism." *The Columbia Encyclopedia*. 6th ed. 2001. Print.

Editions and translations

30. Book with an editor

List an edited book under the editor's name if your focus is on the editor. Otherwise, cite an edited book under the author's name as shown in the second example below.

> Lewis, Gifford, ed. *The Big House of Inver*. By Edith Somerville and Martin Ross. Dublin: Farmar, 2000. Print.

Somerville, Edith, and Martin Ross. *The Big House of Inver*. Ed. Gifford Lewis. Dublin: Farmar, 2000. Print.

31. Book with a translator

Benjamin, Walter. *The Arcades Project*. Trans. Howard Eiland and Kevin McLaughlin. Cambridge: Harvard UP, 1999. Print.

32. Second or subsequent edition of a book

Hawthorn, Jeremy, ed. *A Concise Glossary of Contemporary Literary Theory*. 3rd ed. London: Arnold, 2001. Print.

Multivolume works

33. Multivolume work

Identify both the volume you have used and the total number of volumes in the set.

Samuel, Raphael. *Theatres of Memory*. Vol. 1. London: Verso, 1999. 2 vols. Print.

If you refer to more than one volume, identify the specific volume in your in-text citations, and list the total number of volumes in your list of works cited.

Samuel, Raphael. *Theatres of Memory*. 2 vols. London: Verso, 1999. Print.

MLA Works-Cited List: Periodicals

Journal articles

34. Article by one author

Ekotto, Frieda. "Against Representation: Countless Hours for a Professor." *PMLA* 127.4 (2012): 968-72. Print.

35. Article by two or three authors

Miller, Thomas P., and Brian Jackson. "What Are English Majors For?" *College Composition and Communication* 58.4 (2007): 825-31. Print.

36. Article by four or more authors

You may use the phrase *et al.* (meaning "and others") for all authors but the first, or you may write out all the names.

> Breece, Katherine E., et al. "Patterns of mtDNA Diversity in Northwestern North America." *Human Biology* 76.1 (2004): 33-54. Print.

Pagination in journals

37. Article in a scholarly journal

List the volume and issue number after the name of the journal.

> Bernard-Donals, Michael. "Synecdochic Memory at the United States Holocaust Memorial Museum." *College English* 74.5 (2012): 417-36. Print.

38. Article in a scholarly journal that uses only issue numbers

List the issue number after the name of the journal.

> McCall, Sophie. "Double Vision Reading." *Canadian Literature* 194 (2007): 95-97. Print.

Magazines

39. Monthly or seasonal magazines

Use the month (or season) and year in place of the volume. There is no comma before the date. Abbreviate the names of all months except May, June, and July.

> Barlow, John Perry. "Africa Rising: Everything You Know about Africa Is Wrong." *Wired* Jan. 1998: 142-58. Print.

40. Weekly or biweekly magazines

Give both the day and the month of publication, as listed on the issue.

> Brody, Richard. "A Clash of Symbols." *New Yorker* 25 June 2007: 16. Print.

Newspapers

41. Newspaper article by one author

The author's last name comes first, followed by a comma and the first name.

> Marriott, Michel. "Arts and Crafts for the Digital Age." *New York Times* 8 June 2006, late ed.: C13. Print.

42. Article by two or three authors
The second and subsequent authors' names are printed in regular order, first name first:

> Schwirtz, Michael, and Joshua Yaffa. "A Clash of Cultures at a Square in Moscow." *New York Times* 11 July 2007, late ed.: A9. Print.

43. Newspaper article by an unknown author
Begin the entry with the title.

> "The Dotted Line." *Washington Post* 8 June 2006, final ed.: E2. Print.

Reviews, editorials, letters to the editor

44. Review
If there is no title, just name the work reviewed.

> Mendelsohn, Daniel. "The Two Oscar Wildes." Rev. of *The Importance of Being Earnest*, dir. Oliver Parker. *The New York Review of Books* 10 Oct. 2002: 23-24. Print.

45. Editorial

> "Hush-hush, Sweet Liberty." Editorial. *Los Angeles Times* 7 July 2007: A18. Print.

46. Letter to the editor

> Doyle, Joe. Letter. *Direct* 1 July 2007: 48. Print.

MLA Works-Cited List: Library Database Sources

47. Work from a library database
Begin with the print publication information, then the name of the database (italicized), the medium of publication (*Web*), and the date of access.

> Snider, Michael. "Wired to Another World." *Maclean's* 3 Mar. 2003: 23-24. *Academic Search Premier*. Web. 14 Jan. 2013.

MLA Works-Cited List: Online Sources

Web publications

When do you list a URL? MLA style no longer requires including URLs of Web sources. URLs are of limited value because they change frequently and they can be specific to an individual search. Include the URL as supplementary information only when your readers probably cannot locate the source without the URL.

48. Publication by a known author

> Boerner, Steve. "Leopold Mozart." *The Mozart Project: Biography*. The Mozart
>   Project, 21 Mar. 1998. Web. 30 Oct. 2013.

49. Publication by a group or organization

If a work has no author's or editor's name listed, begin the entry with the title.

> "State of the Birds." *Audubon*. National Audubon Society, 2012. Web.
>   19 Aug. 2013.

50. Article in a scholarly journal on the Web

Some scholarly journals are published on the Web only. List articles by author, title, name of journal in italics, volume and issue number, and year of publication. If the journal does not have page numbers, use *n. pag.* in place of page numbers. Then list the medium of publication (*Web*) and the date of access (day, month, and year).

> Fleckenstein, Kristie. "Who's Writing? Aristotelian Ethos and the Author Position
>   in Digital Poetics." *Kairos* 11.3 (2007): n. pag. Web. 6 Apr. 2013.

51. Article in a newspaper on the Web

The first date is the date of publication; the second is the date of access.

> Brown, Patricia Leigh. "Australia in Sonoma." *New York Times*. New York
>   Times, 5 July 2008. Web. 3 Aug. 2013.

52. Article in a magazine on the Web

> Brown, Patricia Leigh. "The Wild Horse Is Us." *Newsweek*. Newsweek, 1 July
>   2008. Web. 12 Dec. 2013.

53. E-book on Kindle, iPad, or another device

> Morrison, Toni. *Home*. New York: Vintage, 2013. Kindle file.

Other online sources

54. Blog entry

If there is no sponsor or publisher for the blog, use *N.p.*

> Arrington, Michael. "Think Before You Voicemail." *TechCrunch*. N.p., 5 July
> 2008. Web. 10 Sept. 2013.

55. E-mail

Give the name of the writer, the subject line, a description of the message, the date, and the medium of delivery (*E-mail*).

> Ballmer, Steve. "A New Era of Business Productivity and Innovation."
> Message to Microsoft Executive E-mail. 30 Nov. 2010. E-mail.

56. Video on the Web

Video on the Web often lacks a creator and a date. Begin the entry with a title if you cannot find a creator. Use *n.d.* if you cannot find a date.

> Wesch, Michael. *A Vision of Students Today*. *YouTube*. YouTube, 2007.
> Web. 28 May 2013.

57. Posting on social media

Many organizations now use *Facebook* and other social media. Give the author, title, name of the organization, the name of the site, the sponsor (*Facebook*), the date, the medium (*Web*), and the date of access.

> Eklund, Doug. "Dedicated to Myself." *Metropolitan Museum of Art*. Facebook,
> 14 Mar. 2013. Web. 18 Mar. 2013.

58. Posting on *Twitter*

Include the entire tweet and the date and time of publication. Conclude with the medium (*Tweet*).

> Obama, Barack (BO). "It should not be a partisan issue." Utah business
> leaders urge their representative to move on #immigration reform.
> 27 Aug. 2013. 12:02 p.m. Tweet.

59. Wiki entry

A wiki is a collaborative writing and editing tool. Although some topic-specific wikis are written and carefully edited by recognized scholars, the more popular wiki sites—such as *Wikipedia*—are often considered unreliable sources for academic papers.

> "Snowboard." *Wikipedia*. Wikimedia Foundation, 2014. Web. 30 Jan. 2014.

60. Podcast

> Sussingham, Robin. "All Things Autumn." No. 2. *HighLifeUtah*. N.p., 20 Nov. 2006. Web. 28 Feb. 2014.

MLA Works-Cited List: Other Sources

61. Sound recording

> McCoury, Del, perf. "1952 Vincent Black Lightning." By Richard Thompson. *Del and the Boys*. Ceili, 2001. CD.

62. Film

Begin with the title in italics. List the director, the distributor, the date, and the medium. Other information, such as the names of the screenwriters and performers, is optional.

> *Wanted*. Dir. Timur Bekmambetov. Perf. James McAvoy, Angelina Jolie, and Morgan Freeman. Universal, 2008. Film.

63. DVD

> *No Country for Old Men*. Dir. Joel Coen and Ethan Coen. Perf. Tommy Lee Jones, Javier Bardem, and Josh Brolin. Paramount, 2007. DVD.

64. Television or radio program

> "Kaisha." *The Sopranos*. Perf. James Gandolfini, Lorraine Bracco, and Edie Falco. HBO. 4 June 2006. Television.

65. Personal interview

> Andrews, Michael. Personal interview. 25 Sept. 2013.

Sample MLA paper

MLA style does not require a title page. Ask your instructor whether you need one.

Include your last name and page number as page header, beginning with the first page, 1/2" from the top.

Brian Witkowski

Professor Mendelsohn

RHE 309K

3 May 2013

Need a Cure for Tribe Fever?

How about a Dip in the Lake?

Center your title. Do not put the title in quotation marks or type it in all capital letters.

Everyone is familiar with the Cleveland Indians' Chief Wahoo logo—and I do mean everyone, not just Clevelanders. Across America people wear the smiling mascot on Cleveland Indians caps and jerseys, and recent trends in sports merchandise have popularized new groovy multicolored Indians sportswear. Because of lucrative contracts between Major League Baseball and Little League, youth teams all over the country don Cleveland's famous (or infamous) smiling Indian each season as fresh-faced kids scamper onto the diamonds looking like mini major leaguers (Liu). Various incarnations of the famous Chief Wahoo—described by writer Ryan Zimmerman as "a grotesque caricature grinning idiotically through enormous bucked teeth"—have been around since the 1940s. Now redder and even more cartoonish than the original hook-nosed, beige Indian with a devilish grin, Wahoo often passes as a cheerful baseball buddy like the San Diego Chicken or the St. Louis Cardinals' Fredbird.

Use 1" margins all around. Double-space everything.

Cite publications by the name of the author (or authors).

Indent each paragraph 1/2" on the ruler in your word processing program.

Though defined by its distinctive logo, Cleveland baseball far preceded its famous mascot. The team changed from the Forest Citys to the Spiders to the Bluebirds/Blues to the Broncos to the Naps and finally to the Indians. Dubbed the Naps in 1903 in honor of its star player and manager Napoleon Lajoie, the team gained its current appellation in 1915. After Lajoie was traded, the team's president challenged sportswriters to devise a suitable "temporary" label for the floundering club. Publicity material claims that the writers decided on the Indians to celebrate Louis Sockalexis, a Penobscot Indian who played for the team from 1897 to 1899. With a high batting average and the notability of being the first Native American in professional baseball, Sockalexis was immortalized by the new Cleveland label (Schneider 10-23). (Contrary to popular lore, some cite alternative—and less reverent—motivations behind the team's naming and point to a lack of Sockalexis publicity in period newspaper articles discussing the team's naming process [Staurowsky 95-97].) A century later, the "temporary" name continues to raise eyebrows, in both its marketability and its ideological questionability.

Today the logo is more than a little embarrassing. Since the high-profile actions of the American Indian Movement (AIM) in the 1970s, sports teams around the country—including the Indians—have been criticized for their racially insensitive mascots. Native American groups question these caricatured icons—not just because of grossly stereotyped mascots, but also because of what visual displays of team support say about Native American culture. Across the country, professional sporting teams, as well as high schools and colleges, perform faux rituals in the name of team spirit. As Tim Giago, publisher of *The Lakota Times*, a weekly South Dakotan Native American newspaper, has noted,

> The sham rituals, such as the wearing of feathers, smoking of so-called peace pipes, beating of tomtoms, fake dances, horrendous attempts at singing Indian songs, the so-called war whoops, and the painted faces, address more than the issues of racism. They are direct attacks upon the spirituality of the Indian people. (qtd. in Wulf)

Controversy over such performances still fuels the fire between activists and alumni at schools such as the University of Illinois at Champaign-Urbana, where during many decades of football halftimes fans cheered the performance of a student (often white) dressed as Chief Illiniwek. In March of 2007, the University of Illinois board of trustees voted in a nearly unanimous decision to retire the mascot's name, regalia, and image ("Illinois").

Since 1969, when Oklahoma disavowed its "Little Red" mascot, more than six hundred school and minor league teams have followed a more ethnically sensitive trend and ditched their "tribal" mascots (Price). High-profile teams such as Stanford, St. Johns University, and Miami (Ohio) University have changed their team names from the Indians to the Cardinal (1972), the Redmen to the Red Storm (1993), and the Redskins to the Redhawks (1996), respectively. In 2005, the NCAA officially ruled that "colleges whose nicknames or mascots refer to American Indians will not be permitted to hold National Collegiate Athletic Association tournament events" (Wolverton). The University of North Dakota was one of the last holdouts, but in 2012, the citizens of North Dakota voted overwhelmingly to allow the University of North Dakota to drop its controversial "Fighting Sioux" nickname ("UND").

Cleveland's own Chief Wahoo has far from avoided controversy. Multiple conflicts between Wahoo devotees and dissenters occur annually during the baseball season. At the opening game of 1995, fifty Native Americans and supporters took stations around Jacobs Field to demonstrate against the use of the cartoonish smiling crimson mascot (Kropk). Arrests were made in 1998 when demonstrators from the United Church of Christ burned a three-foot Chief Wahoo doll in effigy ("Judge"). Opinions on the mascot remain mixed. Jacoby Ellsbury, outfielder for the Boston Red Sox and a member of the Colorado River Indian Tribes, said in 2007, "I'm not offended [by the mascot]. You can look at it two different ways. You can look at it that it's offensive or you can look at it that they are representing Native Americans. Usually I'll try to take the positive out of it" (Shaughnessy). Nonetheless, Ellsbury still acknowledges that he "can see both sides of [the controversy]" (Shaughnessy). Wedded to their memorabilia, fans proudly stand behind their Indian as others lobby vociferously for its removal, splitting government officials, fans, and social and religious groups.

In 2000, Cleveland mayor Michael White came out publicly against the team mascot, joining an already established group of religious leaders, laypersons, and civil rights activists who had demanded Wahoo's retirement. African American religious and civic leaders such as Rev. Gregory A. Jacobs pointed to the absurdity of minority groups who embrace the Wahoo symbol. "Each of us has had to fight its [sic] own battle, quite frankly," Jacobs stated. "We cannot continue to live in this kind of hypocrisy that says, Yes, we are in solidarity with my [sic] brothers and sisters, yet we continue to exploit them" (qtd. in Briggs).

This controversy also swirls outside of the greater Cleveland area. In 2009, the image of Wahoo was removed from the team's training complex in Goodyear, Arizona ("Cleveland"), while the *Seattle Times* went so far as to digitally remove the Wahoo symbol from images of the Cleveland

Witkowski 4

baseball cap ("Newspaper"). As other teams make ethnically sensitive and image-conscious choices to change their mascots, Cleveland stands firm in its resolve to retain Chief Wahoo. Despite internal division and public ridicule fueled by the team icon, the city refuses to budge.

Cleveland's stubbornness on the issue of Wahoo runs contrary to the city's recently improved image and downtown revitalization. As a native of Cleveland, I understand the power of "Tribe Fever" and the unabashed pride one feels when wearing Wahoo garb during a winning (or losing) season. Often it is not until we leave northeastern Ohio that we realize the negative image that Wahoo projects. What then can Cleveland do to simultaneously save face and bolster its burgeoning positive city image? I propose that the team finally change the "temporary" Indians label. In a city so proud of its diverse ethnic heritage—African American, Italian American, and Eastern European American to name a few examples—why stand as a bearer of retrograde ethnic politics? Cleveland should take this opportunity to link its positive Midwestern image to the team of which it is so proud. I propose changing the team's name to the Cleveland Lakers.

The city's revival in the last twenty years has embraced the geographic and aesthetic grandeur of Lake Erie. Disavowing its "mistake on the lake" moniker of the late 1970s, Cleveland has traded aquatic pollution fires for a booming lakeside business district. Attractions such as the Great Lakes Science Center, the Rock and Roll Hall of Fame, and the Cleveland Browns Stadium take advantage of the beauty of the landscape and take back the lake. Why not continue this trend through one of the city's biggest and highest-profile moneymakers: professional baseball? By changing the team's name to the Lakers, the city would gain national advertisement for one of its major selling points, while simultaneously announcing a new ethnically inclusive image that is appropriate to our wonderfully diverse city. It would be a public relations triumph for the city.

Of course this call will be met with many objections. Why do we have to buckle to pressure? Do we not live in a free country? What fans and citizens alike need to keep in mind is that ideological pressures would not be the sole motivation for this move. Yes, retiring Chief Wahoo would take Cleveland off AIM's hit list. Yes, such a move would promote a

kinder and gentler Cleveland. At the same time, however, such a gesture
would work toward uniting the community. So much civic division exists
over this issue that a renaming could help start to heal these
old wounds.

Additionally, this type of change could bring added economic
prosperity to the city. First, a change in name will bring a new wave
of team merchandise. Licensed sports apparel generates more than
a 10-billion-dollar annual retail business in the United States, and
teams have proven repeatedly that new uniforms and logos can provide
new capital. After all, a new logo for the Seattle Mariners bolstered
severely slumping merchandise sales (Lefton). Wahoo devotees need not
panic; the booming vintage uniform business will keep him alive, as is
demonstrated by the current ability to purchase replica 1940s jerseys
with the old Indians logo. Also, good press created by this change will
possibly help increase tourism in Cleveland. If the goodwill created by
the Cleveland Lakers can prove half as profitable as the Rock and Roll Hall
of Fame, then local businesses will be humming a happy tune. Finally, if
history repeats itself, a change to a more culturally inclusive logo could,
in and of itself, prove to be a cash cow. When Miami University changed
from the Redskins to the Redhawks, it saw alumni donations skyrocket
(Price). A less divisive mascot would prove lucrative to the ball club, the
city, and the players themselves. (Sluggers with inoffensive logos make
excellent spokesmen.)

Perhaps this proposal sounds far-fetched: Los Angeles may seem to
have cornered the market on Lakers. But where is their lake? (The Lakers
were formerly the Minneapolis Lakers, where the name makes sense in
the "Land of 10,000 Lakes.") Various professional and collegiate sports
teams—such as baseball's San Francisco Giants and football's New York
Giants—share a team name, so licensing should not be an issue. If Los
Angeles has qualms about sharing the name, perhaps Cleveland could
persuade Los Angeles to become the Surfers or the Stars; after all, Los
Angeles players seem to spend as much time on the big and small screens
as on the court.

Witkowski 6

Now is the perfect time for Cleveland to make this jump. Perhaps a new look will help usher in a new era of Cleveland baseball and a World Series ring to boot. Through various dry spells, the Cleveland Indians institution has symbolically turned to the descendants of Sockalexis, asking for goodwill or a latter-generation Penobscot slugger (Fleitz 3). Perhaps the best way to win goodwill, fortunes, and the team's first World Series title since 1948 would be to eschew a grinning, life-size Chief Wahoo for the new Cleveland Laker, an oversized furry monster sporting water wings, cleats, and a catcher's mask. His seventh-inning-stretch show could include an air-guitar solo with a baseball bat as he quietly reminds everyone that the Rock Hall is just down the street.

Witkowski 7

Works Cited

Center "Works Cited" on a new page.

Briggs, David. "Churches Go to Bat against Chief Wahoo." *Cleveland Plain Dealer* 25 Aug. 2000: 1A. *LexisNexis Academic*. Web. 19 Apr. 2013.

"Cleveland Indians' Chief Wahoo Logo Left Off Team's Ballpark, Training Complex in Goodyear, Arizona." *Cleveland.com*. Cleveland Plain Dealer, 12 Apr. 2009. Web. 23 Apr. 2013.

Fleitz, David L. *Louis Sockalexis: The First Cleveland Indian*. Jefferson: McFarland, 2002. Print.

"Illinois Trustees Vote to Retire Chief Illiniwek." *ESPN*. ESPN Internet Ventures, 13 Mar. 2007. Web. 26 Apr. 2013.

"Judge Dismisses Charges against City in Wahoo Protest." *Associated Press* 6 Aug. 2001. *LexisNexis Academic*. Web. 19 Apr. 2013.

Kropk, M. R. "Chief Wahoo Protestors Largely Ignored by Fans." *Austin American Statesman* 6 May 1995: D4. Print.

Lefton, Terry. "Looks Are Everything: For New Franchises, Licensing Battles Must Be Won Long before the Team Even Takes the Field." *Sport* 89 (May 1998): 32. Print.

Double-space all entries. Indent all but the first line in each entry one-half inch.

Alphabetize entries by the last names of the authors or by the first important word in the title if no author is listed.

Witkowski 8

Liu, Caitlin. "Bawl Game." *Portfolio.com*. Condé Nast, 21 Oct. 2008.
	Web. 28 Apr. 2013.

"Newspaper Edits Cleveland Indian Logo from Cap Photo." *Associated
	Press* 31 Mar. 1997. *LexisNexis Academic*. Web. 27 Apr. 2013.

Price, S. L. "The Indian Wars." *Sports Illustrated* 4 Mar. 2002: 66+.
	Academic OneFile. Web. 20 Apr. 2013.

Schneider, Russell. *The Cleveland Indians Encyclopedia*. Philadelphia:
	Temple UP, 1996. Print.

Shaughnessy, Dan. "They've Had Some Chief Concerns." *Boston Globe* 12
	Oct. 2007: C5. *LexisNexis Academic*. Web. 19 Apr. 2013.

Staurowsky, Ellen J. "Sockalexis and the Making of the Myth at the Core
	of the Cleveland's 'Indian' Image." *Team Spirits: The Native Ameri-
	can Mascots Controversy*. Ed. C. Richard King and Charles Fruehling
	Springwood. Lincoln: U of Nebraska P, 2001. 82-106. Print.

"UND OK to Drop Fighting Sioux Name." *ESPN.com*. ESPN, 14 June 2012.
	Web. 16 Apr. 2013.

Wolverton, Brad. "NCAA Restricts Colleges with Indian Nicknames
	and Mascots." *Chronicle of Higher Education* 2 Sept. 2005: A65.
	ProQuest. Web. 25 Apr. 2013.

Wulf, Steve. "A Brave Move." *Sports Illustrated* 24 Feb. 1992: 7. Print.

Zimmerman, Ryan. "The Cleveland Indians' Mascot Must Go." *Christian
	Science Monitor* 15 Oct. 2007: 5. *LexisNexis Academic*. Web. 19 Apr.
	2013.

Italicize the titles of books and periodicals.

Check to make sure all the sources you have cited in your text are in the list of works cited.

21 Documenting Sources in APA Style

QUICK TAKE

In this chapter, you will learn to

1. Describe the elements of APA documentation style, including in-text citations and the References list (see below)

2. Identify the basic patterns for APA in-text citations (see pages 287–289)

3. Identify the basic patterns for APA References entries, including entries for books, periodicals, databases, online sources, and nonprint sources (see pages 289–293)

Papers written for the social sciences, including government, linguistics, psychology, sociology, and education, frequently use the APA documentation style. For a detailed treatment of APA style, consult the *Publication Manual of the American Psychological Association*, sixth edition (2010).

Elements of APA Documentation

Citing a source in your paper

APA style emphasizes the date of publication. When you cite an author's name in the body of your paper, always include the date of publication. Notice too that APA style includes the abbreviation for page (*p.*) in front of the page number. A comma separates each element of the citation.

> Zukin (2004) observes that teens today begin to shop for themselves at age 13 or 14, "the same age when lower-class children, in the past, became apprentices or went to work in factories" (p. 50).

If the author's name is not mentioned in the sentence, cite the author, date, and page number inside parentheses.

> One sociologist notes that teens today begin to shop for themselves at age 13 or 14, "the same age when lower-class children, in the past, became apprentices or went to work in factories" (Zukin, 2004, p. 50).

The corresponding entry in the references list would be as follows.

Zukin, S. (2004). *Point of purchase: How shopping changed American culture.* New York, NY: Routledge.

Creating an APA-style references list

To create your references list, go through your paper and find every reference to the sources you consulted during your research. Each in-text citation must have an entry in your references list.

Organize your references list alphabetically by authors' last names or, if no author is listed, by the first word in the title other than *a, an,* or *the.* APA style uses three basic forms for entries in the references list: books, periodicals (scholarly journals, newspapers, magazines), and online sources.

Increasingly, books and articles are accessed online. Because URLs frequently change, many scholarly publishers have begun to use a Digital Object Identifier (DOI), a unique alphanumeric string that is permanent. If a DOI is available, use the DOI. APA now recommends listing DOIs as URLs. Use the new format if available: http://dx.doi.org/10.XXXX/JXXXX.

References entries for books

Orum, A. M., & Chen, X. (2003). *The world of cities: Places in comparative and historical perspective.* Malden, MA: Blackwell.

1. Author's or editor's name.
- List the author's name with the last name first, followed by a comma and the author's initials.
- Join two authors' names with an ampersand.
- For an editor, put (Ed.) after the name: Kavanaugh, P. (Ed.).

2. (Year of publication).
- Give the year of publication in parentheses. If no year of publication is given, write (n.d.) ("no date") : Smith, S. (n.d.).
- If it is a multivolume edited work, published over a period of more than one year, put the time span in parentheses: Smith, S. (1999–2001).

3. *Title of book.*
- Italicize the title.
- Capitalize only the first word, proper nouns, and the first word after a colon.
- If the title is in a foreign language, copy it exactly as it appears on the title page.

4. Publication information.
- For all books list the city with a two-letter state abbreviation (or full country name) after the city name. If more than one city is given on the title page, list only the first.
- Do not shorten or abbreviate words like *University* or *Press*. Omit words such as *Co.*, *Inc.*, and *Publishers*.

References entries for periodicals

Lee, E. (2007). Wired for gender: Experientiality and gender-stereotyping in computer-mediated communication. *Media Psychology, 10,* 182–210.

1. Author's name.
- List the author's name, last name first, followed by the author's initials.
- Join two authors' names with a comma and an ampersand.

2. (Year of publication).
- Give the year the work was published in parentheses.

3. Title of article.
- Do not use quotation marks. If there is a book title in the article title, italicize it.
- Capitalize only the first word of the title, the first word of the subtitle, and any proper nouns in the title.

4. Publication information.
- Italicize the journal name.
- Capitalize all nouns, verbs, and pronouns, and the first word of the journal name. Do not capitalize any article, preposition, or coordinating conjunction unless it is the first word of the title or subtitle.
- Put a comma after the journal name.
- Italicize the volume number and follow it with a comma.
- If each issue of the journal begins on page 1, give the issue number in parentheses, followed by comma. See sample references 18 and 24.
- Give page numbers of the article (see sample references 20 and 21 for more on pagination). Note: APA provides the full numbers for page spans.

References entries for online sources

Department of Justice. Federal Bureau of Investigation. (2004). Hate crime
statistics 2004: Report summary. Retrieved from http://www.fbi.gov/
ucr/hc2004/openpage.htm

1. Author's name, associated institution, or organization.
- List the author's name, if given, with the last name first,
  followed by the author's initials.
- If the only authority you find is a group or organization (as in
  this example), list its name as the author.
- If the author or organization is not identified, begin the
  reference with the title of the document.

2. (Date of publication).
- List the date the site was produced, last revised, or copyrighted.

3. Title of page or article.
- If you are citing a page or article that has a title, treat the title
  like an article in a periodical. If you are citing an entire Web
  site, treat the name like a book.
- If the Web site has no title, list it by author or creator.

4. Retrieval information
- If your source has been assigned a DOI (Digital Object Identifier), list
  it at the end in the format that appears in your source (alphanumeric
  string or URL). Do not add a period at the end of a DOI.
- If the source does not have a DOI, list the URL of the journal's
  home page.

APA In-Text Citations

1. Author named in your text

Influential sociologist Daniel Bell (1973) noted a shift in the United States
to the "postindustrial society" (p. 3).

2. Author not named in your text

In 2012, the Gallup poll reported that 56% of adults in the United States
think secondhand smoke is "very harmful," compared with only 36% in 1994
(Saad, 1997, p. 4).

3. Work by a single author

(Bell, 1973, p. 3)

4. Work by two authors

Notice that APA uses an ampersand (&) with multiple authors' names rather than *and*.

(Suzuki & Irabu, 2013, p. 404)

5. Work by three to five authors

The authors' last names follow the order of the title page.

(Francisco, Vaughn, & Romano, 2012, p. 7)

Subsequent references can use the first name and *et al.*

(Francisco et al., 2013, p. 17)

6. Work by six or more authors

Use the first author's last name and *et al.* for all in-text references.

(Swallit et al., 2014, p. 49)

7. Work by a group or organization

Identify the group author in the text and place only the page number in parentheses.

The National Organization for Women (2001) observed that this "generational shift in attitudes towards marriage and childrearing" will have profound consequences (p. 325).

8. Work by an unknown author

Use a shortened version of the title (or the full title if it is short) in place of the author's name. Capitalize all key words in the title. If it is an article title, place it in quotation marks.

("Derailing the Peace Process," 2003, p. 44)

9. Quotations of 40 words or longer

Indent long quotations 1/2 inch and omit quotation marks. Note that the period appears before the parentheses in an indented block quote.

> Orlean (2001) has attempted to explain the popularity of the painter Thomas Kinkade:
>> People like to own things they think are valuable. . . . The high price of limited editions is part of their appeal; it implies that they are choice and exclusive, and that only a certain class of people will be able to afford them. (p. 128)

APA References List: Books

10. Book by one author

The author's last name comes first, followed by a comma and the author's initials.

> Gladwell, M. (2012). *Outliers: The story of success*. New York, NY: Back Bay Books.

If an editor, put (Ed.) in parentheses after the name.

> Kavanagh, P. (Ed.). (1969). *Lapped furrows*. New York, NY: Hand Press.

11. Book by two authors

Join two authors' names with a comma and ampersand.

> Hardt, M., & Negri, A. (2000). *Empire*. Cambridge, MA: Harvard University Press.

For editors, use *(Eds.)* after the names.

> McClelland, D., & Eismann, K. (Eds).

12. Book by three or more authors

List last names and initials for up to seven authors, with an ampersand between the last two names. For works with eight or more authors, list the first six names, then an ellipsis, then the last author's name.

> Anders, K., Child, H., Davis, K., Logan, O., Petersen, J., Tymes, J., . . . Johnson, S.

13. E-book with DOI assigned

Chaffe-Stengel, P., & Stengel, D. (2012). *Working with sample data: Exploration and inference.* doi:10.4128/9781606492147

14. E-book with no DOI assigned

Burton, R. (1832). *The anatomy of melancholy.* Retrieved from http://etext. library.adelaide.edu.au/b/burton/robert/melancholy

15. Chapter in an edited collection
Add *In* after the selection title and before the names of the editor(s).

Howard, A. (1997). Labor, history, and sweatshops in the new global economy. In A. Ross (Ed.), *No sweat: Fashion, free trade, and the rights of garment workers* (pp. 151–172). New York, NY: Verso.

16. Government document
When the author and publisher are identical, use *Author* as the name of the publisher.

U.S. Environmental Protection Agency. (2002). *Respiratory health effects of passive smoking: Lung cancer and other disorders.* (EPA Publication No. 600/6-90/006 F). Washington, DC: Author.

APA References List: Periodicals

17. Article by one author

Goolkasian, P. (2012). Research in visual pattern recognition: The enduring legacy of studies from the 1960s. *American Journal of Psychology, 125,* 155–163.

18. Article by multiple authors
Write out all of the authors' names, up to seven authors. For works with eight or more authors, list the first six names, then an ellipsis, then the last author's name.

Blades, J., & Rowe-Finkbeiner, K. (2006). The motherhood manifesto. *The Nation, 282*(20), 11–16.

19. Article by a group or organization

National Organization for Women (2002). Where to find feminists in Austin. *The NOW guide for Austin women.* Austin, TX: Chapter Press.

20. Article in a journal with continuous pagination

Include the volume number and the year, but not the issue number.

Engen, R., & Steen, S. (2000). The power to punish: Discretion and sentencing reform in the war on drugs. *American Journal of Sociology, 105,* 1357–1395.

21. Article in a journal paginated by issue

List the issue number in parentheses (not italicized) after the volume number with no intervening space (see entry 18). For a popular magazine that does not commonly use volume numbers, use the season or date of publication.

McGinn, D. (2006, June 5). Marriage by the numbers. *Newsweek,* 40–48.

22. Monthly publication

Barlow, J. P. (1998, January). Africa rising: Everything you know about Africa is wrong. *Wired,* 142–158.

23. Newspaper article

Hagenbaugh, B. (2005, April 25). Grads welcome an uptick in hiring. *USA Today,* p. A1.

APA References List: Library Database Sources

24. Document from a library database

APA no longer requires listing the names of well-known databases. The article below was retrieved from the PsycARTICLES database, but there is no need to list the database, the retrieval date, or the URL if the DOI is listed.

Erdfelder, E. (2008). Experimental psychology: Good news. *Experimental Psychology, 55*(1), 1–2. doi:0.1027/1618-3169.55.1.1

APA References List: Online Sources

25. Article with DOI assigned

You may need to click on a button labeled "Article" or "PubMed" to find the DOI.

> Sharpless, B. A. (2013). Kierkegaard's conception of psychology. *Journal of Theoretical and Philosophical Psychology, 33*(2), 90–106. doi:10.1037/a0029009

26. Article with no DOI assigned

> Brown, B. (2004). The order of service: The practical management of customer interaction. *Sociological Research Online, 9*(4). Retrieved from http://www.socresonline.org.uk/9/4/brown.html

27. Online publication by a group or organization

If the only authority you find is a group or organization, list its name as the author.

> Girls Inc. (2013). Girls' bill of rights. Retrieved from http://www.girlsinc.org/about/girls-bill-of-rights/

28. Article in an online newspaper

> Slevin, C. (2005, April 25). Lawmakers want to put limits on private toll roads. *Boulder Daily Camera.* Retrieved from http://www.dailycamera.com

29. Article in an online magazine

> Pein, C. (2005, April 20). Is Al-Jazeera ready for prime time? *Salon.* Retrieved from http://www.salon.com

APA References List: Other Sources

30. Television program

> Winter, T. (Writer). (2012). Resolution. [Television series episode]. In T. Winter (Producer), *Boardwalk empire.* New York: HBO.

31. Film, Video, or DVD

> Boal, M. (Writer), & Bigelow, K. (Director). (2012). *Zero dark thirty* [DVD].
> United States: Columbia Pictures.

32. Musical recording

List both the title of the song and the title of the album or CD. In the in-text citation, include side or track numbers.

> Lowe, N. (2001). Lately I've let things slide. On *The convincer* [CD]. Chapel
> Hill, NC: Yep Roc Records.

33. Social media (e.g., *Facebook*) page or note

> The Daily Show. (2013, March 18). Political speeches contain much more
> than empty promises. [Facebook page]. Retrieved July 29, 2013, from
> https://www.facebook.com/thedailyshow

34. Twitter update or tweet

> Collins, F. S. (2013, April 30). Check out my NPR interview this afternoon
> with Marketplace's @kairyssdal about #NIH research. [Twitter post].
> Retrieved from https://twitter.com/NIH

Glossary

A

abstract A summary of an article or book

aesthetic criteria Evaluative criteria based on perceptions of beauty and good taste

analogy An extended comparison of one situation or item to another

APA American Psychological Association

APA documentation Documentation style commonly used in social-science and education disciplines

argument A claim supported by at least one reason

assumption An unstated belief or knowledge that connects a claim with evidence

audience Real or assumed individuals or groups to whom a verbal or written communication is directed

B

bandwagon appeal A fallacy of argument based on the assumption that something is true or correct because "everyone" believes it to be so

bar chart Visual depiction of data created by the use of horizontal or vertical bars that comparatively represent rates or frequencies

because clause A statement that begins with the word *because* and provides a supporting reason for a claim

begging the question A fallacy of argument that uses the claim as evidence for its own validity

bias A personal belief that may skew one's perspective or presentation of information

bibliography List of books and articles about a specific subject

blog A Web-based journal or diary featuring regular entries about a particular subject or daily experiences (also known as a Web log)

brainstorming A method of finding ideas by writing a list of questions or statements about a subject

C

causal argument An argument that seeks to identify the reasons behind a certain event or phenomenon

claim A declaration or assertion made about any given topic

claim of comparison A claim that argues something is like or not like something else

cherry-picking the evidence Pointing to individual cases or data that confirm a position while ignoring a significant amount of data that might contradict that position

common factor method A method used by scientists to identify a recurring factor present in a given cause–effect relationship

common knowledge fallacy Similar to the bandwagon appeal, this fallacy assumes what is widely distributed on the Internet must be true.

consequence The cause–effect result of a given action

context The combination of author, subject, and audience and the broader social, cultural, and economic influences surrounding a text

contextual analysis A type of rhetorical analysis that focuses on the author, the audience, the time, and the circumstances of an argument

counterargument An argument offering an opposing point of view with the goal of demonstrating that it is the stronger of two or more arguments

criteria Standards used to establish a definition or an evaluation

critical reading A process of reading that surpasses an initial understanding or impression of basic content and proceeds with the goal of answering specific questions or examining particular elements

cropping In photography, the process of deleting unwanted parts of an image

cultural assumptions Widely held beliefs that are considered common sense in a particular culture

D

database Large collection of digital information organized for efficient search and retrieval

debate A contest or game in which two or more individuals attempt to use arguments to persuade others to support their opinion

definition argument An argument made by specifying that something does or does not possess certain criteria

diction The choice and use of words in writing and speech

E

either–or A fallacy of argument that presents only two choices in a complex situation

emotional appeal An argumentation strategy that attempts to persuade by stirring the emotions of the audience

empirical research Research that collects data from observation or experiment

ethos An appeal to the audience based on the character and trustworthiness of the speaker or writer

evaluation argument An argument that judges something based on ethical, aesthetic, and/or practical criteria

evaluation of sources The assessment of the relevance and reliability of sources used in supporting claims

evidence Data, examples, or statistics used to support a claim

experimental research Research based on obtaining data under controlled conditions, usually by isolating one variable while holding other variables constant

F

fallacy of argument Failure to provide adequate evidence to support a claim. See *bandwagon appeal, begging the question, false analogy, hasty generalization, name calling, non sequitur, oversimplification, polarization, post hoc fallacy, rationalization, slippery slope, straw man*

false analogy A fallacy of argument that compares two unlike things as if they were similar

feasibility The ability of a proposed solution to be implemented

figurative language The symbolic transference of meaning from one word or phrase to another, such as with the use of metaphor, synecdoche, and metonymy

firsthand evidence Evidence such as interviews, observations, and surveys collected by the writer

font The specific size and weight of a typeface

freewriting A method of finding ideas by writing as fast as possible about a subject for a set length of time

G

generalization A conclusion drawn from knowledge based on past occurrences of the phenomenon in question

good reason A reason that an audience accepts as valid

H

hasty generalization A fallacy of argument resulting from making broad claims based on a few occurrences

I

idea map A brainstorming tool that visually depicts connections among different aspects of an issue

image editor Software that allows you to create and manipulate images

intellectual property Any property produced by the intellect, including copyrights for literary, musical, photographic, and cinematic works; patents for inventions and industrial processes; and trademarks

J

journal A general category of publications that includes popular, trade, and scholarly periodicals

K

keyword search A Web-based search that uses a robot and indexer to produce results based on a chosen word or words

L

line graph A visual presentation of data represented by a continuous line or lines plotted at specific intervals

logos An appeal to the audience based on reasoning and evidence

M

metaphor A figure of speech using a word or phrase that commonly designates one thing to represent another, thus making a comparison

metonymy A type of figurative language that uses one object to represent another that embodies its defining quality

MLA Modern Language Association

MLA documentation Documentation style commonly used in humanities and fine-arts disciplines

multimedia The use of multiple content forms including text, voice and music audio, video, still images, animation, and interactivity

N

name calling A fallacy of argument resulting from the use of undefined, and therefore meaningless, names

narrative argument A form of argument based on telling stories that suggest the writer's position rather than explicitly making claims

non sequitur A fallacy of argument resulting from connecting two or more unrelated ideas

O

oversimplification A fallacy in argument caused by neglecting to account for the complexity of a subject

P

pathos An appeal based on the audience's emotions or deeply held values

periodical A journal, magazine, or newspaper published at standard intervals, usually daily, weekly, monthly, or quarterly

periodical index Paper or electronic resource that catalogs the contents of journals, magazines, and newspapers

pie chart A circular chart resembling a pie that illustrates percentages of the whole through the use of delineated wedge shapes

plagiarism The improper use of the unauthorized and unattributed words or ideas of another author

podcast Digital media files available on the Internet for playback on a portable media player

polarization A fallacy of argument based on exaggerating the characteristics of opposing groups to highlight division and extremism

popular journal A magazine aimed at the general public; usually includes illustrations, short articles, and advertisements

position argument A general kind of argument in which a claim is made for an idea or way of thinking about a subject

post hoc fallacy A fallacy of argument based on the assumption that events that follow each other have a causal relationship

practical criteria Evaluative criteria based on usefulness or likely results

primary research Information collected directly by the writer through observations, interviews, surveys, and experiments

process of elimination method A means of finding a cause by systematically ruling out all other possible causes

proposal argument An argument that either advocates or opposes a specific course of action

R

rationalization A fallacy of argument based on using weak explanations to avoid dealing with the actual causes

reason In an argument, the justification for a claim

rebuttal argument An argument that challenges or rejects the claims of another argument

reference librarian Library staff member who is familiar with information resources and who can show you how to use them (you can find a reference librarian at the reference desk in your library)

refutation A rebuttal argument that points out the flaws in an opposing argument

rhetorical analysis Careful study of a written argument or other types of persuasion aimed at understanding how the components work or fail to work

rhetorical situation Factors present at the time of writing or speaking, including the writer or speaker, the audience, the purpose of communicating, and the context

S

sans serif type A style of type recognized by blunt ends and a consistency in thickness

scholarly journals Journals containing articles written by experts in a particular field; also called peer-reviewed or academic journals

secondary research Information obtained from existing knowledge, such as research in the library

secondhand evidence Evidence from the work of others found in the library, on the Web, and elsewhere

serif type A style of type developed to resemble the strokes of an ink pen and recognized by wedge-shaped ends on letter forms

single difference method A method of finding a cause for differing phenomena in very similar situations by identifying the one element that varies

slippery slope A fallacy of argument based on the assumption that if a first step

is taken, additional steps will inevitably follow

straw man A fallacy of argument based on the use of the diversionary tactic of setting up the opposing position in such a manner that it can be easily rejected

sufficiency The adequacy of evidence supporting a claim

synecdoche A type of figurative language in which a part is used to represent the whole

T

textual analysis A type of rhetorical analysis that focuses exclusively on the text itself

thesis One or more sentences that state the main idea of an argument

typeface A style of type, such as serif, sans serif, or decorative

U

URL (Universal Resource Locator) An address on the Web

V

visual argument A type of persuasion using images, graphics, or objects

voice In writing, the distinctive style of a writer that provides a sense of the writer as a person

W

Web directory A subject guide to Web pages grouped by topic and subtopic

Web editors Programs that allow you to compose Web pages

wiki A Web-based application designed to let multiple authors write, edit, and review content, such as *Wikipedia*

working thesis A preliminary statement of the main claim of an argument, subject to revision

Credits

Photo Credits

Text Credits

Index